King James

King James

Pauline Croft

palgrave
macmillan

First published 2003 by
PALGRAVE MACMILLAN
Houndmills, Basingstoke, Hampshire RG21 6XS and
175 Fifth Avenue, New York, N. Y. 10010
Companies and representatives throughout the world

PALGRAVE MACMILLAN is the global academic imprint of the Palgrave Macmillan division of St. Martin's Press, LLC and of Palgrave Macmillan Ltd. Macmillan® is a registered trademark in the United States, United Kingdom and other countries. Palgrave is a registered trademark in the European Union and other countries.

ISBN 0–333–61395–3 hardback
ISBN 0–333–61396–1 paperback

This book is printed on paper suitable for recycling and made from fully managed and sustained forest sources.

A catalogue record for this book is available from the British Library.

A catalogue record for this book is available from the Library of Congress.

10   9   8   7   6   5   4   3   2   1
12 11 10 09 08 07 06 05 04 03

Printed and bound in Great Britain by
Creative Print & Design (Wales), Ebbw Vale

Contents

Preface

My aim in writing this book has been to explore the impact of modern historical research on our understanding of the reigns of James VI and I in his multiple kingdoms. The result is not a biography, but an overview. I have been remarkably fortunate because so many of the historians whose work I have drawn on are also long-standing friends. I owe a great deal – probably even more than I realise – to their intellectual liveliness and sustained interest in sixteenth- and seventeenth-century Europe. In no particular order, Conrad and Elizabeth Russell, Jenny Wormald, Roger Lockyer, Helen Payne, I. A. A. Thompson, Diarmaid MacCulloch, John Morrill, Peter Lake and Michael Questier have been particularly helpful. Andrew Thrush and his colleagues in the 1603–1629 section of the History of Parliament Trust generously shared their unpublished research with me. Linda Levy Peck read the whole text and made constructive suggestions for improvement. Over the years, the Tudor-Stuart seminar at the Institute of Historical Research, University of London, has invited a large number of scholars both fledgling and established to its Monday gatherings. The papers they read, and the discussions that followed, all helped to shape my views and I am grateful to everyone for their contribution. However, I have kept endnotes to publications to a reasonable minimum and, by way of amends, have included a lengthy select bibliography.

My students at Royal Holloway University of London have helped me to understand how dauntingly complex the reign of King James can appear to the non-specialist. I tried to keep that audience in mind while I was writing. Last but not least, all authors rely on their publishers to see their work into print: I owe a great deal to the kindness and professionalism of Terka Acton and her team at Palgrave Macmillan.

Pauline Croft

Introduction

The historian of the reign of King James VI and I is fortunate because there are abundant contemporary sources that can be used to paint a detailed and finely shaded portrait of his life and rule. The king himself frequently (and revealingly) put pen to paper. More government and administrative documents survive for the reign than for that of Elizabeth. There is a rich collection of parliamentary material, together with substantial numbers of private letters and diaries. The wealth of ambassadorial accounts of the Jacobean court – French, Spanish, Dutch and Venetian, to name only the main ones – is extraordinary. Cheap print including sermons and engravings proliferated alongside scurrilous pamphlets and libellous verses. Partly as a result of the profusion of sources, and partly because the reign aroused conflicting opinions from the early seventeenth century onwards, the quantity of later historical writing is immense. Over the last quarter-century, a further outpouring of scholarship has made it particularly difficult for those trying to cut their way through the thicket. This book does not impose one particular viewpoint, but attempts to set out the evidence as fully as possible. Historians can never escape from their own preconceptions, but the aim has been to offer a clear narrative while at the same time weighing the most recent research and presenting balanced conclusions.

The seventeenth century remains the period that arouses most controversy in British history. It still figures at the forefront of both British and American history, and its achievements, built on the foundations laid in Elizabeth's reign, were impressive. Literary heights were scaled. The twin peaks of the English language remain the Authorised or 'King James' translation of the Bible printed in 1611, and the plays of William Shakespeare (1564–1616) collected in the First Folio of 1616. *Othello, King Lear, Macbeth,* and *Anthony and Cleopatra* are all Jacobean; *Measure for Measure* was played before the king in December 1604, *The Tempest* in November 1611. Other playwrights, including Thomas Dekker (1570–1632), Thomas Middleton (1570–1627), John Marston (?1575–1634) and John Webster (1580–1625), produced an unparalleled theatrical feast for London playgoers, including Queen Anne of Denmark. Working under Crown patronage, Inigo Jones (1573–1652) collaborated with Ben Jonson (?1573–1637) on court masques which scaled new heights of musical and dramatic staging in England. Music and musicians enjoyed increasing popularity, with the king, the queen and leading courtiers such as Robert Cecil first earl of Salisbury all spending large sums of money on the finest singers, players, composers and instruments.

Intellectual life flourished. The treatises on the Union produced around 1603–7 demonstrate the lively interest in constitutional and political thought that existed in both England and Scotland. The great Scottish lawyer Sir Thomas Craig of Riccarton, a personal friend of the king, wrote two distinguished tracts, one on the succession, the other on the Union. James himself was a prolific author of poetry, political theory (particularly on the rights of kings), theological disputation and biblical exegesis. The Cambridge-educated Sir Robert Filmer in the 1620s contributed the seminal *Patriarcha* to political ideas, and in 1624 the diplomat Lord Herbert of Cherbury composed the first work of deism, *De Veritate*. The statesman Francis Bacon launched the inductive scientific method, the physician William Harvey discovered the circulation of the blood, the mathematician John Napier invented the present notation of decimal fractions and explained the construction of logarithms. Dozens of gentlemen interested themselves in the history, antiquities and literature of their localities, often writing the first scholarly county histories. Others kept alive the distinctive cultures of the Celtic peripheries: Sir William Glynne of Caernarvonshire followed his father in composing poetry in the strict metres of the Welsh bards who sought his hospitality. In all his dominions, King James ruled over talented and vigorous peoples, reaching out towards a wider world both intellectually and commercially.

Dazzling domestic architecture arose at Hatfield House, Audley

End and Blickling Hall, all of which survive along with dozens of lesser mansions across the country. Lavish townhouses were increasingly erected in London and Westminster. Inigo Jones the co-creator of court masques also built the Whitehall Banqueting House for James I and the Queen's House at Greenwich for Anne of Denmark, the first true Palladian buildings in England. The passion for acquiring paintings, sculpture and other artworks from the continent (particularly Italy) gradually spread among the aristocracy. The king's eldest son Henry Prince of Wales put together one of the most admired collections before his premature death in 1612. From London, the East India Company, the Virginia Company and the Plymouth colony in Massachusetts began to lay the foundations of empire while the Levant Company brought the eastern Mediterranean into Britain's commercial sphere. The new goods they brought back – china tableware, tobacco, luxury fabrics, exotic foodstuffs such as currants and pomegranates – all fostered a striking increase in shopping and consumerism.

Within the British Isles, the year 1603 marked a new beginning of enormous importance. For the first time, the King of England, the King of Scotland, the King of Ireland and the ruler of the principality of Wales were one and the same monarch. In his pacification of the Border shires, the extension of effective central rule into the Highlands and Islands of Scotland, and probably most significant of all his support for the plantation of Ulster, King James made an indelible imprint upon the future of the three kingdoms. Unfortunately, the union of the English and Scottish Crowns immediately placed James under hostile scrutiny. Over the last 300 years the king's reputation has suffered from the acid description of him by Sir Anthony Weldon. A Kentish gentleman from a family that for generations held minor offices in the English royal household, Weldon in 1609 became clerk of the Green Cloth (secretary to the administrators providing food and drink for the court). In 1617 he accompanied James on his return visit to his northern kingdom. Weldon despised the Scots as a 'stinking people' with 'foul houses, foul sheets, foul linen, foul dishes and pots'. He disliked Scotland, 'too good for those that possess it and too bad for others to be at the charge to conquer it'.[1] When the text of his covertly composed satire was discovered, he was sacked. Weldon took his revenge by writing treatises on the courts and characters of King James and his successor Charles I which were published between 1650 and 1659. Often witty and perceptive but also prejudiced and abusive, their status as eye-witness accounts and their compulsive readability led too many historians to take them at face value.

In addition, the longer term historical perspective appeared to support Weldon's hostile account. The catastrophic fall of the Stuart dynasty by 1649 seemed more easily explicable if the first Stuart to occupy the English throne could be ridiculed as drunken, homosexual, timid and duplicitous. Weldon depicted the king as a coward in international relations, crafty only in petty matters, 'insomuch as a very wise man was wont to say he beleeved him the wisest foole in Christendome, meaning him wise in small things but a foole in weighty affairs'. It was widely assumed that the 'wise man' was Henry IV of France, regarded as a far more successful monarch.

Weldon wrote a mercilessly detailed description of a king with unattractive habits. James fiddled constantly with his codpiece; his tongue was too large for his mouth causing him to dribble; he cursed and blasphemed excessively; and he wasted England's wealth in extravagant gifts to his idle fellow countrymen and to sexually deplorable court favourites. The picture was not wholly fanciful, for many of James's less appealing traits can be documented from more objective sources such as ambassadors' letters. There is also plenty of evidence that the Scots were far less hygienic in their habits than the English. However, Weldon's history was entirely one-sided, including no redeeming features that might permit a more balanced verdict. Above all, his work was profoundly xenophobic, drawing on strongly anti-Scottish attitudes that were entrenched in England both before and after 1603. Even Shakespeare, writing *Macbeth* around 1606 to ingratiate himself with the new regime, depicted the Scots as superstitious and violent. However, the fact that Weldon spoke for many Jacobean Englishmen was hardly a satisfactory reason for later historians to accept his highly partisan account.

Weldon was followed by two other writers, Arthur Wilson (1595–1652) and Francis Osborne (1593–1659). Both came from aristocratic circles alienated from the court. They could only dimly remember James from their youth and wrote long after his death. On occasion, both purveyed little more than demonstrably inaccurate gossip from court hangers-on, but their works perpetuated the negative stereotype. Wilson pointed to the king's vast bounty and his unworthy favourites, while Osborne shared Weldon's loathing of the Scots, whom he described as leeches sucking at the English body politic. The composite picture of James derived from three hostile Englishmen was largely endorsed by the king's fellow-countryman the great historical novelist Sir Walter Scot in *The Fortunes of Nigel* (1822). It was finally immortalised in the schoolboy classic *1066 and All That* (1930), which cheerfully categorised James as A Bad King who slobbered and had favourites.

James had some defenders in his own century, including the royalist Godfrey Goodman, Bishop of Gloucester, who detested Weldon. The greatest of all seventeenth century historians, the earl of Clarendon, had little time for those who wished to blame the outbreak of civil war between 1637 and 1642 on events before 1625. Instead, the *History of the Rebellion* described how the Jacobean years brought 'uninterrupted pleasures and plenty'. Clarendon pointed to a heedless younger generation, bored with tranquillity, that began by seeking involvement in the Thirty Years War and ended after 1642 by plunging England, Scotland and Ireland into murderous internal conflict.[2]

The first full scholarly treatment of the reign was written in 1863 by S. R. Gardiner, the great Victorian historian whose views epitomised the so-called 'Whig interpretation' of history. The Whigs were politicans who, after the Glorious Revolution of 1688, aimed to subordinate the Crown to Parliament. Gardiner concentrated on the political record, which he scrupulously researched from original documents. He saw James as an able and intelligent man, capable of great shrewdness and often showing good judgment, but hampered by some fatal flaws. The king did not understand that Spain was intent on European domination and would negotiate duplicitously to achieve her ends. His infatuations with Robert Carr and then George Villiers were deplorable both morally and financially. Above all, Gardiner thought that James never appreciated that the House of Commons spoke for the English nation. The Whig interpretation saw the emergence of nineteenth-century parliamentary democracy as the inevitable and admirable culmination of hundreds of years of English history. Both James I and Charles I held exaggerated notions of the divine right of kings and of the royal prerogative. These viewpoints were at odds both with English common law and with the longstanding English commitment to representative assemblies. Hence, to Gardiner, the Stuarts were swept away by the unstoppable tide of history which would carry Parliament to political supremacy.

The first modern biography, D. H. Willson's *James VI and I* was published in 1956, but largely returned to the seventeenth-century stereotype. The index contains the telling entry, 'Weldon, Sir Anthony, quoted *passim*'. Willson ignored or downplayed the positive aspects of the reign judiciously noted by Gardiner, and concentrated on anecdote. Relating the serious incident when the king was nearly drowned after his horse stumbled and cast him into the icy waters of the New River (a channel cut to bring fresh water to London), Willson jeered that 'there was always a touch of the ridiculous about James'. His concluding chapter began with the scarcely unbiased opinion that 'The King's portraits in his last years are those of a broken, debauched and repulsive old man.' [3]

More recently, historians have returned to reconsidering James as a serious and intelligent ruler. They noted that he left his own coffers empty on his death, but his failure to raise heavy taxation meant that his subjects were considerably more prosperous than they were at his accession. His kingdoms remained enviably neutral while devastating conflicts raged in Europe, since the king to his dying day refused to launch a war against Spain. As for political principles, royal divine right theory as expounded by James was familiar in monarchies across Europe and its threatening novelty should not be exaggerated. Two key figures, Henry Howard earl of Northampton and George Villiers duke of Buckingham received scholarly biographical treatment for the first time, by Linda Levy Peck and Roger Lockyer. In both cases their hitherto low reputations were significantly upgraded. Both were far more than idle courtiers: they devoted much effort to administrative reform and achieved some improvements. On English Parliaments, the researches of Conrad Russell and others produced a more complex and nuanced picture. The Whig stereotype of a monarchy vainly opposing the rise of democracy retreated before a more sophisticated appreciation of contemporary attitudes. The landed gentry summoned to Westminster for intermittent Parliaments saw themselves as partners in the governance of the realm, not as a rising 'Opposition'. They sought harmonious and businesslike transactions, particularly over matters that affected their own localities, and tried to avoid conflicts. The underlying cause of tension in the 1620s appeared to be structural weakness, not political division. The English taxation system was in decay at a time of rapidly escalating military costs, so the Parliaments of the 1620s were left floundering once European war broke out after 1618.

In another attack on traditional views, historians of Scotland argued vigorously for the king's success in imposing his authority on his unruly subjects before 1603. Led by Gordon Donaldson who published *Scotland: James V to James VII* in 1965, scholars such as Maurice Lee Jnr emphasised significant royal achievements. James emerged from a minority which might have left him virtually helpless before an entrenched protestant kirk and a powerful, aggressive nobility. Yet he made himself into a highly effective monarch, balancing factions to his own advantage in both church and state. He went on to cope with the problems of ruling a dual monarchy after 1603 and left his kingdoms at peace in 1625, although at the price of much internal division. The king could hardly be a successful ruler of Scotland until 1603 only to be transformed into a buffoon immediately after crossing the Border.

James the writer, whose treatises were dismissed by D. H. Willson as 'tantrums in print', was rescued by Jenny Wormald. She showed the king's delight in composing works which attempted to analyse the many problems of kingship which he was uniquely qualified to discuss. James was the first ruler since Alfred to combine the theory and practice of monarchy in his own person and open up these mysteries to his reader-subjects.[4] She also pointed to the frequently uncritical acceptance by English historians of their own imperfect institutions. In Scotland, James was accustomed to dealing with a much smaller and more manoeuvrable Parliament, just as he presided over a less bureaucratic government. The king's occasional impatience could be seen as an understandable response to the slowness of English procedures, geared to the running of a larger kingdom but often cumbrous and inefficient. The key issue for most of these historians was the difference between the condition in which the king left his dominions on his death in 1625 and the way in which his son Charles handled that legacy. Like Clarendon, they generally concluded that James was not to blame for the outbreak of civil war.

A greater appreciation of the king's earlier Scottish achievements led in turn to a broader assessment of the reign as a whole. All over Europe, one of the most characteristic and dynamic features of successful early modern state-building was the assimilation of peripheral territories. On this key criterion, the years 1567 to 1625 were crucial in the making of the modern British state. James VI steadily increased his control over previously autonomous areas in Gaeldom, extending the reach of his government into the Western Isles, the Highlands and Orkney. After 1603 he continued efforts made earlier to pacify and reorganise the anarchic Border counties, which became the 'middle shires' of his Anglo-Scottish monarchy. By 1625 the Scottish government in Edinburgh was more securely in command of its distant territories than any of its predecessors. At the same time, although James failed to achieve the full Union that he proposed in 1604, he set in motion long-term trends that steadily brought England and Scotland closer together. When in 1637 the Scots rose in revolt against Charles I, their aim was not to break the link with England, but rather to renegotiate the terms on which the Stuart monarchy dealt with Scottish issues.

More recently, there has been a lively discussion of the complex interrelationship of the three kingdoms, not merely two, over which James ruled. In 1975 the historian of ideas John Pocock called for 'British History . . . a new subject', focusing on what he described as 'the Atlantic archipelago'. The history of England has never been the history of Britain, and the new subject would trace 'a problematic and uncompleted experiment in the creation and interaction of several nations'. By looking at the archipelago's processes of state formation, historians might find many illuminating parallels with the creation over the same period of the states of France and Spain.[5] Pocock's plea took some time to sink in, but from the late 1980s onward, there has been both new research and vigorous disagree-

ment. John Morrill, Nicholas Canny, Jane Ohlmeyer and others eluci-
dated the interactions set in train after 1603. In the process, they often
raised as many questions as they answered, but the reign of James VI
and I already looks very different. The crucial role of Scottish religious discontents in destabilising England after 1637 cannot easily be
assessed without extensive reference to the ecclesiastical policies of
King James, particularly the Five Articles of Perth. Similarly, the Irish
revolt of 1641 which crystallised the defining civil war question of
military command – who should control the army, the king or the
Parliament? – was intimately connected with earlier Jacobean policies. The events that followed the Ulster plantation of 1609 caused
deep fissures in Irish society with acrimonious debates over differing
plantation policies. These in turn dominated the years 1622–41 and
culminated in the overthrow of King Charles's viceroy the earl of
Strafford. These and other inter-kingdom links were already well-
known, but previously were allotted a peripheral role in explaining
what was always viewed as an *English* civil war. Recast as lead players
in the greater drama of 'the fall of the British monarchies' or 'the war
of the three kingdoms', their impact was greatly enhanced. Among
much dispute, there is universal agreement that after 1603, the
Atlantic archipelago was transformed. In this new perspective, the
reign of King James has re-emerged as one of the most crucial in
British history.

1 'The Bright Star of the North'

Minority

James VI and I lived an extraordinary life. Described recently as 'a true novel',[1] it exemplified many of the key developments in England and Scotland between 1566 and 1625. The feckless Mary Queen of Scots, James's mother, spent most of her life in France and was queen consort during the brief reign of her first husband François II (July 1559 to December 1560). During her absence, Scotland experienced the first stage of the protestant Reformation, which culminated with the Parliament held in Edinburgh in the summer of 1560. The mass and papal power were both abolished and a new confession of faith was introduced. When the widowed Mary returned to her hereditary kingdom in 1561, she was a catholic sovereign ruling an officially protestant realm, an unprecedented situation bound to generate friction. In July 1565 she married Henry Lord Darnley, like herself a great-grandchild of Henry VII and a possible claimant to the English throne. Their matrimonial alliance strengthened both their claims and inevitably increased the hostility felt by Mary's distant cousin Queen Elizabeth. To catholics, the Queen of Scots was not just the next heir to the English throne if Elizabeth died childless. In their view, Mary was already the rightful monarch. The papacy never recognised the marriage of Henry VIII and Anne Boleyn, and in consequence the catholic world regarded Elizabeth as a bastard who had usurped Mary's place.

The marriage of Mary and Darnley fell apart with startling rapidity. The queen rapidly became disenchanted with her husband and preferred the sympathetic company of her Italian secretary and musician, David Riccio. The dissolute Darnley, convinced that his six-months-pregnant wife had been unfaithful, was present in March

1566 when Riccio was dragged screaming from a supper party at Holyrood palace and stabbed over 50 times within Mary's hearing. The baby was born in June 1566 and christened James in December at Stirling Castle, with all the splendour the Scottish court could muster including fireworks and masques. Despite the difficult relationship between Mary and Elizabeth, the English queen sent a magnificent gold font as a present since she had agreed to stand as godmother *in absentia*.

Both in Scotland and abroad, the unfounded slander that James was David Riccio's son was spread rapidly and endured for decades. As a child James wept in mortification at it, and in 1600 a hostile Scottish mob shouted at him 'Come down, thou son of Seigneur Davy'. Henri IV of France reportedly commented that King James was rightly called Solomon son of David, who played upon the harp. In the months after the birth of her son, Queen Mary contemplated divorcing Darnley. In February 1567 he was recovering from illness and convalescing at Kirk o' Field, outside the walls of Edinburgh. In the small hours of the early morning, the house was blown up with a tremendous crack, but the body of Darnley recovered outside the rubble revealed that he had been strangled, probably while trying to escape. Mary was widely thought to be involved with the earl of Bothwell, whom she married shortly afterwards. Bothwell was almost certainly the leader of the Kirk o'Field assassination plot; he quickly divorced his own wife and his marriage to the queen was less the result of passion than a deliberate strategy to seize royal power. Mary still had many supporters, but outraged protestant nobles speedily removed the scandalous pair from the throne and declared the queen deposed.

On 19 July 1567 the 13-month-old baby James was carried from Stirling Castle to his coronation in the parish kirk. The circumstances were both dangerous and unpropitious. It was the worst-attended coronation in Scottish history with only a small minority of the nobility present, which suggested that the new regime would not last long. The infant's coronation oath was sworn for him by the earl of Morton. The baptism was performed by the bishop of Orkney, a recent convert to protestantism, while John Knox, the Geneva Calvinist who returned to Scotland in 1559, preached the sermon.

Towards the end of his life, James movingly described himself as 'a cradle king' since he could never recall a time when he had not borne the name and burdens of a monarch.[2]

Mary did not accept the legality of the documents she had been compelled to sign in abdicating her throne. In spring 1568 after escaping from imprisonment, she rallied her supporters against the party that had kidnapped both her son and her Crown. Defeated at Langside, she fled to England expecting to gather further troops and return shortly to Scotland, but instead she was placed under house arrest by Elizabeth. Scotland endured civil war for five more years, but it was clear by 1571 that Mary's partisans had lost. They finally surrendered Edinburgh Castle in 1573. Although the queen's disavowal of her enforced abdication placed a major question mark over the legality of James's accession, she was unable to regain her kingdom. After 1573 the king was still a child, but he was more securely seated upon his throne.

James never saw his mother again after 1567. Effectively an orphan, he endured a lonely and emotionally barren childhood. A household was established for him at Stirling, under the supervision of the earl and countess of Mar. From the age of four he was tutored by the elderly George Buchanan, a brilliant classicist, historian and playwright, but a harsh and demanding Calvinist schoolmaster who subjected the child-king to regular beatings. Buchanan also took every opportunity to blacken the character of Mary, whom he described in print as a tyrant, a murdering woman and a poisonous witch. A second tutor, the 27-year-old Calvinist theologian Peter Young, managed to gain the boy's friendship and also worked hard to build up the royal library for his charge's use. Years later, only weeks after his accession to the English throne, James rewarded Young with the deanery of Lichfield. The child-king also made a lifelong friend of his schoolmate John Erskine, who succeeded his father as earl of Mar in 1572. Along with older members of the Mar family, who were instructed to train the boy in manly sports, they often went riding and hunting. This rapidly became James's favourite form of exercise, but he also learned archery and was presented with many gifts of bows and arrows.

Despite their severe regime, Buchanan and Young somehow suc-

ceeded in implanting in their able pupil a lifelong passion for literature and learning. James grew up to speak fluent Greek, Latin and
French, the language of diplomacy. Latin came first; as he later
remarked, 'They gar [made] me speak Latin ere I could speak Scots.' [3]
Throughout his life James impressed visitors to his court by quoting
classical authors easily from memory. He also mastered an impressive amount of theology, another lifelong passion. James even came
to boast of being tutored by the distinguished scholar Buchanan,
though he never forgot his terror of him. The young king was also
force-fed with Buchanan's political views, which centred on a contractual theory of monarchy and a defence of the subject's right to
resist tyranny, even to the point of slaying a tyrant once he had been
denounced by Parliament. Dedicating his verse drama *Baptistes* to his
pupil, Buchanan explained that the book was a standing witness to
posterity that if James later listened to evil counsellors, or showed an
undue desire for power, the fault rested with the king himself and not
his tutors.

The violence with which Scottish politics was customarily conducted was even more fearful than the discipline of the schoolroom,
and the throne was repeatedly threatened. In the sensational session
of 1560, the Parliament changed the religion of Scotland in flagrant
defiance of the monarchy. This raised the profile of the Parliament,
but the dislocation of political life during the years 1567 and 1573 did
much to diminish it. In May 1571 the lords still loyal to the absent
Mary Queen of Scots met in the traditional place, the Edinburgh
Tolbooth, while those supporting James VI met in the Canongate. A
bombardment from the castle, held by Mary's troops, forced them to
take shelter; their 'creeping Parliament' became a byword and lasted
barely ten minutes. Six rival parliaments were held over the next ten
months, with tit-for-tat seizures of property and executions of supporters.[4]

Closer to home, James's first Regent, the earl of Moray, was assassinated in 1570, and only a year later the five-year-old saw the next
Regent, his grandfather the earl of Lennox, carried fatally wounded
into Stirling castle after a sudden raid by Mary's supporters. The
upheavals continued into his adolescence. James suffered nightmares
after a further terrifying incident early in 1578 when a political coup

restored to power a previous Regent, the earl of Morton. In the course of it, several of the defenders of Stirling castle were killed. Morton was in many ways a constructive Regent, working to keep law and order, especially on the Borders. A friend of John Knox, Morton was seen as a staunch protestant but the increasing hold of Presbyterianism on Scotland perturbed him with its potential to challenge royal power. Although the formal Reformation had been accomplished in 1560, many remnants of the old catholic system organised around bishops, dioceses and parishes still lingered in Scotland until Andrew Melville, the next leading reformer, returned from Geneva in 1574. The Scottish kirk's first *Book of Discipline* of December 1560 had appointed 'superintendants' to take over the functions of bishops, but little had been done. Melville began the establishment of a fully Presbyterian system run by ministers and elders (elected laymen of good standing), who together sat in the kirk-session meeting and supervised the parish. All ministers were regarded as equal, abolishing the traditional hierarchy of bishops and archbishops, and in 1578 the *Second Book of Discipline* called for the final end of episcopal power in Scotland. It also set up autonomous church courts.

These changes were likely to produce, as their adherents wanted, a kirk system separate from that of the state and beyond the control of the Crown. Even worse, in the disturbed circumstances of a lengthy royal minority, the General Assembly of the ministers of the kirk frequently tended to act as if it constituted the sovereign authority of the kingdom. In 1580 it even declared the office of bishop unscriptural. Morton weakened his own case considerably and exacerbated the hostility to bishops by appointing his venal and often corrupt relatives and clients to vacant dioceses, ignoring their unsuitability. However, in an episcopal church, bishops were the natural supporters of royal power, and in 1575 the diplomat Henry Killigrew noted that Morton intended 'conformity with England', suggesting an equivalent royal supremacy over the kirk.[5] Morton rightly saw Melville's advocacy of two mutually exclusive 'kingdoms', one spiritual and ruled by Christ, the other secular and ruled by the king, as a threat to order. He also realised that many laypeople and even clergy disagreed with the extremists' vision of a Scottish kirk modelled closely on Geneva. Bluntly, Morton told Melville that there would never be quiet in Scotland until half a dozen of the most turbulent ministers were either hanged or banished.

Morton made enemies by his own greedy rapacity, and was thought to despise the rest of the Scots nobility. Over the years, he did not bother to build up any relationship of trust or confidence with the young king. As a result, the Regent was very vulnerable to intrigue. Those around James searched for a newcomer to lead Morton's enemies and lighted upon the Frenchman, Esmé Stuart Sieur D'Aubigny, first cousin of James's father Lord Darnley. D'Aubigny was the prospective heir of James's childless great-uncle Lennox, and arguably if James died childless, he would have a claim to the throne itself. In 1579 he visited Scotland, and within a month James abandoned his schoolroom in Stirling castle. Buchanan's rule over his pupil was over, and so in due course was that of the Regent Morton. Severely deprived of family affection, and exposed constantly to the relentless woman-hating of Buchanan (which James absorbed and reiterated in his own early poetry), the teenage king became enamored of his newly discovered cousin. He showered the courtly and cultivated D'Aubigny with lands and offices, creating him first earl, then duke of Lennox. D'Aubigny reformed the court and the royal household on the French model, and also encouraged James in his love of poetry. By his own patronage, D'Aubigny created a circle of court poets, later (perhaps mistakenly) known as the 'Castalian band' and led by Alexander Montgomerie. It was to give the king both lasting pleasure and literary inspiration.[6] James grew up to be an active and committed author, proficient in the fields of political ideas and theology as well as poetry.

To the outspoken and rabidly anti-papist Calvinist clergy, the new duke of Lennox was both a threat to their own position and morally dubious, even though he converted to protestantism. They alleged that he 'went about to draw the King to carnal lust', an impression derived from James's public displays of physical affection in which he would clasp Lennox in his arms and kiss him.[7] In June 1581, having fallen foul of Lennox, Morton was executed on stale but well-founded charges of complicity in Darnley's death in 1567. The judicial murder enraged Queen Elizabeth who had found Morton a staunch ally to

England. Lennox continued to foster relations with the catholic party in France and even with Philip II of Spain. The youthful James went along with these intrigues, assuring Jesuits sent from Spain that he inclined to their side. He thereby gained a reputation for duplicity, particularly in English eyes. However, the Morton faction was re-forming under new leadership in opposition to the apparently all-powerful Lennox. In August 1582, while out hunting, James was lured into Ruthven Castle where he was effectively imprisoned by the protestant earls of Gowrie and Angus.

The kirk exulted at the downfall of the pro-French Lennox, who was forced to leave Scotland, and the Ruthven lords revived contacts with England. The brief political dominance of Esmé Stuart was over, but it seems probable that James's passionate adolescent crush on his elegant and kind-hearted cousin permanently stamped his burgeoning sexuality, just as the kirk suspected. The king poured out his distress in a a long poem, *Ane metaphoricall Invention of a Tragedie called Phoenix*, in which Lennox was transmuted into the 'phoenix rare', coloured with 'heavenly hewes'. Persecuted by harsh birds of prey, the tamed phoenix flew away to Arabia and was immolated on its own pyre. In him, the lonely James lamented, were all his 'kynde, kin and offspring'. He defiantly published the poem in his first book of verses in 1584, as soon as he was free to do so, with a cryptogram revealing that its true subject was 'Esme Stewart Duike' (of Lennox).[8]

Majority

James officially became responsible for the affairs of Scotland before his twelfth birthday in March 1578, during Morton's first brief loss of power. On the earl's return to government a few months later, he did not assume the title of Regent but sent James back to the school-room, demonstrating that he was still a king in title only. Similarly, the downfall of Lennox in 1582 revealed that James was powerless before a noble conspiracy. However, by then the king was 16 and his personal support for any noble faction or councillor was increasingly a political factor of importance. In June 1583 James secretly contacted his friends to help him escape from the hated Ruthven Raid earls, who humiliatingly kept him captive. In alliance with their enemy Captain James Stuart, later created earl of Arran, who had also been imprisoned by the Raiders, James embarked on a programme of enforcing royal authority.

The events of 1582–3 made an indelible mark on the king. He never forgot the General Assembly's accusation that Lennox intended to erect 'a new Paipdome', nor the ministers' rejoicing over his cousin's fall, which they followed by instituting proceedings against the remaining bishops in Scotland.[9] Thereafter, James seems always to have regarded the kirk as the chief threat to strong royal rule. Once freed, he and Arran struck back. Ironically, they were following the earlier policies of the executed Morton and more specifically of his unpopular appointee, Archbishop Patrick Adamson of St Andrews who in 1584 had just returned from England. They began by summoning Morton's old Presbyterian bugbear Andrew Melville before the Privy Council. Melville had preached a sermon comparing the young king to his ancestor James III, whose deplorable favourites were depicted as the cause of his downfall. Melville stood his ground, denying that a secular court had any jurisdiction over sermons; in his view the royal councillors could do no more than complain to the General Assembly. The 'two kingdoms' stance infuriated James, and Melville only escaped imprisonment by fleeing to England.

The confrontation was followed by the parliamentary legislation of 1584, the Black Acts – so named by the kirk – which asserted royal authority over 'all estates as well temporal as spiritual'. It was made treason to deny that the king could sit in judgment on any of his subjects. No one was to assemble the king's subjects without permission (a clause aimed at frequent informal meetings of presbyteries), although kirk synods and twice-yearly presbyteries were approved. Presentations to benefices were to be made by bishops, who were also empowered to decide whether to deprive unworthy ministers. All ministers, readers (lesser curates) and masters of schools were to promise in writing to confirm their submission to the king's majesty and to bishops or other officials appointed by him. The Black Acts made a firm statement of policy, whereby the kirk would become subordinate to royal power. They insisted on the king's control over all his subjects including ministers. The programme bore the stamp of Archbishop Adamson, an admirer of the

English church settlement and influential in drafting the new legislation. Since 1572, bishops had taken an oath that the king was the 'only
lauchfull and supreme governour' in both temporal and religious
matters, a clear echo of Elizabethan usage.[10] In fact, the Black Acts
brought James very near to the limited English royal supremacy as it
existed in 1515 under Henry VIII, with control over the secular functions of the church. The king seems to have kept a similar goal in
mind for Scotland for the next 37 years, although he did not pursue
the policy consistently. For support, he could appeal over the heads
of the extreme Melvillians to many ordinary ministers, who were
prepared to show greater flexibility over government and discipline.
In return they demanded that the king must continue to support true
doctrine and freedom from popery, though there were to be occasions when James forgot the importance of the latter proviso in
retaining their confidence. Similarly, the king won over moderate lay
people, who were averse to the kirk's austere social policies which
included ending traditional festive pastimes, enforcing strict sab-
batarian regulation, and obsessively regulating sexual conduct.

The Black Acts also indicated that the Scottish aristocracy could
expect increasing royal control, as could most of the large burghs
(towns) where the Crown appointed provosts (the equivalent of mayors). It was apparent that James was fast emerging from adolescence
to take control of his monarchy. The king's hand was unmistakeable
in the arrest and execution of Gowrie, who had insulted the royal
sovereignty by the Ruthven Raid. His influence could clearly be seen
when the Parliament called in two of Buchanan's controversial
books, *De Juri Regni apud Scotos* (1579) with its argument that there was
a Scottish ancient constitution that permitted the people to depose
unsatisfactory kings, and *Rerum Scoticarum Historia* (1582) that black-
ened the reputation of monarchs and particularly of the king's mother Mary.[11] James felt confident enough to reveal how profoundly he
disagreed with his domineering old tutor on the key issue of the position and powers of the Crown. Buchanan had succeeded only in
angering his young charge, not brainwashing him.

Ever since 1567, the king had been an object of scrutiny to the
ambassadors of foreign powers, but by 1584 his personality and viewpoint were becoming internationally significant. His mother, who

had not seen him since babyhood, was currently intriguing to promote a scheme known as the Association, whereby she would be
released from captivity in England and return to Scotland, associated
in a dual monarchy with her son. One of the most detailed reports on
James was written just at this time in August 1584, its author the
French agent Fontenay reporting back to Mary's secretary. Fontenay
described James as timid from being brought up in fear, but also
intellectually able. He grasped and understood quickly. He judged
carefully and with sensible discourses, he retained much and for a
considerable time. He was learned in many languages, sciences and
affairs of state, not only those of his own realm. In appearance James
was unimpressive, and as a result of lacking good instruction, very
rude and uncivil in speaking, eating, manners, games and entertainment in the company of women. He hated music and dancing but
was restless, never standing in one place and taking particular pleasure in moving around. His carriage was bad, with erratic and
vagabond steps. Grave in speech, he was 'un vieulx jeune homme',
old in a young man's body, but on the other hand he was lazy, too
devoted to his pleasures, especially hunting which he loved above all.
At such times he left his affairs to be managed by his councillors, particularly the newly created earl of Arran and the secretary John
Maitland of Thirlestane. This was excusable at his age, Fontenay
thought, but if the habit became engrained he would end up like his
Merovingian forebears leaving everything to the mayors of the
palace.

Yet James was also full of self-confidence, insisting privately to
Fontenay that no affair of any importance happened which he did
not know about, and that he had spies who watched the court, morning and evening. Despite his constant hunting, he asserted that he
could do as much business in one hour as others in a day, because
simultaneously he listened and spoke, watched and acted, sometimes
doing five things at once. He needed his recreation for health not just
pleasure, for if he attended to his affairs for six or seven days without
a break, immediately afterwards he always fell ill. James was acute in
his analysis of the Scottish political situation, explaining to Fontenay
that the power of the great lords had increased because for 40 years
or more they had had only women and little children to govern them,

or traitorous and avaricious regents. During the divisions and troubles of his minority, the nobility had become so audacious that it was
not possible to subdue and reduce them immediately to their duty;
but James promised that little by little he would have them in good
order. Describing his powerful ministers, particularly Arran, he
boasted that he could always ruin them as easily as he had made
them.

Unconvinced, Fontenay commented on James's ignorance and
lack of knowledge, of his little strength, promising too much of himself and despising other princes. He warned Mary not to send her son
any money since he was extravagant and lived only by borrowing. He
also noted that James was emotional and loved indiscreetly and
opiniatedly, taking no account of his subjects' reactions.[12]
Nevertheless, the downfall of Arran in 1585 gave more credibility to
James's assertions of control as well as marking the beginning of his
personal rule, for no other nobleman replaced Arran. The pragma-
tism of 'little by little' was coming to characterise his style of governance. At the same time, the curious combination of ability and
complacency, idleness and shrewd judgement, warm emotions and
lack of discretion so well described by Fontenay remained typical of
James throughout his life.

In the years between 1584 and 1603, the king worked hard to re-
establish royal control in Scotland. He was aided by a profound
social change already under way, whereby educated laymen drawn
from the laird (landowning gentry) and burgess (townsmen) classes
took over the predominant role in government and administration.
The lawyers, above all, created a new milieu of professionalism and
definition. James's secretary, the immensely capable Maitland of
Thirlestane who was promoted to chancellor in 1587, epitomised the
trend. Steadily, he built up an effective bureaucracy from the ranks of
the lairds (his own class), the urban lawyers and the junior members
of great houses loyal to the Crown. The lairds and the townsmen
tended to be strongly protestant, as was Maitland himself. Allying
with them, he strove to bring increasing royal control and domestic
peace to Scotland, and to end the violent gangsterism, private wars
and organised raiding, particularly on the Borders, that still infested
Scottish society. Maitland was in power for nine constructive years

until he was driven from court in 1592, and his work in making royal rule effective was a major contribution to James's ultimate success. Not surprisingly, the widening of the circle that served central government accelerated the degree of jockeying for patronage and position among the lairds, but their ambition was increasingly to find a place in royal service rather than to live on their lands. The same was not true of the nobility, who mostly regarded Maitland as an enemy and retained their power-bases in the regions.

The Succession to England

As the decades went by and Elizabeth remained unmarried, James steadily emerged as her most likely successor. After the collapse in February 1582 of the negotiations for the Anjou match, the queen's last flirtation with matrimony, it was widely assumed that James was effectively her heir, just as his mother Mary Queen of Scots had hoped at his birth. Unlike Henry VIII who in 1544 revived Edward I's claim to suzerainty over Scotland, Elizabeth never advanced any similar theory of dominance since she was well aware of its offensiveness to Scots. Nevertheless, James was sharply conscious of previous English pretensions, and in 1583 during a long and heated interview, he reminded the English secretary of state Sir Francis Walsingham that he was 'an absolute king', meaning that he owed allegiance to no other monarch.[13]

From 1560 onwards an Anglophile faction grew up at the Scottish court. Initially, its leaders looked south for support from their fellow protestants in England against the catholic Queen Mary. However, just as James began to reassert royal influence at home, he was faced with acute problems in foreign policy which affected Scotland's relationship with England. In 1584 William the Silent, Prince of Orange and leader of the rebellion against oppressive Spanish rule in the low countries, was murdered at Delft. The assassin was a fanatic seeking the prize money that Philip II had placed on Orange's head. In 1585 Elizabeth reluctantly concluded a formal alliance with the Dutch rebels, thereby making a Spanish attack on England virtually inevitable. It would be essential to secure Scotland, so often described as England's postern gate, against any Spanish blandishments.

After two years of manoeuvres by Elizabeth's diplomats sent north to assess James and his kingdom, a treaty was signed in 1586 between England and Scotland. It established a defensive alliance and provided for mutual assistance in the event of invasion. The treaty was reinforced by a letter from Elizabeth agreeing that while James continued friendly to England, she would support him with an annual pension, later around £3000 sterling. She also promised not to undercut any right or title that might be due to James, then or in the future. The pension was valuable in view of the king's chronic financial difficulties, and he constantly strove to get the queen to increase it. Her letter, with its oblique comments about James's rights and titles, became more important as the years wore on since it discreetly alluded to his claim to her throne. Significantly, James had the letter formally registered by the Scottish Privy Council in 1596.

When the Anglo-Scottish treaty was made, Mary Queen of Scots was still alive. Then, in February 1587 after years of imprisonment in England, Mary was executed at Fotheringhay Castle in Northamptonshire for her complicity in the Babington plot to murder Elizabeth. James wrote to protest against the English trial of a Scottish monarch, forcefully describing it as 'the late preposterous and strange procedure'. He shrewdly urged Elizabeth not to set the monstrous example of one crowned head putting another to death. Sovereign princes should not be 'the example-givers of their own sacred diadems' profaning', a view he knew she personally shared.[14] There was a surge of Scottish nationalist feeling against English presumption in executing their former queen, and on hearing of Mary's death, James broke off diplomatic relations. Initially, he even refused to receive the ambassador sent from London to explain the circumstances. However, there are indications that privately the king felt relief. Mary's continued survival in English hands inevitably weakened the security of his own position. Scotland 'could never have bene without factions if she had beene left alive', he wrote.[15]

As regards the English throne, Elizabeth refused to go beyond her letter of 1586, and to James's intense annoyance never proclaimed him officially as her heir. She also dribbled out the pension, varying its amount and frequency from year to year in a way that skilfully underlined the king's reliance on her continued goodwill.[16] But it was clear that after 1586–7, England had replaced France as Scotland's key ally. The 'auld alliance' was dead, an outcome that reassured Scottish protestants. Moreover, by not taking any further hostile action on Mary's death in 1587, James reinforced his status as Elizabeth's nearest relative, 'Madame and dearest sister' as he addressed her in their renewed correspondence. In August 1588, at the height of the Armada crisis, he wrote assuring her of his support, 'as your natural son and compatriot of your country'.[17] These broad hints showed James's confidence that, as a committed protestant, he was acceptable to English opinion in a way that the catholic Mary had never been. His future prospects as Elizabeth's heir added considerable lustre to his position as the monarch of a poor and relatively marginal European power.

The years between 1587 and 1589 made an immense impact on James, and just as he had written *The Phoenix* to express his feelings about Esmé D'Aubigny, he turned again to discourse to help himself cope with stress. As J. H. Burns has emphasised, with the gathering of the Spanish Armada the European scene became essentially an apocalyptic one. The young king used the language of scriptural prophecy, denunciation and exhortation, writing an elaborate paraphrase of the biblical Book of Revelation. He continued in 1588 with *Ane Fruitfull Meditatioun* on the text, which speaks of the final overthrow of Satan. In 1589 he composed another *Meditatioun*, this time on the Old Testament book Chronicles I, in which he assumed the unity of 'the Ile' of Britain against the enemy. He also attributed to 'our virtewe' the divine support that led to the scattering of the Armada by God's 'michtie wind'. By associating Scottish godliness with the English naval campaign to prevent the Armada from landing, James was able to present the events of 1588 as a victory for 'Britain' and a defeat for the pretensions of the papacy rather than for Philip II.[18]

Marriage and the Scottish Succession

A suitable marriage alliance would also reinforce the king's international standing. Throughout his youth, James showed little inclination for women and was praised for his chastity, unlike his royal ancestors who frequently sired bastards. After the departure of

D'Aubigny, James continued to prefer male company and in 1589 it was rumoured that he was 'too much carried by young men that lie in his chamber and are his minions'. Yet a royal match was esssential to preserve the Stuart line, and in the same year after hesitating over a French protestant candidate supported by Queen Elizabeth, James married Anne of Denmark. Scotland and Denmark conducted a profitable trade and the country was acceptably reformed in religion, although Lutheran rather than Calvinist. After the princess's first efforts to cross the North Sea were thwarted by storms, James gallantly travelled to Denmark in October 1589 to collect his bride. They returned in April 1590, after a winter's entertainment which included a speech by James to the theology faculty of Copenhagen University and a visit to the great astronomer Tycho Brahe. The king was inspired to write poems both to his young wife whose 'enchanting fame' transported him over 'the stormie seas', and to Brahe whose researches revealed how God 'pitch'd eache Planet in his place'.[19]

Anne was anointed and crowned in May 1590 in the abbey church at Holyrood. Her relationship with James tended to alternate between affection and estrangement, but so did many of the arranged marriages of the sixteenth and seventeenth centuries. Between 1593 and 1595 the king was romantically linked with at least one young woman, Anne Murray later Lady Glamis, to whom he wrote a lengthy poem addressing her as 'my mistress and my love'.[20] The queen herself was occasionally the subject of scandalous rumours, but more significant in the royal marriage was the king's action in 1594 when he deprived Anne of the maternal care of their first-born son. At barely six months old, Prince Henry was taken to Stirling Castle and left in the care of the earl and countess of Mar. James regarded the Erskine family as hereditary custodians of the royal heir and recalled his own childhood there. Placing the baby in a loyal noble household safely away from court faction was a Scottish tradition, but it was utterly different from the close family upbringing Anne had enjoyed in Denmark. Her anger and distress at the removal of her first child were never entirely assuaged, and in 1600–1 she was even suspected of plotting against the king's life.

The queen also gradually became estranged from her husband on religious issues, converting from her native Lutheranism to a discreet, but still politically embarrassing catholicism which alienated many ministers of the kirk. However, these marital tensions did not prevent Anne from giving birth between 1594 and 1607 to seven children, of whom three survived into adulthood. She also suffered three miscarriages. Together the royal couple amply fulfilled their duty of providing enough children for a settled succession. James himself was the first adult male monarch of Scotland since the death of James V in 1542, so the birth of Prince Henry was greeted with an outpouring of rejoicing. In 1600 when his younger brother Charles was born, Scotland gained a further promise of dynastic stability.

Queen Anne was also a political and diplomatic asset. Despite frequent friction with James both in Scotland and later in England, she often behaved with graciousness and charm as befitted her birth and royal breeding. Extravagance was her greatest fault, although it must be remembered that she brought a substantial dowry that was not exhausted for some years. The king prided himself that her lineage brought honour to Scotland, for, uniquely in Europe, his queen was the daughter, sister and wife of kings. James was made a knight of the Order of the Garter before his accession to England, but in 1603 to show respect to Anne, the chapter of England's oldest and grandest order of chivalry promptly elected her brother Christian IV of Denmark and her son Henry to its membership.

The royal relationship mellowed over time. The couple showed some fondness for one another and much affection towards their three surviving children (a daughter Elizabeth was born in 1596, between Henry and Charles). In 1603 on his way to England, James ended a letter to Anne, 'Praying God, my heart, to preserve you and all the bairns, and to send me a blithe meeting with you and a couple of them.'[21] The family warmth of his greeting is unmistakeable.

Witchcraft

The king's visit to Denmark in 1589–90 had one unexpected and ultimately tragic consequence. Witchcraft prosecutions before the Reformation in Scotland were extremely rare, but in the years between 1560 and 1706, particularly between 1590 and 1662, between 1000 and 1500 people perished, mostly women. This was a far higher percentage of Scotland's population of under one million than the equivalent persecutions in England. Witchcraft was included in 1563 among the business of the pre-Reformation courts, now to be subsumed under either the jurisdiction of the state or that of the new Presbyterian kirk. The state took it over, but the interest of the kirk in the matter rose steadily. Seeing witchcraft as a disease of the body politic comparable to drunkenness or adultery, it repeatedly badgered the secular power to take action. James took little notice until a group of witches at North Berwick, with whom his enemy the earl of Bothwell was closely associated, claimed in 1591 to have raised storms in an attempt to destroy the king on his Danish voyage. The North Berwick trials launched a period of persecutions with two peaks in 1590–1 and 1597. James himself played a central role and at least 70 and perhaps more than 100 witches were tortured, tried and executed.

Denmark was a country already familiar with witchhunts, since Lutheran reformers all too often adopted the expedient of labelling their conservative opponents as witches. Danish churchmen were also familiar with the developed demonology of the continent, which considered the core of withcraft practice to be the demonic pact – the personal arrangement between the devil and each witch. It seems highly likely that on his Danish visit James became familiar with ideas about witchcraft, which then formed the crucial background in triggering the Scottish persecution. Social historians have suggested that the period between the mid-sixteenth century to the 1660s was particularly dangerous for women, as male society became obsessed by the fear of disorder. Women were increasingly seen as unruly and resentful of their proper subordination to men. This fear of females was closely linked to the steady deterioration in the economic conditions suffered by the poor, from amongst whom most of the women victims emerged. All over Europe, economic instability and increasing poverty were major ingredients of witchcraft persecutions.

In 1597 James wrote the *Daemonologie*, a tract in dialogue form attacking the scepticism about witchcraft displayed by the English writer Reginald Scot and the German Johann Weyer. As the witches had threatened the royal couple, the treatise was an expression of James's belief in divine right monarchy, and it was linked to another

of his intellectual interests since he considered the study of witchcraft
to be a branch of theology. The tract is pervaded by an intense belief
in the reality of the devil and the royal publication gave further sanc-
tion to the prosecution of witches in Scotland, which continued well
into the eighteenth century.

James concluded that the likely end of the world drew near, causing Satan 'to rage the more in his instruments'.[22] He was not alone in
this apocalyptic belief: in a book published in 1593, the great mathematician John Napier of Murchiston also argued for the imminent
end of the world. However, it seems that although in 1597 the king
was still theoretically convinced of the existence of witches, he was
losing his enthusiasm for persecution and he revoked the standing
commissions on witchcraft authorised in 1591. The *Daemonologie*
warned the magistrate of his duty to protect the innocent as well as
punish the guilty. Sometime after 1599, James wrote to Prince Henry
to congratulate him on 'the discovery of yon little counterfeit wench.
I pray God ye may be my heir in such discoveries.'[23] A degree of disbelief was already creeping in which would increase after 1603.

The King and the kirk

James still had much to do in Scotland itself. The smack of firm government promised in 1584 was for several years more a hopeful statement of policy than an actuality. In 1585 James was persuaded into
making a conciliatory gesture, denying any intention of placing himself at the head of the kirk, but defending bishops as sanctioned both
in the Bible and in the early Christian church. In the General
Assembly of 1586, a compromise was reached, allowing a diminished
form of episcopacy whereby men were honoured by the Crown with
the title of bishop but also acted as ordinary ministers. However, in
the following year their status was diminished when a parliamentary
act of annexation allocated the secular revenues of ecclesiastical
benefices, principally those of episcopal and monastic properties, to
the Crown in support of its rising costs. The burgeoning adminstra-
tion created by Maitland needed patronage and pensions to nourish
it, but any longer term aims of strengthening episcopacy were dealt a
serious blow.

At the same time presbyteries continued to be set up, synods and General Assemblies met regularly and were given jurisdiction over all ecclesiastical causes. In the Parliament of 1592, James in addition consented to what was later known as the Golden Act (again from the kirk's point of view) annulling most of the Black Acts of 1584 and confirming all the kirk's liberties, privileges, immunities and freedoms. Chancellor Maitland pressed the king to show greater acceptance of the kirk and in many ways the act acknowledged a *fait accompli*. The regular meetings of kirk sessions led by ministers and elders were increasingly effective in controlling the lives of their parishioners, and were becoming a bulwark of orderly society. By 1593 presbyteries covered all Scotland except the Hebrides and the western mainland. In 1579 the kirk had also been given its first significant statutory responsibilities in the enforcement of the emerging system of poor relief, made necessary by a steadily rising population checked only by recurrent famines. Much of the kirk's poor relief was paid for by the fines levied for fornication and adultery, so both the state and the community at large benefited from the strictness of its often-criticised severity over sexual standards. By 1592 James could not deny that Presbyterianism was deeply entrenched in Scotland. He set out to use it as an instrument of his own royal polity rather than oppose it.

By contrast, episcopacy seemed to be dying. The king did not succeed in appointing any new bishops between 1585 and 1600, and when Archbishop Adamson, that invaluable royal ally, died in 1592, he was not replaced at St Andrews. Yet from 1586 on, James continued to make stealthy moves to increase his control over the sessions of the General Assembly. In 1586 he obtained a brief adjournment for his own convenience; in 1588 he called for a special meeting; and in 1591 he politely asked that an Assembly might be moved to Edinburgh to make it easier for him to attend. There was some unease at this infringement of kirk autonomy, but pleasure at the king's personal interest, always one of his most effective strategies, outweighed it. James also mollified the General Assembly of 1590 by describing them as 'the sincerest kirk in the world', far superior to the still half-popish English church.[24] The Golden Act of 1592 provided further reassurance to the kirk, although the legislation was more

Erastian than appeared at first sight. It did not annul the first of the Black Acts setting out the royal supremacy, and it also specifically reserved to the Crown the right to name the time and meeting place of General Assemblies, ending the kirk's previous freedom to summon.

In 1596, at a time of great political tension and popular fear of resurgent catholicism at home and abroad (see p. 35), trouble broke out again, and an interim commission met at Cupar, claiming to be appointed by 'the Generall Assemblie to sie to the dangers of the kirk at all occasiones'. Delegates, led by Andrew Melville, were sent to demand action against the turbulent catholic nobles, but the king reacted angrily, complaining that they had assembled without his permission. Melville then famously told James that he was but 'god's sillie [weak] vassall' and that in Scotland 'thair is twa Kings and twa Kingdomes'. In the kingdom of Christ and the kirk, James was 'nocht a king, nor a lord, nor a heid, bot a member'.[25] Such extreme two-kingdom language had not been heard for more than a decade, and the situation was further inflamed by the trial of David Black, minister of St Andrews, who delivered an inflammatory sermon attacking James, his queen and Queen Elizabeth. He concluded that 'all Kingis wer the devillis childrene'. Later, in *Basilicon Doron*, James reminisced about the attacks he had endured from those Presbyterians 'because I was a King, which they thought the highest evill'.[26]

A near-riot in Edinburgh was calmed by the intervention of the provost, but next morning James and the court left the capital in protest and the central lawcourts were ordered to Linlithgow. Edinburgh was a far smaller place than London and its dominance over the realm was much less entrenched; its merchants and traders could not afford to alienate the king in this way. The town council made an abject apology which was only accepted by James when accompanied by a substantial sum of money. The king also called an extraordinary General Assembly to meet him in Perth, to underscore both his sole right of summons and, by implication, the privileges he could bestow on towns other than Edinburgh.

However, the tumults of 1596 seem to have convinced both the king and the mainstream membership of the kirk that a working consensus must be rebuilt. Thereafter, James paid the expenses of

moderate ministers to ensure that they attended meetings of the
General Assembly, while after 1600 the pattern of delegation was
altered to ensure a more representative gathering. The extremists
were isolated, since the kirk had no real constituency among its godly
supporters for political turmoil which disturbed the reign of an
assuredly protestant monarch. Nor was there much support for
those ministers who aimed at an unpopular theocracy. However
much they might dislike some of the king's policies, the ministers
had to live with the reality of royal authority and there were no more
attempts at illicit General Assemblies. From the late 1590s, the Privy
Council also interfered increasingly with the kirk's power of excommunication, which on occasion could embarrass the king's leading
courtiers and their families. The compliance of the kirk in these measures was linked to its serious manpower problems, for the first generation of protestant parish clergy was passing away. In some areas
there were more vacancies than there had been in the difficult years
immediately following the Reformation. At the same time, soaring
monetary inflation and rising food prices were impoverishing ministers and parish readers on small fixed salaries. To the majority of clergy facing these problems, cooperation with the Crown seemed more
constructive than confrontation. After the winter of 1596–7, a steady
change of attitude set in, from which both sides benefited.

It seems also to have been those dangerous few months that decided James that he must move more vigorously to revive episcopacy.
He had never been enthusiastic about the egalitarian organisation of
Presbyterianism, but at last he took effective action to reinvigorate
the office of bishop in the Scottish church. 'The king will have it that
the bishops must be', noted the English agent at Edinburgh.[27] It is
worth emphasising that James was not intent on simply copying the
English system. In 1598, arguing in the General Assembly held at
Dundee for the need for clerical representation in Parliament, the
king promised that he did not intend to bring in 'Papisticall or
Anglican' bishops.[28] Cleverly, he sweetened his policy by indicating
that it could be to the financial benefit of the kirk, which would
acquire extra revenues from the prelacies that had fallen earlier into
secular hands. He spent time throughout 1599 in lengthy conferences
intended to build consensus. Renewed harmony gradually emerged,

which paved the way in 1600 for the king's creation of three bishops. The move was linked to both the undermining of the Presbyterian insistence on the equality of ministers, and also to the royal desire for the presence in Parliament of bishops as representatives of the most moderate wing of the kirk. By July 1606 at the Parliament held at Perth, every diocese had a bishop for the first time since 1586.

Scottish bishops were appointed by the Crown, but they were drawn from the General Assembly and still remained answerable to it. In their dioceses they worked with the local courts, synods and presbyteries. The revived Scottish episcopate which James worked hard to establish was a far cry from the English model, and showed no sign of the increasing tendency of some English bishops and theologians to claim that episcopacy was *jure divino*, that is, originally established by divine right. The king's bishops were to prove themselves good stewards, vigorous in their efforts to improve the quality of the kirk's ministry.

Scottish Politics, 1585–1603

Noble faction remained a serious problem after 1585 although James received increasing cooperation from many members of his aristocracy. The king was deeply conservative in his social outlook and strongly encouraged the presence of noblemen at his court, on the Privy Council and in Parliament. Nobles had privileged access to the king and the right to give him counsel. James was well aware of their turbulence, but as he later wrote to his son, 'virtue followeth oftest noble blood'.[29] It was advantageous to involve magnates in central government, since it strengthened the Crown's link with the localities which noblemen largely controlled. Instead of confronting them, the king followed the traditional royal policy of persuading his noblemen to identify with his rule. In the important act of 1598 against feuding, James preferred to leave much of the older system of kin conciliation in place, only taking cases of murder out of the hands of local lords. In contrast, his lawyer-administrators wanted to extend the formal rule of law into all areas. James also left virtually untouched the old feudal jurisdictions that added so much to noble powers in the localities. Feuding continued amidst the landed elite as a whole, not just the nobility, until well into the early seventeenth century, but from the 1590s onward curtailment of the practice was as much the product of increasing consent, the internalisation of obedience, as of royal repression. The strength (and the social values) of central government slowly made themselves felt and it can be argued that the king's 'little by little' policies were once again the most realistic way forward.

James was careful not to alienate nobles unneccessarily, and personally devoted time and effort to reconciling major disputes. In 1595 he involved himself at length in the problematic succession to the earldom of Atholl, and around 1603 he devoted much time to reconciling the worst of all aristocratic feuds, that between the earls of Huntly, Argyll and Moray, by creating a network of family intermarriages. The king also used the gift of pensions and other forms of patronage to cement the bonds of loyalty between the Crown and leading noblemen. The 1590s were an exceptionally difficult decade economically, and James genuinely desired to prevent Scots noble houses from falling into ruin, although his generosity exacerbated his own financial difficulties (see pp. 40–1).

The problem of unruly nobles was made more complex as a result of James's pursuit of allies in his quest to succeed Queen Elizabeth. He was convinced that the central difficulty would lie in reconciling both the English catholics and also the catholic powers abroad, especially Spain, to his accession. Known across Europe as a protestant monarch, he was nevertheless anxious to avoid the papal excommunication which had made Elizabeth so vulnerable to catholic assassination attempts. James was still insecure and inclined to look for help outside England, since even at the peak of the Armada crisis the queen had not confirmed him as her heir, and she later rescinded promises of increasing his pension. In consequence and despite her annoyance, James maintained contact with the catholic states of Europe, even dangling before them the prospects of future pro-catholic policies once he ascended the English throne. He strengthened his ties with Henri IV of France (after 1594 a convert to catholicism) and built contacts with lesser catholic powers such as Tuscany. Making no specific promises, James was successful throughout the 1580s and 1590s in presenting himself as friendly and well disposed towards the European catholic world, and even to the papacy itself. As a result, although Pope Clement VIII did not endorse his claim to England, he equally did not denounce it.

At home James pursued a policy of friendship towards his catholic aristocrats, above all the anti-English earl of Huntly, the richest and most powerful catholic landowner in Scotland. His grandfather, known as 'the king of the north' was a supporter of Mary Queen of Scots, always a significant factor with James who cherished his mother's old friends. Huntly was a handsome man with elegant French manners, who was married in 1588 to Henriette Stuart, the daughter of James's dear cousin Esmé D'Aubigny duke of Lennox. Henriette was a devout catholic with royal blood whom the king held in personal esteem, and she was a close friend of Queen Anne. Her brother Ludovic was brought to Edinburgh to be invested with his late father's dukedom, becoming the premier nobleman in Scotland and a lifelong friend of the king. The Huntly-Lennox wedding ate up over 5 per cent of the royal household's annual expenditures, a sign that James regarded them as part of his wider family. He called Huntly his 'good sonne' and even signed some of his letters 'your Dad, James R', as he was to do in later letters to Buckingham.[30] In short, Huntly was a favourite.

Like most of the nobility, Huntly had little love for Chancellor Maitland who occupied an office previously reserved for members of the nobility. In 1587 Huntly and the protestant earl of Bothwell (nephew of Mary Queen of Scots' third husband) called unsuccessfully for Maitland's dismissal. At the height of the international crisis of 1588, James appointed Huntly as the captain of the royal guard, only to learn in 1589 that Huntly and the catholic earls of Errol and Angus were in treasonous correspondence with Spain. James removed Huntly from his office and marched north against him when he and the others rebelled. Huntly's forces melted away, but James refused to take any further action beyond putting Huntly and his associate Bothwell (who joined the rebellion out of hatred of Maitland) briefly in prison.

In February 1592 Huntly again outraged opinion by killing the protestant and popular earl of Moray in a raid. The feud between the two families was longstanding and James chose to treat the incident as another episode of clan warfare. However, his attempt to ignore the murder increased the unease of both the kirk and the English government, concerned by James's easy-going attitude towards pro-Spanish catholics. In December more evidence of Huntly's treasonable conspiracies with Spain came to light. The 'Spanish blanks' were sheets of paper signed by Huntly and other catholic peers inviting Philip II to set out his terms for another invasion. James still took no firm stand. The kirk and the English government then threw their support behind the factious but protestant earl of Bothwell.

Bothwell had been well received at court in the 1580s, but James conceived an obsessive hatred of him in 1591 when he was accused in the North Berwick affair of using witchcraft to conjure up storms to drown the king. Twice, in December 1591 in Edinburgh and again in 1592 at Falkirk, Bothwell tried to seize James in a misguided attempt to gain access to the royal presence and return to favour. On both occasions, the king was saved by the support of the local people who flocked to assist him. The conviction that Bothwell was his greatest enemy blinded James to the dangers posed by the charming but unreliable Huntly. In February 1593 the king again marched north against the catholic nobles, but again the outcome was indecisive. Queen Elizabeth continued to support Bothwell and in July 1593, the earl forced his way into the privy chamber of the palace at Holyrood and dramatically proffered his sword in token of submission. James controlled his instinctive panic sufficiently to dictate his terms for accepting Bothwell back to favour, but realised that he must recall Chancellor Maitland who had left court in 1592.

Thereafter, the king and Maitland began to regain control of the situation, pressing for Bothwell's exile and also taking seriously the threat posed by Huntly. By appearing to condone treasonable dealings with Spain, James risked losing the support not merely of his own protestant subjects and the anti-Huntly nobles, but also of Elizabeth. A similar combination of forces had brought ruin to his mother. In 1594 James again marched north, this time accompanied by Andrew Melville to demonstrate the royal rapprochement with the kirk. In an extraordinary misjudgment Bothwell joined Huntly in rebellion, but was excommunicated by the kirk and lost his popular support. Outright rebellion was an unambiguous form of violence far easier for James to handle than clan feuding. By March 1595 the northern catholic earls had surrendered and were allowed to go into exile. In April Bothwell joined them; he ended his days years later in Naples, where he was 'famous for suspected negromancie'.[31]

This seemed to mark the end of the years of noble faction, particularly as another invasion scare was whipping up anti-Spanish feeling. However, in July 1596 Huntly returned secretly from exile and again James did nothing. The anxieties of the kirk began to mount and the crisis of 1596, in which the king confronted strong Presbyterian hostility in Edinburgh and elsewhere, was shot through with accusations that he was punishing the ministers of God's word while showing favour to treacherous catholics. Finally, Huntly agreed to accept a token conversion to protestantism in 1597. His estates, currently in the hands of his brother-in-law Lennox, were returned. In December 1597 he and the two other catholic earls were reinstated with impressive ceremony at the end of the Parliament, when Huntly carried the sceptre in front of the king.[32]

Huntly enjoyed enduring royal favour despite his repeated proven treachery. The conciliatory approach preferred by James can be defended as pragmatic and in line with his policy proclaimed in 1583 that he would 'draw his nobility to unity and concord . . . as a universal king impartial to them all'.[33] The king was worried that he could easily create another endless quarrel by over-harsh punishments, and by the later 1590s the kirk was already leading a fairly thorough campaign to curb bloodfeuds and related violence. Moreover, Huntly was very powerful and friendship with him facilitated royal control over the Highlands. James perhaps also hoped that Huntly's links with Spain might be useful in lessening the hostility of Philip II to his claim to succeed Elizabeth. In Armada year, Philip planned to place his daughter the Infanta Isabella on the English throne once his forces succeeded in deposing the queen. He told Sixtus V that James as a heretic could not inherit the succession rights of Mary Queen of Scots, while Isabella, through her mother, was a descendant of John of Gaunt. In 1594 the publication of the Jesuit Robert Persons's book *A conference about the next succession to the Crowne of Ingland* repeated Isabella's claim, dismissing that of James. Could Huntly help to persuade Spain otherwise?

Nevertheless, the hope was no more than a straw to set in the scales against Huntly's repeated treachery, particularly as he had access to Spanish funds in his defiance of royal authority. The saga demonstrates one of James's major weaknesses of judgment. Personal affection together with an innate respect for magnate blood and status led the king to overlook outrageous conduct. He thereby united dangerously powerful strands of public opinion against him. The straighforward view of the English envoy in 1589 that James had 'a strange, extraordinary affection to Huntly' seems as persuasive as any other analysis.[34]

The Scottish Parliament

As James emerged from his minority, the Scottish Parliament was a small unicameral body (all sitting in one chamber), drawn from the three estates (landowners, bishops and burgesses) with fewer than 100 members. Sessions were short, no more than a few days, often badly attended and relatively unimpressive. James made efforts in 1587 to emphasise the dignity of Parliaments and even designed suitably formal apparel for members, but the full robing for the ceremonial opening and closing was not revived until 1605, after James had seen the more elaborate English parliamentary ceremony. Conventions of estates, informal bodies that met without the 40-day summons required for a Parliament, could also levy taxation and legislate, though it was increasingly accepted that their decisions ought to be ratified by a Parliament. Between 1588 and 1603, James called fairly regular Parliaments (five) and very frequent conventions (49). After 1585 there was a marked increase in the number of statutes passed, and as factionalism declined, attendance slowly increased. James urged his nobles to attend Parliaments and set a regular example himself. In 1587 an earlier act of 1428 was revived to ensure that two representatives drawn from the landed classes were elected from each shire. This increased the role of the lairds, Chancellor Maitland's preferred class, but the impetus seems to have come from the lairds themselves rather than the Crown. After 1581 James's government was regularly raising much more taxation than its predecessors and the demand for representation resulted, although the electorate was still tiny.

The king was particularly active in the 1580s and 1590s in his attempts to control parliamentary business. Scottish Parliaments began by electing a committee, 'the lords of the articles', which sifted legislation before presenting it to the full House. It thereby set the agenda, and up to the 1580s the committee was supposed by its geographical spread to reflect different parts of the country. This balance faded as James increased royal control by bringing in his officers of state and Privy Councillors as non-elected members of the articles committee. In 1587, 12 of the 30 lords were councillors, and in 1592, 17 out of a total of 31. Privy Councillors also played an important role in conventions, which were more open to management by the Crown. In 1588 all 16 of the non-burghal members of the convention were councillors, and in 1594, 23 of the 33 non-burghal members. James attended the committee of the lords of the articles, and often spoke. The king further ensured that unwelcome business was not put forward by making the procedure for accepting petitions slower and more regulated. After 1594, petitions had to be handed in to the clerk register within three days, and in future a committee was to meet 20 days before a Parliament to weed out any items deemed unsuitable or time-wasting. All petitions were to be signed and those that survived the vetting were printed in a book and put before the lords of the articles. By contrast, the king could raise matters at any time, giving him the invaluable power of the initiative which further reinforced his role as an active participant. Yet all these controls did not reduce the Scottish Parliament to a rubber stamp. James spent time and effort on management because he wished to ensure that Parliament worked effectively for him rather than being hijacked by any other group such as the kirk.

In addition to the lords and commoners (representatives of the burghs), the clergy in theory formed the third estate. However, since the Reformation they had been superseded by the commendators, laymen of noble families who had acquired ecclesiastical titles and estates. This reinforced the power of the nobility and left the kirk without any voice in Parliament, an absence which might well work to the disadvantage of both the kirk and the king if he wished to balance his aristocracy. In 1597, capitalising on his victory over the Edinburgh Presbyterians, James managed to get the General

Assembly to petition the Parliament for the clergy's restoration as one of the three estates. By 1621 the 11 bishops in the Parliament formed the most solid phalanx of royal supporters.

Parliamentary taxation became more regular after 1556, and beginning in 1581 there was a further large increase in both its frequency and burdensomeness. As a result of debasement (see pp. 39–40), the pound Scots was dropping sharply against the English pound, from 1 : 5.5 in 1567, to 1 : 7.33 in 1587 and 1 : 12 by 1600. In 1581 £40,000 Scots was demanded in Parliament; in contrast, the largest exaction of the Morton period had been £12,000 Scots. In 1588 the sum of £100,000 Scots that was asked for the king's forthcoming marriage was far larger than any previous vote of supply, and moved the level of taxation on to a new plane. So did the vote of £100,000 Scots in 1594 for the baptism of Prince Henry; James's own baptism in 1566 raised only £12,000. Conventions of estates remained easier to manage on matters of taxation than Parliaments, and the tax of 1597 was the first since the civil war to be granted by a Parliament rather than a convention. In 1599 when James again asked for money, the convention declined on the grounds that its numbers were too small and its session too brief. This forced the king to put his future requests for finance before either a Parliament or a convention of estates which approximated to a Parliament in composition and numbers. Subsequently, James faced increasing opposition to his demands for taxation, and resistance to royal interference was to grow after 1603.

The collection of tax monies was dependent on archaic methods of assessment which prevented the Crown from extracting too much of Scotland's real wealth. Vested interests ensured that collection was slow and painful since there were endless disputes over the liability to pay. However, from the mid-1580s a semi-permanent network of regional collectors and sub-collectors was constructed by Archibald Primrose, clerk of the taxations, a talented administrator still in Crown service in 1625. Unfortunately, in Scotland as in England, the 1590s were blighted by atrocious weather, with four disastrous harvests that raised food prices and brought severe hardship to the poor. Heavy taxation at such a time was bound to cause further economic dislocation. Despite this, James and his Privy Councillors successfully raised the royal tax income to new heights, and the fiscal intrusion of government into the localities was gradually if unwillingly accepted. At the same time the novel and widespread use of print to promote acts of Parliament, along with treatises on the nature of kingship and histories of Scotland, were slowly increasing the level of national political consciousness. The Scottish Parliament's place in that consciousness was still low, but it was rising.[35]

The rise in national taxation was the result of the chronic problem of royal expenditure, and opposition to taxation was hardly surprising. The heavy demands were unprecedented, while the king's personal extravagance and fiscal mismanagement did not suggest that the money would be well spent. A probably apocryphal story described a stratagem employed earlier by the royal schoolmaster Buchanan. Irritated by the young king's lack of restraint in signing grants, he presented a deed which James signed then realised too late that it did not simply give away money, but created his tutor monarch for a fortnight. His absurd prodigality was described by an English observer in 1588: 'He gives to everyone that asks, even to vain youths and proud fools the very lands of his crown or whatever falls, leaving himself nought to maintain his small, unkingly household.' A memorandum presented to the estates in 1587 pointed to the danger that the king might tax 'sa oft as he pleases upon collorit causes'.[36]

The king's government had long been in desperate financial straits. In 1572 the regency resorted to the heavy debasement of the silver content of a new coin, the half merk piece (worth 6s 8d Scots) with the young king's head on it. Under Morton (1572–80) there was a decisive upswing in trade, bringing new prosperity to merchants and landowners, but at the same time severe inflation was fuelled by further deliberate depreciations. The profits made by the government between 1583 and 1596 were worth at least £100,000 Scots, as the Mint accustomed itself to acting as part of the revenue-raising machinery. The calling in of old money or foreign coins and their replacement by new coin was profitable to the government, but inflationary and unpopular with everyone else, particularly as James's inability to act responsibly in financial matters was resented. However, the recoining enabled the king to uphold the high standard of design enjoyed by the Scottish coinage, which utilised the style and idiom of Renaissance Europe far more than the English coinage.

James also used his coins to communicate his political stance. The famous motto *Nemo me impune lacessit* (no-one wounds me with impunity) appeared for the first time, as did *Florent sceptra piis regna his Iova dat numeratque* (sceptres flourish with the pious, God gives them kingdoms and numbers them). In 1603 the motto *Henricus rosas regna Jacobus* announced that Henry VII had united the red and white roses, but James the two kingdoms – a greater feat.

The king had other sources of income besides taxation and debasement. The customs brought in rising revenues from trade, amounting to £5399 Scots in 1582, and were raised sharply in 1597 to boost income further. Fortunately, trade was booming and lucrative enough to support the building in Edinburgh of handsome residences for merchants. Growth areas such as salmon, salt and coal, where exports were particularly buoyant, helped to bring in customs revenues of £11,575 Scots in 1598. Out of the merchant class emerged a number of contractors, led initially by the remarkable Thomas Foulis who offered the king invaluable banking services, making loans and discharging large payments. A recognisable financial sector was forming. After 1586 James also received a pension from Elizabeth, which was usually £3000 sterling per year. Between 1586 and 1603, he received some £58,000 sterling which was helpful, but barely replaced the French jointure enjoyed by Mary Queen of Scots in the 1560s. Meanwhile, the costs of government rose massively. The feuing (hereditary renting-out) of Crown lands by both James IV and James V had steadily dried up much of the Crown's traditional landed income. The reluctance of James VI to part with Crown land forced his generosity to the nobility to take the form of pensions. Noblemen were slipping into greater debt between 1590 and 1609, borrowing heavily to offset the effects of inflation and poor harvests as well as to fund their increasingly lavish lifestyles. As James became a pensioner of England, so his nobles increasingly became dependent on their royal pensions. The king believed in rewarding his nobility as an ingredient of good kingship, persuading noblemen to identify their interests with those of the Crown. Increasing royal control over the finances of the most politically volatile group in Scottish society accelerated the decline in noble violence, but at the same time put immense strain on royal resources. The problem was all too apparent by 1591, when James confessed to Maitland, 'I have offended the whole country, I grant, for prodigal giving from me.' In December the king demanded information on his royal possessions from his Exchequer officials only to receive a blistering reply, telling him 'in all humilitie' that he must 'begyne to prove als cairfull of your own necessitie as your majestie hes done and daylie dois of utheris'.[37] Officials could not control the royal largesse; that was the king's responsibility.

Maitland died in 1595 and James wrote a tasteful sonnet for his memorial tablet. He kept the chancellorship vacant for three years, but in 1596 an eight-man commission, the Octavians, was given the task of reform. Aiming to raise royal income by at least £100,000 Scots per year, in 1597 they steeply revised the customs rates outward and imposed a novel import duty. They also investigated the traditional sources of revenue such as Crown lands and feudal duties. They controlled James's spending by insisting on the consent of at least five of the eight Octavians to each item. The royal household was pruned, as were noble pensions. The commission was based in the Exchequer and headed by Alexander Seton, a trained lawyer and the younger son of a lesser noble family conspicuously loyal to Mary Queen of Scots. The reforms had some impact but not enough. James was still critically dependent on heavy regular taxation and also massive credit from merchants. He was occasionally forced to sell or pawn some of his jewels, but at the same time could not be dissuaded from buying new ones. He spent a large part of the parliamentary grant of 1596 on entertaining Queen Anne's brother-in-law the duke of Holstein, with banqueting, sports and frequent drinking sessions which left the king's health distempered. The waste of taxation caused deep disquiet both in the country and among the more responsible courtiers. A kingly court was essential to impress the nobility and foreign visitors, but its excesses were also the cause of much hostility. It was not only the kirk that objected to the extravagance and luxury surrounding the king and queen, but also taxpayers and merchants whose credit was exploited.

James was impressed by Alexander Seton's abilities and later created him earl of Dunfermline, but he inevitably made enemies among the courtiers and nobles whose income and perks he cut. He was also a catholic who in 1596 openly supported the return from exile of the treacherous Huntly. Thereupon, the kirk joined the growing number of Seton's opponents, and the troubles in Edinburgh in December 1596 were exacerbated by allegations of popery hurled at him and other Octavians. James concluded that the reformers were a political liability and by the end of 1597 the commission was disbanded, although individuals retained their posts in the royal administration. In January 1598 a cynical royal bankruptcy left Thomas Foulis and his partner, who had been acting as the state's bankers, owing huge debts to their own creditors. The manoeuvre temporarily undermined the merchant classes, but enabled James to survive until 1603. The earl of Cassillis was treated with similar cynicism in 1599 when James appointed him treasurer in an attempt to mulct the wealth of his wife.

Later efforts at retrenchment were even less successful. The English agent reported in September 1599 that the king was at his palace at Linlithgow, 'these three days past very busy with his Council about finding the means for the maintenance of his estate, yet little done'.[38] In many ways the king was a victim of the struggle for patronage that characterised all early modern courts, for the Crown was expected to distribute rewards for service. Nevertheless, the royal bounty had to operate with a degree of commonsense restraint, if only to prevent the alienation of other powerful groups such as merchant creditors. James's inability to exercise any sustained and effective control over his financial affairs, a hallmark of his reign in both Scotland and England, was his Achilles' heel.

In areas other than finance, the Privy Council was more successful. Unlike its English equivalent it retained considerable legislative and judicial powers, and lawyers found it difficult to distinguish the authority of a parliamentary act from that of a council ordinance. James reconstituted the council from 1598, with 32 working councillors over whom he held powers of appointment. He was an assiduous attender, a fact which added to the prestige of a conciliar place and encouraged the nobility to participate. The strengthening of his council after 1598 served James well in the years of absentee kingship after 1603.

Last Years in Scotland

After 1597 James could justifiably consider that his hold on Scotland was unchallengeable. A dozen years after emerging from his long minority, the threat from the kirk was fading; he had regained control over his nobility; and the likelihood of his succeeding to Elizabeth's throne grew greater with every passing year. In 1597–8 he returned to his study and to the pattern of authorship he had begun to develop in the 1580s. His two works, the brief and predominantly scriptural *Trew Law of Free Monarchies* and the longer *Basilicon Doron* ('the king's gift' intended for Prince Henry) are uniquely the reflections of a king on kingship (see pp. 131–5). Amidst weightier matters, James could not resist recommending to Henry the sport of hunting with running hounds, his favourite form, as 'the most honorable and noblest'. Hunting was kingly, since 'it resembleth the warres'.[39] From his youth the king was constantly in the saddle, and his endless hunts kept him fit and active, able to cope with his frequent travels about his kingdom. These journeys often delayed official business, but they ensured he was well informed about local affairs and were valuable in showing the king to his people. His visible presence was a necessary reassurance after a minority, and allowed him to impress his vigour upon his nobility. Hunting trips managed to combine business with pleasure and James was able to display one of his greatest accomplishments, the deft personal kingship that he had brought to a fine art.

As the 1590s drew to a close, one intractable problem increasingly troubled the king. Despite his long amity and correspondence with Elizabeth, he was no nearer to being proclaimed her heir. He had the strongest hereditary claim, but there were several obstacles. Under the English statute of 1351, no foreigner was permitted to inherit English lands; how then could he inherit the Crown itself? James pressed the queen in vain for a grant of the confiscated English estates of his Lennox (Darnley) grandparents, which would have negated the statute. James's cousin Lady Arbella Stuart, daughter of Darnley's brother, had been born and educated in England; did that make her a serious contender? The English succession statute of 1544 made no provision for any heir beyond Elizabeth, but the will of

Henry VIII explicitly debarred the Scottish line descended from his sister Margaret, queen of James IV, in favour of the children of his younger sister Mary, the duchess of Suffolk. Her great-grandsons inherited her claim, but their parents' marriage had been annulled as illegal, probably debarring them. One final threat was the act of 1585 that provided that if any claimant should conspire against Elizabeth, then the claimant and his or her heirs automatically forfeited any rights of inheritance. Was James tainted by his mother's involvement in so many plots?[40] Amidst this uncertainty, the king grew increasingly agitated.

In December 1596 James was misled by reports that the queen and the English Parliament had spoken against his title and acted disrespectfully towards the memory of Mary Queen of Scots. He harangued the Scottish Parliament about Elizabeth's 'false and malicious and envious dealing'[41] and made vague threats of sending ambassadors around foreign courts to drum up support for his claim. The queen sent a furious letter and Sir Robert Cecil the English secretary of state discreetly intimated that James damaged his standing in the eyes of other princes by speaking on the basis of mere rumours. The king was forced to backtrack, but continued to worry about any secret device that might deny him his inheritance. After the peace of Vervins between France and Spain in 1598, the possible revival of the Spanish claim of the Infanta Isabella began to unnerve him.

In late 1599, as preliminary discussions were under way about a peace between England and Spain, James's concerns increased. The Infanta, now married to her cousin the Archduke Albert, arrived in Brussels to rule over the war-torn Spanish southern Netherlands. They were both anxious to promote a peace with England. Yet from Brussels, Isabella would be worryingly well placed to assert her claim when Elizabeth died. In November James invited his Scottish subjects to subscribe to a General Band (bond) for the maintenance of his title to England and Ireland without prejudice to the rights of Elizabeth in her lifetime. Scots, in turn, heard rumours that if the English throne went to another candidate, an English army would descend on Scotland to suppress James's superior claim. Other rumours from Brussels indicated that Albert's brother would marry Lady Arbella

Stuart to push her claim. James began to see Sir Robert Cecil as an enemy. Since Cecil favoured the peace process, he presumably must also favour Isabella's claim, assuming that 'such as wished the peace would also wish the Infanta'.[42]

Meanwhile, the king was trying to build up a party of supporters in England. He responded to the earl of Essex, who as early as 1589 began making overtures towards him as Elizabeth's most likely successor. Essex was deeply anti-Spanish and strongly opposed to Cecil's peace policy, but he was a bad choice of ally since after 1598 he was losing the favour of the queen. In Scotland, James called conventions of his subjects and tried to extract heavy taxation to boost his military power, in case he should need to assert his claim by force. In June 1600 the estates of the burghs and barons (the towns and lairds) pointed instead to the folly of trying to conquer England and refused to support him. The king raged at them but deadlock resulted.

Amidst all this concentration on the English succession, the king must have assumed that the years in which his royal person had been in danger of capture were long over. He was wrong, for in August 1600 the most obscure of all Scottish noble conspiracies took place. After a day's hunting the king dined at Gowrie House, the seat of the Ruthven family. After dinner James was found in a turret, apparently being assaulted by the earl of Gowrie's younger brother. The page John Ramsay ran the assailant through, then turned on the earl himself. James at once proclaimed his escape from mortal danger and to the end of his life kept 5 August as a feast day to celebrate his survival. Ramsay later became earl of Holderness and profited greatly from his timely aid to the king. Others were not convinced by James's version of events, noting that he had no cause to love the Ruthvens and also that he was very heavily in debt to them. The truth about the episode was impossible to discover since the king was the sole survivor of the fracas. It seemed unlikely that the Gowries were trying to exert their control over James by capturing him, since he was no longer a minor. However, it is possible that the family were trying to bring pressure to bear over their money, the king panicked, and Ramsay over-reacted. When the ministers of the Edinburgh kirk showed their disbelief in James's story, they were banished from the city. Gowrie Day became an annual holiday and James never forgot the shock of the event.

The disturbances of August 1600 were not repeated, and by September it was clear that the peace negotiations held at Boulogne between England, Spain and the Spanish Netherlands had broken down. This assuaged James's fears that he might be out-manoeuvred by another claimant, either the Infanta-Archduchess or Lady Arbella. The following year, the English diplomat and author Sir Henry Wootton visited the king's court. He described James as of medium height with short hair and a kindly manner. He was fond of literary discourse, especially of theology, and at dinner anyone might enter to observe the king. He conversed with those about him, 'listening to banter and merry jests in which he takes great delight'. He was familiar and easy with his gentlemen of the chamber and the domestics (who wore caps while they served him, never permitted at the English court). He was grave with the great lords. He had no guard, but was surrounded by a large number of gentlemen who scrutinised newcomers. The picture catches James at his best: relaxed, unpretentious (at least to English eyes), intellectually alert and at the centre of a court full of loyal subjects.[43]

In his last years in Scotland, James could take pride in his achievements. Emerging from the extremely difficult circumstances of a long minority, he successfully reasserted royal power. Historians of Scotland have disagreed, however, about the extent of his achievements. Gordon Donaldson extolled him as the most remarkable king of his dynasty; more recently, Jenny Wormald has argued for his 'stupendous' success. By contrast, the more sceptical view of Michael Lynch, while not denying that James was one of Scotland's more effective kings, describes the strategies of the reign as 'random, fussy and intrusive – like the king himself'. Lynch points to some significant weaknesses. The double pressures of unprecedentedly heavy taxation and systematic debasement of the coinage were applied in the 1590s, a time of extremely harsh economic conditions when food prices reached new heights. Rampant inflation produced disaffection, not least because 'the many layers of the middling sort felt the weight of governance but few of the benefits of royal patronage.'[44] There is consensus, however, that the later English caricature of James has no foundation in his early years. On the contrary, he demonstrated his effectiveness as a politician both at home and in his relations with foreign powers. As he told Prince Henry, whatever the outcome of the English succession he could take pride in the ending of centuries of Anglo-Scottish hostilities and the growth of a more constructive relationship. James handled the kirk with skill, gradually outwitting the Melvillian extremists and fostering the support of moderate ministers. Noble violence declined and there was increasingly widespread support for the king. His literary achievements in poetry and political ideas were notable in themselves and highly unusual in a monarch.

On the other hand, obvious flaws were visible in both his character and his approach to kingship. His personal affection for the treacherous, violent Huntly nearly led to a major crisis. His lack of concern for his finances was notorious, unsustainable and showed signs of alienating his subjects in and out of Parliament. His court had already acquired a reputation for profligate expenditure and heavy drinking on festive occasions. Towards the last years of Elizabeth's life, he was tempted to intervene by force to assert his right to the English throne, a policy that – as his Scottish subjects recognised – would have proved disastrous. For the future, one point emerged as the most critical. James had succeeded best through making effective personal contacts, still vitally necessary in Scottish kingship. The kirk and the nobility both needed constant royal oversight. The Scottish monarchy was only gradually moving towards the more impersonal and institutional style of governance long established south of the Border. If James succeeded in his lifelong aim to mount Elizabeth's throne, the lack of his presence in his native kingdom might undermine his recent achievements. At the same time, James's distinctive style of personal kingship, which had proved its worth in Scotland, might not suit the English. Whatever happened on Elizabeth's death, both England and Scotland would be open to grave risks of instability.

2 *The English Throne*

Accession and Peace

In spring 1601 a secret revolution took place in Anglo-Scottish affairs. The attempts made by James in 1599–1600 to levy Scottish taxes for a possible invasion force and his objections to the peace feelers from Spain made it clear to Sir Robert Cecil, Elizabeth's most trusted minister, that he was growing dangerously restive. Then, in February 1601, the earl of Essex led a band of discontented young noblemen and their followers in a short-lived but alarming rising in London. Essex was in disgrace after abandoning the English army sent against the Irish rebels led by Tyrone (see p. 52) and his chaotic revolt was a rash attempt to evict his enemies from court in order to regain his influence with the queen. Instead, he was hustled to the block after a brief trial two weeks later.

Essex had been the king's chief informant at the English court for at least three years, so his death left a void. James realised that he must attract wider support from the Privy Council, particularly Cecil whom he described as 'king there in effect' after the removal of his rival Essex. Cecil politely rebuffed earlier attempts to win him over, since as secretary of state he could not assist a foreign power, but Essex's rising together with James's obvious frustration decided him to act. Some Englishmen were already conducting a secret (and legally treasonous) correspondence with Scotland. The most notable letter-writer was Lord Henry Howard, a crypto-catholic and former partisan of Mary Queen of Scots. Cecil joined in the secret correspondence, so after spring 1601, James – as the strongest contender for the throne – was acting in concert with Cecil, the leading member of the English Privy Council. This was a clear indication that the remaining legal barrier to the king's accession, his status as an alien, would be disregarded. Swiftly, Cecil increased the Scottish pension to £5000 per annum.

Reassured that his claim was accepted, James stopped sabre-rattling and assured Cecil that 'good government at home, firm amity with the Queen, and a loving care in all things that may concern the weal of that state [England] are the only three steps whereby I think to mount upon the hearts of the people.' The king repeatedly expressed his high regard for 'the travails of so great worth and inestimable value' undertaken on his behalf by the assiduous secretary.[1]

In March 1603, observing Elizabeth's steady decline, Cecil drafted the proclamation that would announce her death and the transfer of her Crown 'absolutely, wholly, and solely' to James.[2] Secretly, he sent it north for the king's scrutiny and approval. The ports were closed and extra watchmen patrolled London, but there were no signs of trouble. In the early hours of 24 March 1603, the queen died at her palace of Richmond outside London. On a previously agreed sign, the courtier Sir Robert Carey slipped away and out-rode the official messenger, arriving in Edinburgh three days later. The youngest son of Lord Hunsdon, Elizabeth's cousin by a Boleyn mother, Carey was attempting to win favour under the new dynasty and continue his family's senior place at court. He epitomised many ambitious Englishmen now turning to James.

By the time Carey reached Holyrood, the king had been proclaimed in both Whitehall and London where the announcement was received calmly and without opposition. On hearing the good news, James immediately sent a trusted envoy to take over the key English Border fortress of Berwick. He wrote a moving letter to Cecil, praying God would make him 'equal and answerable to that place your state hath called us unto'. He thought no previous age had seen such efforts for the peaceful 'translation of a monarchy'.[3] Imbued with the sense of his own regality and believing passionately in the divine right of kings, James was deeply conscious that his inheritance of the English throne placed on him an extraordinary responsibility. On 5 April the king left Edinburgh, reassuring his anxious people that he would return every three years, in line with his advice in *Basilicon Doron* that a king should tour all his kingdoms every three years. He borrowed a final 10,000 merks (£6660 Scots) from the burgh of Edinburgh to pay for the journey.

The ride south became a triumphant progress, with James feasting and hunting amidst his new subjects who flocked to see him. Later, he recalled how 'all the ways betwixt Berwick and London were paved with people'. He was delighted by their welcoming 'sparkles of affection' and 'sounds of joy' which he would never forget. He did not sufficiently appreciate that apart from natural curiosity, their overwhelming emotion was relief. Sir George Carew writing to Cecil from the midlands confessed that he had feared 'many distempers in the State' but instead thanked God for the miraculous outcome which confounded those 'who for many years past trembled to think of her Majesty's decease, as if instantly upon it the kingdom would have been torn asunder'. Cecil's half-brother Thomas Lord Burghley, lord president of the Council in the North, expressed his relief that all had gone quietly despite the fears of the common people that 'their houses should have been spoiled and sacked'.[4] The joyous reception followed the realisation that the death of Elizabeth had triggered neither civil war nor foreign invasion.

When the cavalcade eventually reached the outskirts of London, James was met by a gifted lawyer and orator, Richard Martin, most of whose speech had been concocted in advance with Cecil. After briefly mourning the queen, Martin acclaimed an experienced king whose 'princely and eminent virtues' had brought Scotland 'to order in Church and Commonwealth'. In turn, England looked for 'an admirable goodnesse and particular redresse' under 'an uncorrupted king'. This was an unmistakeable allusion to the many problems burdening the country. Oppressive monopoly grants and cynical lawyers both needed reform; the open selling of church livings must stop; so must the exploitation of the poor by heavy taxation. Honest trade (not the privateering for which the English had become notorious) should bring 'well-gotte treasure'. James must not 'shut himselfe up . . . from his people' as the ageing queen had tended to do. Closing with a gracious reference to *Basilicon Doron*, written for Prince Henry and newly printed in England, Martin pointed to the benefits of a settled succession after decades of worry about Elizabeth's childlessness.[5]

Martin's speech shows that Privy Councillors were well aware that the previous regime had bequeathed problems to its successor. Cecil had already drafted a proclamation suspending the monopolies that Martin denounced; it was announced immediately to demonstrate that the king listened to the grievances of his subjects. James himself probably paid less attention. He was greatly impressed by English wealth displayed in the lavish hospitality offered him by the nobility. It has been calculated that Scottish peers by comparison were worth only about the same as the better-off Yorkshire gentry. For years the king had worked towards his accession to the English throne, and now he intended, as the Venetian ambassador noted ironically in June 1603, 'to enjoy the papacy ... [and] dedicate himself to his books and to the chase'.[6]

Before leaving Edinburgh, James confirmed all the English Privy Councillors in their posts. He intended this to be a message of reassuring continuity, but it alienated some of those who had not received much favour in the 1590s and were hoping for change. As Cecil observed, when James did not immediately give them all they desired, their loyalty vanished. Sir Walter Raleigh and Lord Cobham, among others, became involved in the obscure Bye and Main plots of later 1603, intended to kidnap or threaten James. The conspiracies were a warning not to mistake the smoothness of the succession for a universal welcome. However, James was aware that the English Privy Council had grown dangerously narrow in the 1590s, and he promptly promoted his long-standing correspondent Howard (soon to be earl of Northampton), together with his nephew Lord Thomas Howard, naval hero and future earl of Suffolk. James also added five Scots nobles, led by his Stuart cousin Lennox and including Mar, the diplomat and trusted guardian of Prince Henry. These appointments were more symbolic than real, and the Scots treated them as honorific rather than administratively burdensome. Even so, the English Privy Council grew accustomed to the presence of one or two Scots at its meetings. In any case with experienced Englishmen such as Secretary Cecil, Lord Chancellor Ellesmere and Lord Treasurer Dorset, the day-to-day government of the realm was in safe hands. James could enjoy his leisure pursuits while reserving his efforts for big issues, particularly foreign policy and his scheme for a closer union between England and Scotland.

The breakdown of the Boulogne peace talks of 1600 between England, Spain and the Spanish Netherlands did not end all diplomatic contacts, but the central problem was the continuing rebellion

in Ireland. It escalated in August 1598 when the earl of Tyrone inflicted a major defeat on English forces. Despite leading the largest
English army so far sent to Ireland, in 1599 Essex failed to reverse
Tyrone's victory. The rebels were in league with Spain and in 1601
Spanish troops landed at Kinsale in southern Ireland. Philip III hoped
to divert English forces and so weaken their support for the Dutch
rebels, but the new commander Lord Mountjoy forced the Kinsale
garrison to surrender in January 1602. The Irish rebellion collapsed,
and in 1603 Tyrone surrendered to Mountjoy who knew (as the rebel
earl did not) that the queen had just died. Already in 1602, the English
Privy Council was largely agreed that there would be no remaining
obstacle to peace with Spain once the revolt was over. The financial
position was increasingly desperate and relief from the high costs of
war would be very welcome. However, James, in their secret correspondence, persuaded Cecil that the possibility that the Infanta
Isabella might assert her remote claim to the throne required that no
negotiations should commence with Spain until after his own safe
accession.

   Once Tyrone was beaten and James securely established, the way
forward was clear. In June 1603 he forbade his English subjects to
prey on Spanish shipping. As king of Scotland, he had never been at
war with Spain and the proclamation signalled his peaceful intentions. The Archdukes Albert and Isabella seized the moment, sending
an envoy to congratulate James on his accession and also sound out
his views. The archduchess had no interest in asserting any claim to
Elizabeth's throne and she and Albert urged the government of Philip
III to join them in negotiations with England. These began in May
1604 and finally concluded in August, bringing the long Armada war
to an end.

   However, Cecil's tough negotiating stance conceded none of
Spain's most cherished aims. Philip III and his chief minister the duke
of Lerma were hoping for freedom of worship for English catholics,
the banning of English trade with the New World (which Spain
regarded as her exclusive possession) and the breaking of English
links with the rebel Dutch. They disliked sending envoys to London
and would have preferred neutral territory, perhaps northern France.
Cecil insisted on London. He offered only vague concessions. If

James received a reasonable Spanish offer for the Dutch cautionary towns (held by English garrisons as security for the huge sums of money lent to the rebels by Elizabeth), then he might sell them. But James would decide on whether the offer was reasonable. The Dutch would continue to recruit English volunteers to their cause (still popular among committed protestants), but the archdukes would also be allowed to recruit. Cecil smoothly ensured that the contentious issues of New World trade were discussed, but set aside. The treaty was a triumph of diplomacy. By stimulating the export of goods, it enhanced economic growth in England, Spain and the Spanish Netherlands. Burgeoning trade also increased customs duties, benefiting each ruler and employing an expanding merchant marine. At the same time, the treaty helped to clear the seas of freebooting pirates, to the benefit of all legitimate merchants. Despite initial grumbles by traders who found conditions in the Iberian markets tougher than they expected, over the next decade London's trade boomed with Spain and the Mediterranean. James left all the details of the negotiations to Cecil aided by Northampton, but he returned from hunting to host the grand banquet concluding the treaty. It was during the celebrations that the idea of a future marriage between a Spanish Infanta and Prince Henry was first mooted.

The king's own great project was not peace with Spain, although he was pleased by it, but the creation of a fuller union between England and Scotland. His accession created a dynastic or regnal union, but, with all the vagaries of possible succession crises, there was no guarantee that it would be permanent. The dynastic link between England and Normandy had not lasted long. James was convinced that his accession created a literally God-given opportunity, and for himself a divine obligation, to bring the two realms together in perpetuity. He emphasised repeatedly that he was not a foreign king but the descendant of the first Tudor. Before the royal entry into London in March 1604, a special commission spent months ensuring the traditional correctness of every detail. The office of Constable of the Realm was briefly revived to ensure that the procession conformed to medieval precedents in order to emphasise dynastic continuity.[7] The occasion was more impressive than any in which James had previously participated, and its defining moment came when he encountered Henry VII painted in imperial robes leaning down to give him a sceptre. In John Speed's military map of England and Scotland, drawn in 1603–4, the king and queen were seated at the top of a genealogical tree rooted in William the Conquerer. The accession medal proclaimed James as Imperator (Emperor) of Britain, the coronation medal hailed him as Caesar Augustus of Great Britain, and the new coinage of 1603–4 also used the title King of Great Britain.

In the proclamation of May 1603 ordering his subjects on the English and Scots Borders, renamed 'the middle shires', to cease raiding one another, James asserted that 'in the hearts of all the best disposed subjects of both the Realms', there was 'a most earnest desire that the sayd happy Union should bee perfected'.[8] He was far too optimistic, for it rapidly emerged that on both sides of the Border the Union aroused fear and distaste. Many English lawyers still saw Scotland as an inferior kingdom, while the Scots defensively emphasised the need to maintain their laws and their kirk as the touchstones of their nationhood. The greater purity of the reformed kirk of Scotland by comparison with the Church of England was a matter of particular pride and concern. Numerous tracts were written and circulated, but there was little consensus. Those who wanted Union, apart from the king himself, were a small minority in both countries.

Amidst all his efforts to present the attractions of a greater union to his English subjects, James was well aware that he must not appear to forget his own countrymen. The departure of his court left Edinburgh semi-deserted and most of the Scottish aristocracy were very conscious of their king's absence. A monarch lived and conducted the business of government within his court, traditionally an important point of contact for those who sought his favour or his intervention in their problems. Although the significance of the court north of the Border was much less than in England – it has been argued that Scotland was virtually all country and no court – it remained the centre of decision making and the source of patronage. Scottish nobles were attuned to the importance of keeping in contact with the king, whether over a specific issue such as a lawsuit, or the broader but more vital matter of convincing their kinsmen and clients that they wielded influence. After 1603 Scottish aristocrats could no longer speak easily with James at Edinburgh or Stirling. They were forced instead to apply for a Privy Council licence to travel, then make a round trip south and back of at least 800 miles. They endured considerable inconvenience, as well as having to spend time in a notoriously expensive foreign city. James must ensure that the new situation did not provoke discontent, since he could not afford to have an alienated Scottish nobility plotting behind his back.

The king brought south with him a coterie of trusted advisers and courtiers. They were followed shortly afterwards by another royal progress, led by Queen Anne and Prince Henry. In May 1603 with James already in London, Anne successfully demanded the custody of her 9-year-old boy (whom she had hardly seen for five years) by refusing to cross the Border without him. The king wrote to Henry from England that he would be joining him soon, but apparently made no specific arrangements. The queen's forceful maternal action was politically significant, since after May 1603 Henry immediately made the transition to the English court and to an English rather than a Scottish upbringing.

The royal consort was a novelty in 1603. No-one could remember either Philip II, husband of Mary Tudor, or Catherine Parr, last wife of Henry VIII. Queen Anne has traditionally been regarded with condescension by male historians who emphasised her extravagance and triviality. Recent studies have pointed instead to her influence, certainly as long as her marriage (despite its obvious frictions) remained a reality. Two daughters were born to the royal couple in England, though neither survived. The last baby, who arrived in June 1607, was christened Princess Sophia after Anne's mother, the late queen of Denmark. The name emphasised Anne's royal birth, a fact underscored by the two visits of her brother King Christian, although the first degenerated into a drunken route at Theobalds. Anne played an important role in embodying to ambassadors and others the high status of the new Stuart dynasty with its links to Danish royalty. James highlighted her distinction by rebuilding Somerset House for her between 1609 and 1614 and renaming it Denmark House. It was the largest and most expensive single royal architectural work undertaken between 1603 and 1640, although by the time of the formal opening in 1617 in James's presence, the influence of his wife had faded.

Anne rapidly came to be regarded as the head of the realm's noble-women, and places at her court were prized. Intelligently, she used them to reach out to leading members of the English nobility, whose wives and daughters gathered in her circle. In this way the queen helped to break down the barriers between the two aristocracies of her husband's realms. She came to love the London theatre, which offered far more variety than was available in Edinburgh. In 1604 Cecil sent his close associate Sir Walter Cope to hunt for players to amuse her. Cope found that Anne had already seen all the new plays, but fortunately, he wrote in a note to Cecil, the actor-manager Richard Burbage told him that his company had just revived an old production. It was entitled *Love's Labour Lost*, 'which for wit and mirth he says will please her exceedingly'.[9] Very soon Anne established herself as a significant cultural patron, staging a new art form, the masque, at court entertainments. Part ballet part drama, with music and scenery, the masque showcased Anne's female court, separate from that of the king. She perceptively employed men of outstanding talent such as Ben Jonson and Inigo Jones. Masques underscored the civilising feminine presence of the queen and her entourage in a royal circle that otherwise tended to be dominated by James's hunting companions. Anne also helped to form the cultivated and cosmopolitan tastes of her son Henry, who by 1610 was emerging as a collector and patron of discrimination. Anne and Henry commissioned artists such as Mytens, van Somer, van Mierevelt and the miniaturist Isaac Oliver, whose work stamped English taste for a generation. The king had few cultural (as distinct from intellectual) interests so all the evidence suggests that Anne played the central role in creating, in the words of her biographer, 'a rich and hospitable climate' for the arts at the Jacobean court.[10]

At the same time, it seems clear that in England Anne increasingly deplored her husband's behaviour. In 1604 she observed caustically to the French envoy Beaumont that 'the king drinks so much, and conducts himself so ill in every respect, that I expect an early and evil result'.[11] The queen wanted greater control over Henry, since if James met an early death her son might become king during his minority. Her extraordinarily indiscreet comment indicates not only her irritation with her husband, but also her understandable fears that she might soon be faced with widowhood in a country where she had barely settled.

James seems initially to have envisaged a court equally divided between the English and the Scots as another expression of Union. This soon proved impractical, especially after he reappointed all the Elizabethan Privy Councillors. The senior officials of the regime remained reassuringly familiar to the English, although a court with a married monarch and a young royal family was very different from that of an elderly spinster queen. To balance the English monopoly of office, James ensured that his immediate court entourage, the Bedchamber, was staffed almost exclusively by Scots. It was essentially a continuum of the Scottish chamber with only one Englishman, Sir Philip Herbert later earl of Montgomery, admitted in July 1603. There was little change until the rise of another favoured Englishman, George Villiers, who was admitted to the Bedchamber in 1615.

The presence of the Scots around James probably stemmed initially from his instinctive desire to be surrounded by familiar faces, but it soon assumed greater significance. The entourage at Whitehall provided the invaluable point of contact whereby Scottish nobles and lairds might still have access to their king, who remained the fount of honour. This helped assuage worries that after 1603, James might grow completely out of touch with their affairs. Even the great Scottish lawyer Sir Thomas Craig of Riccarton when urging the Union could give way to panic that 'Our kings will be Englishmen, born in England, residing in England. They will naturally prefer Englishmen as their attendants and courtiers.' Cocooning the king in a Scottish ambiance in his private quarters, the Bedchamber offered reassurance that on the contrary, he would not become totally Anglicised. The system has even been described with some exaggeration as 'a serious constitutional mechanism for dealing with the problem of an absentee king'.[12]

Bedchamber contacts enabled Scots to gain access to the royal bounty that might compensate for the departure of their monarch and his court. For most of the Scottish aristocracy, already struggling with financial difficulties linked to the sharp price rise in late sixteenth-century Scotland, the high cost of prolonged residence in

London was unsustainable, but the Bedchamber made it less necessary by providing the means of access via friends and relatives. This
perception of the importance of the entourage increased as the number of Scots who had rushed south began gradually to decline. James
took measures in 1604 to halt their influx, tightening the regulations
again in 1611. The darker aspect of the Bedchamber was that it was
precisely the easy and privileged access enjoyed by a small number of
Scots that gave them innumerable opportunities to petition for
favours. Already in the 1590s, the king's willingness to sign grants
and commissions for the members of his Chamber caused his financial officers to despair. After 1603 the problem was exacerbated by his
readiness to use English money to pay Scottish pensions. James felt a
genuine sense of royal responsibility to support Scottish noble houses, under pressure to emulate the grander lifestyles of their English
equals. Unfortunately, the king's generosity was fed by his easy
assumption that the resources of his new realm were inexhaustible.
England was a much richer kingdom than Scotland, but the king
failed to appreciate that any substantial diversion of resources away
from Englishmen would inevitably be resented.

Parliament and Union

A major outbreak of plague in London deferred the meeting of the
first English Parliament of the reign until March 1604. The king
expected that the Union would be the central topic and devoted his
opening speech to it. It was manifest 'that God by his Almightie
Providence hath preordained it so to be'. The divine hand was clear in
genealogy, since James was the direct descendent of Henry VII. It was
also obvious in geography, since the two realms inhabited one island
and were divided at the Border only by shallow rivers. In religion,
they shared the protestant faith, while culturally they shared both
language and manners (although this was only true for southern
Scotland and not the Gaelic north).[13] A true Union would subsume
the ancient identities of England and Scotland into a new monarchy
of Great Britain, a title coined in the mid-sixteenth century amidst
plans to marry the young Edward VI to the infant Mary Queen of
Scots.

The royal speech was sweeping in its implications, but the government's initial proposals were modest. Acting almost certainly on Cecil's advice, James asked only for a commission with powers to discuss the issues relating to the Union and to report to the next Parliament. This passed with relative ease. The other proposal for a change in the royal style to King of Great Britain proved more controversial. In one sense it simply stated a fact – that James was king of both kingdoms – and the language of Great Britain was steadily growing more familiar. However, to the House of Commons the laws and freedoms of England were inextricably bound to the king's title and to their own terms of representation. An English Parliament made laws for England. Who, they asked, could make laws 'to bind Britannia'?[14] James reasonably referred the matter to the judges, but was shocked when they agreed with the Commons that the laws of England would be immediately extinguished if the king's title were changed.

The royal rhetoric was splendid but often vapid. James repeatedly pressed for a union of hearts and minds, using the homely image of a married couple: 'I am the Husband and all the whole Isle is my lawfull wife.' More grandly, he urged 'Unus Rex . . . Unus Grex and una Lex' (one king, one people, one law). He told the House of Commons that he hoped to leave behind him 'one worship to God, one kingdom entirely governed, one uniformity in laws'. He did not spell out the legal and constitutional details of his vision, perhaps because he intended to be as flexible as possible. In any case, none of the composite monarchies currently surviving in Europe – Castile, Aragon and Portugal: Poland and Lithuania: the Scandinavian kingdoms that alternated between combinations of Finland, Sweden, Denmark and Norway – offered an entirely satisfactory model of union. Perhaps James looked only for an expression of agreement in principle. The most precise statement he made was in a private letter to Cecil in November 1604: 'I mean specifically . . . the uniting both of the laws and Parliaments of both the nations.' Even then he gave no indication of what the united institutions might look like, and added that they 'should be left to the maturity of time, which must piece and take away the distinction of nations'.[15] Clearly, the king aimed to be tactfully gradualist.

James was distressed by the Commons' unhelpful attitude. At the opening of the session, they spent considerable time on a disputed election concerning rival candidates for Buckinghamshire. To the Lower House it was important that they made the final decision on such disputes, but when the king involved himself in it, eventually producing an acceptable solution, they politely sent a delegation to thank him. However, his speech urging them to move forward to discuss the Union met with little response. Instead of enthusiasm for his vision, James found himself faced with ingrained suspicion and distrust, despite assurances that he would do nothing to undermine his subjects' liberties. They must surely have been misled by a few giddy heads, as he described them in a pained letter to the Speaker. In fact, the Commons were influenced primarily by the charismatic Sir Edwin Sandys. An experienced Elizabethan member of Parliament who emerged in 1604 as a natural leader, Sandys proved exceptionally skilled in articulating the Commons' disquiets. He became one of the most influential Parliament men of the next 20 years, and his concern for the privileges and protocol of the Lower House was nearly always at odds with James's high sense of the royal prerogative. Ironically, Sandys' emergence was due to a large extent to the lack of effective Privy Council leadership in the Commons. This was a novel problem stemming from James's generous awards of noble titles to his councillors, who thereafter attended the Lords.

There were major differences of approach, not least because the king asserted that all the Commons' privileges derived from the Crown and he could withdraw them at will. By contrast the Commons deeply believed their privileges were theirs by ancient right and inheritance. James was also emphatic that the institution of monarchy was of divine origin and older than all representative assemblies. This view was at odds with the Commons' sense of their historic responsibilities and importance and some of their members including Sir John Dodderidge, the Solicitor-General and a prominent antiquary, were convinced that the English Parliament went back to pre-Roman times. The conviction was misplaced, but served as a potent and sustaining myth. Many members of the Lower House were lawyers who felt a duty to preserve the balance of constitutional powers. In the fifteenth century, the great lawyer Sir John

Fortescue distinguished between absolute monarchies, *dominium regale*, and limited monarchies where the Crown could rule only by laws assented to by the people, *dominium politicum et regale*. To Englishmen, England was the supreme example of the latter, with its liberties resting on the 1215 grant of Magna Carta as well as later statutes limiting the powers of the Crown whilst enshrining the property rights of the subject. It was the Commons' obligation to see that their new king did not undermine these hard-won and long-cherished liberties.

Tactfully, the Commons replied to the king's letter that he was misinformed about their contrary intentions. One major issue they were debating concerned the unpopular royal rights of wardship and purveyance. Wardship arose because there was no concept of freehold in early modern England, and great landowners were technically tenants-in chief of the Crown, who in return could be called upon to provide military service. If a landowner died before his heir was of age, the estate reverted temporarily to the Crown. The wardship was then sold off by the court of Wards to the highest bidder, who was often not a member of the same family and might exploit the estate ruthlessly until the heir came of age. Purveyance allowed the Crown's agents, the Greencloth, to requisition the large supplies of food and drink consumed by the court at artificially low prices. Cecil was willing to bargain for purveyance and at first indicated that he was willing to end wardship in return for financial compensation for the Crown. Then, under pressure from his subordinates in the court of Wards, he changed his mind and dropped the scheme. This left the Commons feeling that they had been misled and exposed to the king's anger, and their indignation over this issue along with others decided them to compose *The Form of Apology and Satisfaction*. Intended as a justification of their proceedings, it reminded the king of the 'very fundamental privileges of our House . . . from time immemorial'. They pointed to 'the ancient and long continued use of Parliaments' although they admitted that they had not been so assertive about their rights and privileges under the late queen. That was because of her age and sex, 'which we had great cause to tender', since disputes might have imperilled the succession. Above all, the *Apology* expressed the essential conservatism of the Commons' view of their functions: 'The prerogatives of princes may easily and do daily grow. The privileges of the subject are for the most part at an everlasting stand. They may be by good providence and care preserved, but being once lost are not recovered but with much disquiet.' [16]

Far from attempting to win the initiative from the Crown, as historians once believed, the Commons saw themselves as defending the ancient *status quo* from an all-too-innovative monarch. James diverted a possible confrontation by sending them a 'comfortable' message that he acknowledged their loyalty. The Commons did not formally present the *Apology*, but the king knew what it said and disliked their action in composing it. His servants also made some discreet soundings about the possibility of a vote of taxation by the Commons but were quickly rebuffed. On 7 July, after months of mostly fruitless discussion and no money, he prorogued the Parliament. James thanked the Lords, but most of his speech was sharp and pointedly addressed to the Lower House.

I will not thank where I think no thanks due . . . You see I am not of such a stock as to praise fools . . . You see how in many things you did not well. The best apology maker of you all, for all his eloquence, cannot make all good. You have done many things rashly . . . I wish you would use your liberty with more modesty in time to come.[17]

Members could be in little doubt as they went back to their counties that the initial euphoria of the king's accession was over.

Clearly, the king had formed a low view of the Commons and it came as a shock that an English Parliament was so different from a Scottish one. The Scottish Parliament acted on an agenda set by the lords of the articles. Parliaments were small, with little tradition of oratory, and the calling of frequent conventions (on some occasions little more than an enlarged Privy Council) gave the king an additional power to legislate and tax. By contrast the English Parliament with its two distinct Houses, Lords and Commons, was much the largest representative assembly in Europe, with 78 lords and 467 commoners assembling in 1604. The Commons could usually be guided by skilled Privy Councillors, but it was far too large to be packed. In England each House largely discussed what it chose;

speeches by members were often carefully composed and there was rising interest outside Parliament in what was said there. Members of the Commons saw debate and the sifting of proposals as an essential part of their function, not as obstructionism. As they recorded in the *Apology*, they had taken their time over the Union because 'the propositions were new, the importance great, the consequences far-reaching and not discoverable but by long disputes'. The king might view this with impatience, but in England, Parliament was the sole forum available for legislation and taxation. It was imperative that the monarch made every effort to manage it constructively, since there were no alternative bodies.

Hostility to the Union proved impossible to overcome despite the king's flexibility over detail. On both sides, the first session of 1604 powerfully shaped attitudes for the rest of the reign, although it must be emphasised that they were attitudes of misunderstanding, and even incomprehension, rather than outright hostility. On one issue, James would not accept defeat. On 20 October 1604, a proclamation 'by the cleerenesse of our Right' proclaimed him King of Great Britain.[18] His vision was reiterated as 'evident to sense': the island had 'one common limit or rather Gard of the Ocean Sea, making the whole a little world within itself'. It seems highly likely that James was emphasising his grandeur as the ruler of multiple monarchies in order to impress foreign sovereigns, particularly Philip III with whom he had just concluded the Treaty of London. The new title was to be used on all coins, but not to extend until further notice to any legal documents or proceedings. The compromise was reasonable, but aroused widespread fears that the king might routinely use similar proclamations if he felt thwarted by Parliament.

In December 1604 the elderly Archbishop Matthew Hutton of York, who had attended the House of Lords, wrote to Cecil to emphasise that there was widespread criticism of the king's extravagance and his obsessive devotion to hunting. Copies of the letter began to circulate and so Cecil felt bound to compose a stiff reply, but Hutton was articulating deep-seated disquiets that had emerged barely 18 months after the king's accession. One of the king's greyhounds named Jowler was kidnapped at Royston, and returned with a message around its neck asking James to go home and cease burdening the countryside with his sporting companions. Public support for the new king was gradually cooling, a factor that did not encourage the Commons to view the Union any more warmly in the next session. However, the horrifying discovery of the Gunpowder Plot, on the night of 4/5 November 1605 just as Parliament was about to reconvene, stirred a strong feeling of national relief at the preservation of the king and the two young princes, who would have been present at the opening ceremony. Cecil, recently created earl of Salisbury, skilfully used the wave of emotional loyalty to extract the very generous vote of three subsidies and six fifteenths and tenths (an additional fixed sum) from the Commons. This was only one subsidy less than the largest vote of taxation granted to Queen Elizabeth in wartime, and brought in around £450,000. Besides making a major contribution to the financial situation, the subsidy seemed to promise a better relationship between the king and his people represented in Parliament.

Nevertheless, by the end of the third session of 1606/7, it was apparent that problems remained. There were culture clashes: to many English courtiers, even the Scots aristocrats appeared dirty and uncouth in their habits. Latent English hostility to the king's followers emerged in the Commons in 1607, when the Scots were attacked as 'all beggars rebels and traitors', who regularly murdered their kings and had nearly succeeded in assassinating James himself in the Gowrie plot. Significantly, the outburst came only a week after it was confirmed that James had undertaken to repay the enormous debts of two Bedchamber Scots, Hay and Haddington, together with the English Bedchamberman Montgomery, to the tune of £44,000. 'In the meantime', the London letter-writer John Chamberlain commented laconically, 'his own debts are stalled', to be paid in two years' time.[19]

The royal act of largesse was widely regarded as an outrageous waste of the generous grant of parliamentary taxation voted in 1606. Few incidents did more to make the Bedchamber the object of acute suspicion, and also to increase the unwillingness of the king's English subjects to hand over their money in taxes. Some of the many libels (sardonic little poems) against James and his Scots seem to date from this incident, including

> The Scotchmen are but beggars yet,
> Although their begginge was not small.
> But now a Parliament doth sitte,
> A subsidy shall pay for all.

The rhyme circulated throughout James's reign and popular resentment of the Scots continued until 1625. As late as the 1650s, the memory of the 'bludy Scots' plunder of English taxation was still vivid.[20] The king frequently acknowledged that his bounty had gone too far, commenting in 1607 that his first three years had been like a Christmas. Yet he never learned to control his spendthift ways and, to the end of his life, he granted expensive gifts of pensions and lump sums of money to his many friends. By 1607 the House of Commons had formed the strong impression that taxes granted to the king would almost certainly be wasted.

In February 1607 two speakers reminded the Commons that statutes from the fourteenth century, long ignored but still technically binding, required annual meetings of Parliament. The point was never made under Elizabeth because it was never thought necessary, but confidence in James's willingness to work with Parliament was already lessening. Then, in March 1607, the king went out of his way to praise the Scottish Parliament, emphasising its members' limited right to speak and his own control over the agenda. The English Parliaments were so long, and the Scots Parliament so short, 'that a Mean between them would do well'.[21] He presumably intended to underline in a good-humoured way the practical value of a tight agenda with less time wasting, but to his hearers it indicated once again that he did not care for the proceedings of the Commons and would like to change them.

By 1607 the scheme for the Union was effectively dead. The Lords dutifully tried to get the Commons to confer about it, but an act rescinding the hostile laws (which made the Scots aliens in England and *vice versa*) symbolised merely token progress. Sandys was once again brilliantly in control of the Lower House and his call for a 'perfect Union' saw the end of the project. To Sandys, the only scheme worth having was a union whereby the Scots were ruled by English laws. He knew this was a political impossibility.[22] The king, in his closing speech, again pleaded that Union did not necessarily mean immediate uniformity, but Sandys had delivered the fatal blow. For their part, the Scots in 1607 made it clear that they would not be governed by an appointed deputy, but insisted on retaining their independence. The dual monarchy, one king ruling two separate kingdoms, was the only way forward.

In 1607 the Commons clashed with the judges over the question of naturalising the '*post nati*', those young Scots born after James's accession to the English throne. In 1604 Cecil assumed that the naturalisation of Scotsmen would have to be by Parliament, although until then individual cases might be dealt with by charter under the great seal. The hostility of the Lower House left naturalisation in limbo, but after the end of the session, Cecil devised another way forward. A legal test was deliberately concocted and brought before all the judges in the Exchequer chamber in 1608. Their verdict in Robert Calvin's case established that Scots born after 1603 were effectively naturalised English. There was some resentment that the case bypassed the Commons, but at the time it seemed a practical and relatively low-key method of solving the dispute. It was only in the 1620s that the case of the *post nati* became one of the complaints of the Commons against a judiciary that they increasingly saw as too compliant with the wishes of the Crown.

James also remained intent on bringing his two aristocracies together. Salisbury echoed the king by speaking of a union of nobility, and marriage was a method of integrating at least some Scots into the English upper classes. Eleven Scottish gentlemen who began their careers as royal household servants found wealthy English wives after 1603. Several English aristocrats married Scots, most famously the elderly earl of Nottingham who in 1603 married a teenage relative of James. The following year, Nottingham gave his widowed daughter in marriage to another distant Stuart relative. Some fathers took a low view of possible Scottish sons-in-law, whereupon James occasionally intervened. When his favourite Sir James Hay made little headway in his pursuit of the daughter of Lord Denny through her mother, a Cecil, he gave Hay extra perquisites . After the king showered favours on the reluctant Denny, the marriage took place. The earl of Ormonde was imprisoned in 1614 to prevent him from blocking the marriage of his heiress daughter to the Scottish Lord Dingwall. But outside the court circle of those who saw the king regularly, relatively few Scottish nobles married in England and the level of assimilation at court was far less than James hoped. While Englishmen like Sir John Holles grumbled in 1610 that 'the Scots monopolise his princely person, standing like mountains betwixt the beams of his grace and us',[23] a contrary perception grew up in Scotland. There, the court at Whitehall increasingly symbolised all they disliked about the British link: a tolerance of catholicism, a leaning towards arbitrary government, corruption and unpopular fiscal expedients that stemmed from excessive royal expenditure. Probably such suspicions on both sides were unavoidable, for the situation was intrinsically very difficult, but James must at least be given credit for his consistent attempts to improve Anglo-Scottish social relationships.

The king always accepted that a true union would take time. He graciously apologised in Parliament in March 1607 for his error in assuming that the Union would go through speedily. He wisely emphasised that the most valuable aspect of the new relationship was that it brought to an end centuries of war between two ancient kingdoms. Time was to show that despite all the tensions, after 1603 there were very few in either England or Scotland who wanted to break the regnal link. Across Europe those composite monarchies that were loosely knit proved more successful in the long run in reconciling unity with diversity than those constrained by formal constitutions. Meanwhile, the king's proposals gave a high profile to previously vague notions of 'Britishness'. His insistence on his new title as King of Great Britain, and the use of it on coins, was a subtle form of propaganda that gradually familiarised his subjects with the concept. So did the creation in 1606 of the common flag that was to evolve into the Union Jack. Economic progress also assisted the convergence of the two kingdoms. Scottish coastal trade to London grew steadily as did cross-border trade. The commissioners for the Borders began to tackle the problems of endemic lawlessness and cross-border raiding that worsened the poverty of the 'middle shires'.

James took a personal interest in the rebuilding of Berwick Bridge, a wooden structure largely swept away by floods in 1608. Knowing its importance to commerce as well as its symbolism, the earl of

Dunbar planned to replace it with a stone bridge and after his death in January 1611, Salisbury set aside money for the project. Work started in June, but proceeded slowly and the bridge was still not finished in 1617. In 1620 James expressed the hope that it would be 'in all points fit for so royal a monument of blessed union', but the bridge was only completed a year after his death.[24] The bridge may stand as a symbol of Jacobean rule, for the king had done more than he realised in his lifetime. Despite the failure to obtain the constitutional Union he had set his heart on, he laid sound and enduring foundations for the future Great Britain. Yet his own trust in his new subjects was permanently shaken by the hostility that the Union project had aroused, and his disenchantment with the English Parliament was never removed.

3   Early Years in England

After the first heady months following the king's accession it became clear that despite the private wealth acquired by some Scots, they did not wield much executive power in England. Cecil remained as secretary of state and master of the court of Wards (probably the most lucrative single office in the royal gift). His rivals hoped that Cecil might lose influence and become only one among several senior advisers, but his great administrative abilities and extraordinary attention to detail rapidly made him as indispensable to James as he had been to Elizabeth. Cecil was granted a barony in 1603, made Viscount Cranborne in 1604 after negotiating the peace with Spain, and earl of Salisbury in 1605. In 1606 he became a knight of the Garter, but James, ever a devotee of ancient nobility, had already granted the honour to the earls of Southampton (a former follower of the rebel earl of Essex), Pembroke and Northampton, and the Scots aristocrats Lennox and Mar before honouring his chief councillor. In response Salisbury staged a magnificent procession from London to Windsor, where the Garter was conferred, that reportedly surpassed the coronation procession itself.

The Privy Council was very different from its predecessor before 1603, since it was dominated by an inner core of four men who were closer to the king than the rest of the council. By the end of 1604, Salisbury as the dominant minister was ably supported by the earl of Northampton and the earl of Suffolk, while the earl of Worcester, as master of the Horse, acted as liaison between the Privy Council and the king while he was away hunting. They adapted to the new monarch's idiosyncrasies, including his habit of discussing issues while walking around in circles with his odd gait; James jokingly christened these sessions his 'deambulatory councils'.[1] However, by 1605 the king was spending about half the year out of London, mostly on visits to his favourite hunting lodges at Royston and Newmarket. This left the councillors at Whitehall in charge of most government business and dependent on postal communication to ascertain the royal wishes, which often slowed down decision making. James quickly came to dislike his capital city and tried to minimise his time there, but he enjoyed his visits to Theobalds where a vast game park surrounded the palatial house built by Lord Burghley to entertain Queen Elizabeth. Salisbury spent much of his childhood there and inherited the estate in 1598, but after several royal visits he thought it politic to offer Theobalds to the king who obviously coveted it. In return Salisbury was given the smaller royal estate of Hatfield, where he built the splendid but compact brick mansion still inhabited by his descendents. Both Hatfield House and his opulent London residence, Salisbury House in the Strand, possessed handsome gardens and were designed to offer bountiful hospitality to the royal family, underpinning Salisbury's political leadership. He was an obsessive builder and his other projects included the smart commercial centre in Westminster, the first outside the City itself, which was named Britain's Burse by James at its opening ceremony in 1609.

Aware of the threats he might face in the new Anglo-Scottish polity, Salisbury was careful to cultivate the friendship and support of the earl of Dunbar. One of James's most trusted and longstanding ministers in Scotland, after 1603 Dunbar served as virtually a lord deputy, though without the title. Together, Salisbury and Dunbar built an effective working relationship that ensured administrative stability in both countries in the decade after the regnal union. When Salisbury's heir William married in 1608, the most valuable wedding gift of plate came from Dunbar. On the English Privy Council, the academic and intellectual Northampton gradually emerged as the second most diligent and influential minister. He and Salisbury collaborated conscientiously together on state business, although after his colleague's death, Northampton revealed a deep personal antipathy which he had suppressed previously. In 1608 on the demise of the earl of Dorset, Salisbury was also promoted to Lord Treasurer without losing either of his two other great offices. This gave him an unparalleled monopoly of power not seen since the days of Cardinal Wolsey and further increased the envy of many of his rivals including Northampton.

Promotion to the lord treasurership in 1608 brought Salisbury face to face with the worsening problem of the royal finances. Before 1585 Elizabeth not only balanced her books, but also built up a substantial reserve. However, the long war against Spain between 1585 and 1604 proved enormously expensive, particularly with Tyrone's rebellion in Ireland. In 1602 Cecil was desperately worried that expenses were far outstripping revenues, but since the expenditure resulted from military campaigns, it was hoped that the deficit would be temporary. Elizabeth sold Crown lands to limit the burden of taxation she was forced to ask from Parliament, but this inevitably diminished future royal income. On her death in 1603 she left debts of around £300,000. The significance of these is often exaggerated. The triple subsidy voted in Parliament in 1601 was still being collected when she died and was worth at least another £200,000. Elizabeth lent very large sums of money to both Henri IV and the Dutch United Provinces during the war, and she expected the greater part to be repaid. Salisbury managed to extract a considerable amount by 1612. When these factors were taken into account, the queen died more or less solvent, an extraordinary achievement after 18 years of grinding war.

There was no doubt, however, that over the course of the sixteenth century, the English Crown was growing steadily poorer. From the 1540s onward, inflation was undermining the purchasing power of the relatively static royal income, as well as eating into the value of the parliamentary subsidy. At some point these long-term weaknesses would have to be addressed, but in 1603 with peace on the horizon, it seemed reasonable to expect that the worst was over. The navy and the ordnance would need far less money, while the levying, feeding, clothing and transporting of troops would cease. Experience was to show that the military establishment still required in Ireland would be costly to maintain, but the winding-down of the war was a huge relief to the Exchequer.

In France, civil strife had ravaged the country in the second half of the sixteenth century with disastrous effects on royal income, but after victory in 1598, Henri IV and his able treasurer Sully were speedily able to repair the damage. Once peace was assured, England could hope to follow France in returning to solvency, but the first imperative was a period of consolidation and frugal government.

The more senior Privy Councillors were already aware that in Scotland James had shown himself to be profligate and incompetent in financial matters. It was also to be expected that the king would require a larger income than Elizabeth. As a married man with a family, he would have to provide his queen and the royal children with suitable establishments. The Anglo-Scottish court created by the dual monarchy would also entail higher outlays than previously. The king's journey from Edinburgh was expensive even though most of the hospitality was paid for by his aristocratic hosts, and the coronation which took place the year after his arrival in London was another unavoidable expense. Many of these were one-off charges, so there seemed little reason to fear a financial crisis, but the Privy Council shouldered the task of seeking economies and increasing the royal revenues.

The customs dues were one of the essential components of the Crown's income. Granted to each monarch for life in the first Parliament of every reign since 1461, the duties increased in value whenever trade flourished. They suffered in the 1590s from the trade depression caused by war, but with peace they would generate much more income. In addition, the valuations on which the duties were assessed were mostly unchanged from the Book of Rates published under Mary Tudor. In 1604 Lord Treasurer Sackville, appointed originally by Elizabeth and about to become earl of Dorset, uprated the customs valuations in line with inflation. The increase in revenues paved the way for another reform aimed at maximising income from trade. In the same year, a new contract was made between the Crown and those London merchants experienced in collecting or 'farming' various branches of the customs. Different syndicates offered bids and in return for a guaranteed annual revenue, the Crown handed over its customs administration to the successful farmers, who were associated with Salisbury. The Great Farm enriched the winning merchants, but the trade revenues flowing into the Exchequer also rose steadily. Salisbury reduced the farmers' percentage both in 1607 and again in 1611 when it became clear that the Great Farm was even more profitable to them than he had anticipated.

As trade flourished, it was tempting to place further burdens on it. Since the mid-sixteenth century, a few extra duties, known as impositions, were collected on luxury imports such as wine. Their legal status was ambiguous since they were not included in the Tonnage and Poundage Act by which Parliament voted customs to the Crown. In 1605 Lord Treasurer Dorset alerted Salisbury to the possibility that recent problems in the Levant Company could be turned to good account. The most valuable commodity imported from the Levant was currants, but merchants were opposing the additional duty charged on them. They pointed out that it was originally not a levy paid direct to the Crown, but had covered the unusually high costs of the company's trade, which required the merchants to maintain an ambassador at Constantinople and make expensive presents to the Turkish court. John Bate, a leading Levant merchant, caused a riot at the Thames waterside in 1606 when he refused to pay the royal currant levy and was placed in prison. A test case in the Exchequer – masterminded by Dorset and Salisbury – found Bate guilty, and established the vital precedent that the Crown at will could place extra impositions on selected goods.[2] Judge Fleming, chief baron of the Exchequer, elaborated the verdict by outlining a new view of the royal prerogative. Distinguishing between its 'ordinary' and 'absolute' aspects, he attributed the levying of impositions to the king's absolute or legally unfettered prerogative. Merchants were dismayed at the verdict's long-term consequences for trade, while lawyers were alarmed at the expansion of the prerogative. Salisbury brushed aside both arguments and promptly drew up an extensive new list of impositions on luxury imports. Published in 1608, it rapidly increased the Crown's rising revenues from commerce.

Meanwhile, the king seemed intent on distributing money and favours as extravagantly as possible. By 1605 he was beginning to listen to complaints about his profligacy, and the Privy Council composed a careful but forceful letter. Like all their contemporaries, they fully accepted that bounty or generosity was an intrinsic part of kingship, but reminded James that his unregulated giving in response to 'importunity of suitors' was dangerously weakening his own estate. It also made their task of re-establishing the postwar royal finances almost impossible.[3] In February 1606 Dorset addressed a joint committee of the Lords and Commons in Parliament and set out the king's debts. These had risen to £735,000, while the ordinary receipts fell short of the outgoings by £81,000 annually. Much of the initial debt of 1603–4 should already have been offset by the parliamentary subsidy voted in 1606 which brought in £450,000. Moreover, by 1607–8 the ordinary revenue had risen to around £366,000 per annum, an increase of more than £100,000 or around 28 per cent from the annual revenue at the king's accession.[4] Prudent management should have kept James solvent thereafter, especially as his income from the customs dues and impositions was also rising steadily, but, instead, his expenditure increased relentlessly.

Salisbury was the guiding hand behind the 1605 Privy Council letter and after his elevation to the lord treasurership in 1608, he set about a thorough reform programme, building on what he and Dorset had already accomplished. He sat regularly in the Exchequer court and instituted a search for old debts. His admiring subordinate Sir Julius Caesar, the chancellor of the Exchequer, noted that in a single day's work on the leases of lands belonging to convicted recusants, Salisbury 'got for the king . . . £9402'. Another day's work pursuing subsidy collectors who owed money reclaimed a further £9647 1s 11d.[5] Salisbury also effected economies, which included trimming the expanding household of Prince Henry. Steadily, he reinvigorated the hidebound administration of the Exchequer and drove down the deficit.

The Crown lands, the other major component of royal income alongside customs, were diminished by wartime sales. Traditionally, they were used more as a source of patronage to bestow on courtiers and other suitors than as a source of income. On the other hand, they could yield much higher revenues if they were properly administered. Salisbury tackled the conservation and management of the royal woods, expanding the income from sales and rents. He raised the entry fines and increased the price paid by purchasers of royal estates. After selling off some small properties that were uneconomic to administer, he persuaded James in 1609 to accept a fresh entail on the Crown lands that would limit his ability to give them away. Salisbury also instituted a system whereby the grants available to suitors were listed in a Book of Bounty, so instead of badgering the king personally, courtiers and others were referred to a regular weekly session in the Exchequer presided over by Salisbury and his trusted officials.

The Great Contract

With two years of exhausting work behind him, by 1610 Salisbury was prepared to embark on his next project for increasing the royal revenues. Deeply imbued with the ethos of Elizabethan England, he was convinced that the only lasting solution must lie with Parliament. Economies were necessary, but so also was a new supply of revenue to set the Crown on a secure footing. Inflation continued to erode the royal income and Salisbury was appalled on taking over in 1608 to find that there were no reserves in the Exchequer for an emergency. With some difficulty, over the autumn of 1609 James was persuaded to call another parliamentary session. The lord treasurer wrote a remarkably frank series of tracts in which he tried to make the king recognise that his reckless extravagance was a fundamental cause of royal indebtedness. Salisbury pulled no punches, listing events such as the Cornish tax revolt of 1497 and the disaster of the Amicable Grant in 1525. He pointedly praised the disciplined, well-organised Henry VII from whom James so proudly derived his claim to the English throne. The conclusion was stark: 'It is not possible for a king of England . . . to be rich or safe, but by frugality.' James was well aware of his rising debts and as early as October 1605, he lamented that the 'glorious sunshine of my entry here should be so soon overcast with the dark clouds of irreparable misery'.[6] Yet these moments of gloom soon passed and had little effect on his usual prodigality. Salisbury in his treatises tactfully suggested that settled pensions should be provided for Scots courtiers, hoping to restrain the king's unceasing gifts to his fellow-countrymen. By 1610 they had amassed an astonishing £88,280 in cash, a potential £144,100 in old debts to be collected and £11,093 in annuities. Most of this went to 11 Scotsmen, while many others went home empty-handed. The king's bounty was extremely unevenly distributed.[7] The problem really stemmed from the fact that as in Scotland, James at heart believed that finance was not a problem for him, but for his Privy Councillors. Salisbury was risking grave royal displeasure in urging the king to face up to his personal responsibility.

Members of Parliament assembled at Westminster in February 1610 and Salisbury proposed to the Commons (since they and not the

Lords voted taxation) a sweeping new financial scheme. Known as the Great Contract, it was crafted by Salisbury and his Exchequer colleagues over the summer and autumn of 1609. The contract proposed that in exchange for ten royal concessions, Parliament should grant a lump sum of £600,000 to pay off the king's debts and provide an emergency reserve. In addition Salisbury asked for a regular annual grant of £200,000, which would require initial parliamentary approval, but then continue without further authorisation. The ten concessions were designed to be attractive to the king's subjects, but not too expensive to the Crown, since that would be counter-productive. Most of them were burdensome legal rights deriving from the royal prerogative. James in future would agree to be bound by the statute of limitations (the time-scale during which legal action might be taken), which already applied to his subjects. This would remove a great royal advantage. Crown leases of land found to have a minor flaw would not be automatically cancelled, but interpreted favourably for the lessee. The most tempting offer was the abolition of purveyance, the royal right already complained of by the Commons in earlier sessions.

In addition, Salisbury offered significant reforms in the practice of the court of Wards, of which he was master. The Commons had already criticised the highly commercialised system (see p. 61). Wardship caused a great deal of emotional and financial damage to families, and not surprisingly the gentry who formed the majority of the Commons looked for its removal and not merely reform, however sweeping. In the bargaining Salisbury was forced to increase his offer, so that the outright abolition of the court of Wards became part of the Great Contract.

Speaking to a Commons committee, Salisbury expounded his conservative political philosophy: 'All wise princes, whensoever there was cause to withstand present evils or future perils . . . have always addressed themselves to their Parliaments.'[8] He briskly dismissed accusations that the king's extravagance was to blame for the crisis. Instead, Salisbury emphasised unavoidable expenditures such as the late queen's funeral and the arrival of ambassadors to greet the new king. He pointed to the security of the realm, which was integrally related to the solvency of the Crown. Salisbury also noted that in the later years of Elizabeth's reign, her tightfisted refusal to show generosity to her servants was resented. The king's subjects had welcomed the new era of royal bounty after 1603. This public approach was studiedly different from the one set out in his private treatises only a few months earlier, which unhesitatingly pointed the finger at James himself.

The Commons were far from convinced, and it was quickly apparent that attitudes as traditional as Salisbury's own, but far less receptive to royal needs, still dominated members' views on taxation. The Crown was at peace, the king's extravagance was too well known and his excessive gifts to his Scottish cronies were deplored. In debates they harped on extensive medieval precedents, all insisting that Crown expenditure was to be supported only when incurred in the national or 'commonwealth' interest. James was compared to a leaky cistern: money given to him would simply pour out again. Most members were gentlemen who ran their own estates and understood the disciplines of living within their income. They thought the king should do the same.[9]

James was annoyed by their frankness and by the slowness of proceedings, particularly when the Commons moved on to censure Dr John Cowell, regius professor of civil law at Cambridge. In 1607 Cowell published *The Interpreter*, a dictionary of common legal terms in some of which he maintained that the king was an absolute monarch above the law. The same themes were reiterated in a sermon preached by Bishop Samuel Harsnett at court in 1610. To limit controversy James condemned Cowell's book in a proclamation, although he supported Harsnett. In a speech to Parliament on 21 March, he emphasised the divine right of kings, 'God's lieutenants upon earth', but accepted that in a settled kingdom, kings would voluntarily conform themselves to the law. He also went out of his way to praise the English common law despite his own background in the Scottish civil law. James defused the crisis over Cowell and his speech was well received, but for those members of the the Lower House who found the king's oratory both absolutist and boastful, it did little to incline them to the Great Contract.[10]

The Commons haggled for several weeks before breaking off in June 1610 for the installation of the 16-year-old Henry as Prince of

Wales. Salisbury expended much effort on arranging a splendid investiture, which uniquely took place in the midst of the Westminster session. He hoped that by showcasing the popular young prince, he would loosen the Commons' purse-strings as well as ingratiating himself with the youth who would be Henry IX. Shortly before the ceremony, shocking news arrived of the assassination of Henri IV, which plunged France into a dangerous minority. Members of Parliament were reminded that their own security depended on the Stuart dynasty, and were urged to appreciate their good fortune in possessing both a mature king and a promising heir. After the installation of Prince Henry, they returned to the discussion of the Great Contract with increased willingness.[11]

During the session, however, tempers were steadily soured by the re-emergence of the issue of impositions. Both Salisbury and the king assumed that the precedent established by Bate's case settled the matter, but the Commons would not accept that the currant levy, unique to the Levant trade, provided a sufficient precedent for the extension of impositions on to other commodities. Fleming's ill-advised discourse on the Crown's absolute prerogative also affronted the lawyers. They led a powerful attack, but James sent a message warning the Commons not to dispute his prerogative since impositions had been settled by the Exchequer court. This seemed to limit freedom of speech, and the Lower House was not pacified when the king despatched a softer message agreeing that they could discuss any individual imposition that presented a problem. Instead, on 23 May the Commons drew up a petition asserting 'the ancient and fundamental right of the liberty of the Parliament in point of exact discussing of all matters concerning them and their possessions, goods, and rights whatsoever'. Without discussion in the law courts as well as in Parliament, 'it is impossible for the subject either to know or to maintain his right and property to his own lands and goods'. The judgment in Bate's case applied only to John Bate, and technically it could be reversed upon a writ of error, a form of appeal. It could not be construed as a binding and universal precedent.[12]

James replied soothingly that he had been misunderstood, since he would never meddle with property rights. He urged them to concentrate on more important issues, meaning the completion of the Great

Contract. Undeterred, the Commons spent two weeks debating impositions and extracted a royal promise that any future imposition would be put to Parliament for prior consent. To Salisbury this was a damaging concession since he had confidently expected that impositions could be easily extended whenever new luxuries appeared. James had no particular love for impositions and was willing to give them up in return for financial compensation. For him the question was purely monetary, whereas to the Commons it was a constitutional issue about the property rights of the subject. Salisbury had not foreseen that impositions would raise major legal issues, and the conflict caught him unprepared.

By the time of the summer recess in July 1610, the Commons had agreed in principle to that part of the Contract providing an annual levy of £200,000, but it was worth less to the king than Salisbury originally calculated because the Commons did not offer to compensate for the lost revenues of the court of Wards – now to be abolished, not reformed. They voted only a single subsidy and one fifteenth, worth around £107,000, and never discussed the Contract's request for a lump sum of £600,000. Returning home, members of Parliament found that their neighbours disliked the idea of an annual levy of taxation. They also objected strongly to impositions. When Parliament met again in October, attendance was poor in the Lords and disgraceful in the Commons, where 'not above 100' out of 497 members were present.[13] Those unwilling to be associated with the Contract were voting with their feet. The reluctant members spun out the debates inconclusively despite the pleas of Sir Julius Caesar, Salisbury's henchman: 'the King's need bleeds, the commonwealth bleeds, let us take reality, not *verba* (words).' James reminded them that he needed the lump sum to wipe out his debts, a vital part of the Contract since he was paying heavy interest charges. The king asked for a reduced £500,000, and also refused to offer job compensation to the officers of the wards (some of them in the Lower House) who would be unemployed when the Contract went through. The Commons thereupon broke off negotiations, and after it was reported that a move was afoot to petition the king to send all the Scots home, he angrily dissolved the Parliament.

There were, of course, valid reasons to argue against the Contract.

To the country, there seemed little reason to pay higher taxes for an ill-regulated court and in the absence of foreign threats, there was no sense of national emergency. The argument from medieval and Elizabethan precedents, that Parliament should pay only for the expenses of the commonwealth, was persuasive. The annual levy would presumably have been spread evenly across the tax-paying classes, but relief from wardship would only benefit a limited number of greater landowners. Similarly, purveyance was mostly a grievance in the southern counties where the king was usually resident. The Crown's offers seemed uneven. To courtiers, the Contract's abolition of wardship and purveyance removed significant sources of patronage from which they had benefited. The more financially sophisticated worried that in an age of inflation, the king would be tied to fixed revenues negotiated in Parliament. Nevertheless, Salisbury was right in sensing that the Crown's weaknesses must be addressed, and there was no better scheme on the drawing-board.

James was already furious at the lengthy and fruitless negotiations in which he had been enmeshed by his lord treasurer. The bargaining spirit of the Commons, intent on extracting retribution instead of freely offering supply, offended his deepest sense of fit responses to a king. He turned on Salisbury, whose recent behaviour had shown signs of great strain, and told him to look for 'the next best means how to help my state, since ye see there is no more trust to be laid upon this rotten reed of Egypt, for your greatest error hath been that ye ever expected to draw honey out of gall'. Everybody else, said James, had despaired of the Parliament, but Salisbury had been blinded by 'the self-love of [his] own counsel' in continuing discussion.[14] Salisbury was out of favour, but only briefly, for James still relied on him somehow to solve his financial problems. He remained indispensable and by February 1611, the king returned to his usual practice of communicating with the Privy Council almost exclusively through the lord treasurer.

Even though Salisbury survived the crisis, the failure of the Great Contract was a turning-point. The scheme, at once far-sighted and conservative, attempted to restore the Crown to the levels of financial safety that Elizabeth achieved in her middle years. Salisbury had no intention of abolishing parliaments. The proposed annual revenue of

£200,000 would only cover ordinary expenditures and any threat of war would require additional Commons votes of taxation. The Crown must achieve an accommodation with Parliament, since without taxation the country could not be adequately defended at home, nor go to the assistance of allies abroad. Salisbury wrote bluntly to James after the failure of the Contract that without parliamentary help, little more could be done, 'seeing that place hath ever been the only foundation of supply to those princes whose necessities have been beyond the cares and endeavours of private men'.[15] Salisbury based his analysis on English history, but James made no further attempt to build a new relationship with Parliament. When the ministers of Charles I attempted to do so in 1641, it was too late.

Meanwhile, Salisbury surveyed a number of other schemes that might bring in money although not on the scale of the Contract. The most promising was the sale of the new title of baronet, a hereditary knighthood designed to be passed on to eldest sons. Candidates paid £1095, designated for the expenses of pacifying and resettling Ulster. Eighty-eight baronetcies were bestowed between May and November 1611 and strikingly, around a quarter of the gentlemen who came forward were recusants or were catholic-related. Four were closely connected to the families of the Gunpowder plotters of 1605. The willingness of the king and Salisbury to accept these catholic baronets indicated more than just a general offer of a degree of tolerance to peaceable recusant landowners. The transaction silently acknowledged that the powder plotters had been extremists whose crimes were disavowed by their catholic relatives. James acknowledged their loyalty by permitting them to buy an expensive honour.[16]

In December 1611 Salisbury suffered an illness that compelled him to hand over the day-to-day running of the Treasury to Sir Julius Caesar. It proved to be the onset of terminal cancer and although he continued to work obsessively, it was clear that his days were numbered. James was ill-advised to assume that any single individual, however able and diligent, could carry such a crushing workload. Some jobs were inevitably left undone and Salisbury's premature death in 1612 was due in part to his Herculean efforts in royal service, undermining his fragile health. Thereafter, the king's financial advisers attempted to put forward measures of economy and efficiency rather than trying to restructure the system. Salisbury's moves to place greater taxes on trade (a more elastic source of revenue than the subsidy which was rigidly assessed on land) were not followed up. Inefficiency and corruption grew steadily worse throughout the administration. When Salisbury wrote to James in 1611 that he felt constrained to warn him 'how the storm comes before it breaks', he was more prescient than he would have wished.

Foreign Policy

Foreign policy was a more crucial aspect of James's kingcraft in England than in Scotland, and he took his responsibilities seriously. After 1603, despite his increasingly lengthy absences from the capital, he insisted on remaining fully briefed on foreign affairs. Regular correspondence passed between Westminster and the royal hunting lodges. The rest of the Privy Council played little part in the formulation of foreign policy, which was the preserve of the king and Salisbury until the latter's death. James took pride in his role as a European peacemaker, and told his Parliament in 1604 that with the Anglo-Spanish negotiations then in progress, they enjoyed 'outward Peace . . . peace abroad with all forreine neighbours'.[17] Yet major conflicts remained, particularly in the low countries where Philip III's armies were still attempting to reverse Dutch independence. The archdukes as governers of the Spanish low countries were desperately anxious to end the war that brought economic ruin to their provinces. Meanwhile, until 1610 Henri IV continued his aid to the Dutch in an effort to weaken Spain, while the English pressed both the Dutch and the French for the payment of the extensive loans made by Queen Elizabeth. Slowly, the people of the low countries took charge of their own affairs. Fighting between the northern and the southern provinces gradually petered out: interim truces were made, and finally in 1609, the United Provinces (as the Dutch state was known) signed a 12-year truce with Spain.

Peace in the low countries was a great gain, but religious division was still destabilising Europe. After the Reformation, the German territories of the Holy Roman Empire were split between catholic and protestant states, and tensions were considerable. In 1608 a protestant union was formed under the leadership of Frederick IV of the Palatinate, a Calvinist state along the lower Rhine. In response, the following year saw the creation of a Catholic League led by Duke Maximilian of Bavaria, polarising the situation. Then a succession dispute broke out in the principality of Cleves-Julich near the Dutch border, where the protestant faction appealed both to James I and Henri IV for support. The French response was much stronger. Although a catholic convert, Henri remained fiercely opposed to the Spanish Habsburgs, cousins of the Austrian Habsburgs in Vienna with whom the Catholic League was closely allied. Henri decided to challenge Habsburg dominance of Europe and began to mobilise France for war over Cleves-Julich. Then the king was assassinated in May 1610 and in the vacuum created by his death, the princes of the Protestant Union appealed to James for protection. A small expeditionary force of English troops was sent out, but both financial constraints and James's cherished reputation as a peacemaker prevented England from taking further action. Gradually, the crisis died down without an outbreak of war, but it drew attention to the precariousness of peace in Europe.

Throughout these years King James was actively reinforcing his diplomacy by his pen. The enjoyment of authorship, so manifest in his earlier works written in Scotland, did not fade after 1603. His first major treatise was on the Oath of Allegiance that he devised for catholics after the Gunpowder Plot of 1605 (see p. 161), and his book was entitled in Latin, *Triplici Nodo Triplex Cuneus: or an Apologie*. It appeared anonymously in 1608 and Latin and French translations were published soon after. James was concerned to refute the argument that the papacy possessed God-given powers to depose princes, a claim he thought constituted a threat to all lawful monarchs both catholic and protestant. He followed up the *Apologie* in 1609 with a longer treatise, the *Premonition* or warning, addressed to the Holy Roman Emperor Rudolph II and all other European kings and princes, whom he described as cousins and friends. English diplomats were instructed to present copies to the heads of those states where they were accredited, an order that created much embarrassment in catholic courts. In the original controversy over the papal deposing power, James had been answered by Cardinal

Bellarmine, who reiterated the papal claim to be able to depose kings as well as to excommunicate them. This, argued James, was a usurpation of power contrary to 'the rule of all Scriptures, ancient Councels, and Fathers'. Such papal claims were a threat to European stability, and should alarm catholic monarchs even more than protestant ones, since many of them had large numbers of catholic clerical subjects whose secular allegiance, the king argued, was unreliable. The king used the *Premonition* to urge a General Council of the Church, another of his favourite schemes (see pp. 173–5) but unfortunately he devoted a lengthy section of his treatise to a discussion of whether the papacy was the Biblical Antichrist. This was surely a tactical error since catholic sovereigns were almost bound to find the tone offensive.[18] However, perhaps the chief interest of the *Premonition* is that it conveys the strength of the king's conviction that the estate of monarchy, and the need to defend the divinely bestowed powers of monarchs, created unshakeable bonds of unity between all European rulers. James thought that such royal bonds transcended the catholic–protestant divide, and it was in this spirit that he approached the question of finding a consort for his son.

After the murder of Henri IV, France was ruled by Queen Marie de Medicis acting as regent for her young son Louis XIII. Faced with a factious nobility at home, she had no desire to continue her late husband's warlike plans. Instead, she concentrated on building links with Spain through double marriages, which took place in 1615 when Louis married the daughter of Philip III and Marie's daughter Elizabeth married the future Philip IV. Like Queen Marie, James saw foreign policy as intrinsically dynastic, a matter for the royal houses of Europe. Linked to the protestant princes by both religion and treaty obligations, he wished to balance those commitments by arranging a catholic marriage for Henry, which would also reinforce his personal links with other European sovereigns and demonstrate his ecumenical goodwill.

Negotiations with Spain at first seemed promising, but when Philip III welcomed instead the overtures of France, he offered James only the younger Infanta Maria. Still a child, she would keep Prince Henry waiting for too many years. Angry at what he regarded as Spanish duplicity, the king turned his attention to the second-ranking catholic states of Savoy and Tuscany, both of which were wealthy enough to offer a substantial dowry. A match with either of them would replenish the royal coffers and reinforce James's credentials as a wise Solomon bridging the European religious divide.

Throughout 1611 and early 1612, James and Salisbury jointly conducted marriage negotiations for Henry. Then Salisbury died in spring 1612 before anything was finalised. Tensions were rising between father and son, for Henry was a committed protestant and filled with distaste at the prospect of a catholic bride, Spanish or not. He did not share his father's view that the estate of monarchy transcended religious barriers. Significantly, the pulpits of London and protestant opinion generally were already voicing deep hostility towards all the suggested catholic matches. In November 1612 the 18-year-old prince died suddenly, probably of typhoid fever. Time was to show that in the matter of his marriage, Henry was more in touch with public opinion than his father, but with his death the agitation over the catholic match died down. Instead, there was an outpouring of grief, indicating none too tactfully that English public opinion was already disenchanted with James and had looked forward to the prospect of the Anglicised, upstanding young prince.

One aspect of Henry's death, however, was quietly welcomed by the king's hard-pressed Privy Councillors. Henry showed every sign of becoming as heedless of money as his father and his love of art collecting and cultural display led him to spend beyond his means. The expensive separate court created for him in 1610 was disbanded, ending a heavy and increasing strain on the royal finances. Prince Charles was not installed as Prince of Wales until 1616 and his household costs were modest. The unexpected financial relief of Henry's death provided a breathing space.

The deaths of Dunbar, Salisbury and Prince Henry in 1611–12 brought the first and most successful era of Jacobean rule to a close. For all the setbacks over the Union and the Great Contract, these years contained solid achievements. James's trouble-free accession and the beginnings of *rapprochement* between the English and the Scots laid the foundations for a lasting union of the Crowns. Peace with Spain ended the crushing financial burdens carried by England since 1585 and led to a trade boom. The assured succession guaranteed by the king's young family was a great relief after the years of uncertainty under Elizabeth. Queen Anne and later Prince Henry invigorated the cultural life of the court with their patronage of artists, actors and musicians. Playwrights began to celebrate a new concept of empire and British national consciousness in plays such as Shakespeare's *Cymbeline*. Perhaps most significant, in these early years the king put into effect his broad-based, inclusive policies on religion. By well-chosen appointments and discriminating clerical patronage, he successfully guided the Church of England into the middle ground on both doctrine and liturgy. He encouraged the inclusion of moderate Puritans as well as crypto-catholics prepared to conform, thereby defusing the twin threats of radical Puritanism and militant catholicism (see pp. 155–60). All these varied achievements added lustre to the first part of the reign, but although they did not fade immediately, after 1612 Jacobean rule lost much of its early sparkle. In the absence of statesmen of the stature of Salisbury and Dunbar, its political successes were also far fewer.

4 The Rise of the Favourites

The Earl of Somerset

In his early years in England, James promoted court favourites such as the Scot Sir James Hay and the Englishman Sir Philip Herbert, whom he created earl of Montgomery. These men were boon companions rather than sexual intimates and they were of little political importance. The situation changed in 1607 when a young, blond Scot named Robert Carr (or Ker) was injured competing in a court tournament. James visited him during his recovery and gradually Carr became the new favourite, far closer to the king than his predecessors. Among those who were drawn to the rising star was the ambitious and able Englishman Sir Thomas Overbury, who urged Carr to aim at power, not just prominence at court. Late in 1610 Carr was involved in some dubious manoeuvres in Parliament and was apparently responsible for circulating the story that the Commons were calling for all Scots to be sent home (see p. 79).

After the deaths in quick succession of both Dunbar and Salisbury, Carr seized the opportunity of expanding his political influence. James was increasingly enamoured, bestowing gestures of physical affection upon Carr in public, as he had done with D'Aubigny years before. Carr received a peerage in 1611, a place on the Privy Council in April 1612 and the earldom of Somerset in 1613. The death of Salisbury forced James to take more business into his own hands and Carr acted as his private secretary. Carr was also effective in screening him from the endless press of suitors. The king despised many of those who pestered him, remarking cynically in 1610 that if Judas had been convicted of Christ's murder some courtier would be found to beg his pardon. Yet James found it difficult to deny them, so Carr's presence at his side afforded a measure of protection.

James decided not to replace Salisbury as lord treasurer, but to put the Treasury into commission. The commission was led by Northampton and his nephew Suffolk, together with Sir Julius Caesar, the experienced chancellor of the Exchequer. The able Northampton also took over the day-to-day handling of government business formerly despatched by Salisbury. Northampton made efforts to revive the reforming navy commission over which he presided in 1608, though James had not carried out its recommendations. To Northampton's disappointment the king showed no greater interest in 1613. He was more successful in his efforts to raise extra income from trade, bringing in the London merchant Lionel Cranfield whose insider knowledge led to the renegotiation of several of the customs farms on better terms for the Crown. Cranfield's statistical flair and commercial experience became a valuable asset to James's government.[1]

Carr contined to enjoy privileged access to the king and, after 1611, was the most significant new presence on the political scene. His influence increased after the death of Prince Henry, who showed every sign of resenting the favourite's monopoly of his father's affections. Princess Elizabeth, the king's second surviving child, was of marriageable age. Since James was still looking to catholic states for a bride for his heir, a protestant match for Elizabeth would balance English policy abroad. James made a defensive alliance with the German Union of Protestant States in March 1612 and agreed that his daughter should marry the Union's leader, the Elector Frederick V of the Rhineland Palatinate. Frederick was also a grandson of the Dutch protestant hero William the Silent. He crossed to England in September 1612 and after dazzling celebrations at court, the couple were married in February 1613. After the death of Henry, Elizabeth was a more significant figure than she had been when the match was originally agreed. Prince Charles was not robust; if he predeceased the king, then the princess was the next heir. In 1614 James sombrely noted the possibility that the Electress or her children might succeed to what he called 'this imperiall Crown'.[2] Elizabeth remained her younger brother's presumptive successor until the birth of the future Charles II in May 1630.

The Palatinate marriage left the king well placed as a mediator amongst protestant states. Through Queen Anne, James had close links with Denmark; while through his son-in-law the Elector he had family links with the King of Sweden, the Eelector of Brandenburg and the Duc de Bouillon, the usual spokesman for the French Huguenots. In January 1613 James facilitated a peace between Sweden and Denmark. Deeply imbued with a sense of dynasty (partly the result of his long wait to inherit the English throne), the king tended to think of the legal rights of rulers as the central aspect of foreign policy. His approach was often successful in peacetime, but became less relevant after the outbreak of European war in 1618.

With the death of Henry and the departure of Elizabeth for the Rhineland, the king's emotional links to his family were weakened. Queen Anne detested the newly created earl of Somerset, since his emergence demonstrated publicly that her influence over her husband had waned. From then on, the queen retreated more into the shadows; she staged her last known masque in February 1614 and her female court ceased to attract the service of English noblewomen. James was entranced by his favourite, but Somerset fell in love with the court beauty Frances Howard. She was a daughter of the earl of Suffolk and already wedded to the young earl of Essex, but Frances was desperate to free herself from her unhappy marriage. With the king's support, she obtained an ecclesiastical annulment after a salacious public hearing which branded Essex as impotent. The verdict was widely seen as reflecting badly on James (who had enthusiastically involved himself in the case, opposing Archbishop Abbot) and on the immoral behaviour of his whole court.

Meanwhile, Somerset's political adviser Overbury was growing increasingly restive. He grew to loathe Frances and disliked the way in which the relationship brought Somerset closer to the Howards, undercutting his own influence. Equally, the king disliked Overbury's hold over Somerset, so when Overbury refused a pressing royal offer of an ambassadorship abroad, he was sent to the Tower in April 1613. He died there five months later.

The wedding of Somerset and Frances in December 1613 was another brilliant court spectacle, paid for by the king. James was never jealous of his favourites' wives, but Frances was to prove a uniquely disruptive influence. The marriage aligned Somerset with the Howard group led by Northampton and Suffolk. Although the family did not form a political bloc, they were seen as favouring pro-Spanish policies, and in the case of Northampton, disliking frequent parliaments. In June 1614 after the death of Northampton, James appointed Suffolk as lord treasurer. In July Somerset succeeded his father-in-law as lord chamberlain. The Howards' control over patronage had never been greater.

The more protestant-leaning Privy Councillors, led by the earl of Pembroke and George Abbott who succeeded Bancroft as archbishop of Canterbury in 1611, were put on the defensive. Their position was undermined further by the failure of the Addled Parliament in spring 1614 (see p. 93–4) They decided on the hazardous gamble of attempting to distract the king's attention from Somerset and by serendipitous chance lighted upon George Villiers, a charming young country gentleman who was presented to James on progress in August 1614.

The relationship between Somerset and the king was still close, but the favourite's rise to power had gone to his head. Somerset treated James with scarcely concealed disrespect and personal coldness. It seems likely that his own passion for Frances made him spurn the king's advances. James, in letters of extraordinary frankness, complained of his 'insolent pride . . . with a settled kind of induced obstinacy', his 'continual dogged sullen behaviour' and his 'long creeping back and withdrawing . . . from lying in my chamber, notwithstanding my many hundred times earnest soliciting you to the contrary'.[3] Villiers was increasingly in the royal presence despite Somerset's efforts to block his rise at court. James wanted to recall Somerset to his former affectionate conduct, sadly acknowledging that his own love for him had been 'infinite' and asking that he 'might be met then with your entire heart, but softened with humility'.[4] In summer 1615 the king tried to arrange that his old and new favourites should come together, but when Villiers courteously called on Somerset, all he got was a promise to break his neck. Shortly afterwards, the news broke that before her marriage, Frances Howard Somerset had been instrumental in arranging for the death by poisoning of Sir Thomas Overbury in the Tower.

James was shocked and in October 1615, he appointed commissioners to investigate. He showed both sense and courage in telling Somerset that the investigation must go ahead: 'In a business of this nature I have nothing to look unto but first my conscience before God, and next my reputation in the eyes of the world.'[5] As Frances was the daughter of Lord Treasurer Suffolk and her husband was lord chamberlain, the affair reached into the heart of the court. The couple were tried and found guilty in 1616, then sentenced to death, although it remains unclear whether Overbury died from the substances administered to him or from disease contracted in the Tower. From the sensational annulment of Frances's first marriage through the celebrations of the Somersets' nuptials, and concluding with the appalling evidence presented at the murder trial, the sordid story dominated the years 1613 to 1616. Ambassadors in London sent detailed accounts back to their own rulers. The court was exposed as never before and a rash of salacious libels resulted. There was a strongly misogynistic flavour about much of the reportage which exemplified the dismal anti-women rhetoric of the period. Frances was exaggeratedly depicted as the quintessence of female villainy, but her involvement in the poisoning plot was beyond doubt.

The king commuted the death sentences, but the Somersets remained in the Tower until 1622, later retiring to the country. However, James showed no compunction in allowing the lesser fry to hang. These included Mrs Turner, Frances's confidante, and Richard Weston, Overbury's gaoler in the Tower, who rightly feared that those in power would 'make a net to catch little birds and let the great ones go'.[6] Popular feeling followed Weston and in 1616 a crowd nearly lynched the queen's coach when it was thought that Frances and her mother were inside. James did not disgrace Somerset who even kept his Garter, and imprisonment in the Tower was made comfortable by a large domestic staff. The king pardoned Frances soon after the trial and Somerset in 1624, but their reputation was beyond repair. The trial was a turning-point and from then on, courtiers came under increasingly scurrilous attack.[7]

The Parliament of 1614

As the Anglo-Scottish court lost much of its lustre, the English

Parliament also seemed to be failing. The three sessions of 1604–7 achieved few of the king's objectives, but at least in 1606 a large grant of taxation was voted. The failure of the Great Contract in 1610 together with the determined attack on impositions further soured James's attitude. The sole financial outcome of the 1610 session was a single subsidy. Impositions were already bringing in around £70,000 per year and this would rise steadily with the expansion of trade, so the inadequacy of parliamentary supply was thrown into sharp relief. James became increasingly obsessed by the idea of a marriage dowry to help him out of his financial difficulties. Diplomatic overtures began for a marriage between Prince Charles and the 6-year-old Christine of France. The king was hoping for around £240,000, a substantial sum that would almost halve the Crown's debts. Despite promising beginnings the negotiations floundered when the internal situation in France deteriorated. By late 1613, the Duc de Bouillon and the Prince de Conde, second in line to the throne, were on the brink of raising a noble rebellion in protest against Marie de Medicis. As a result Anglo-French discussions ended in winter 1614.

Those advisers who in any case disliked the prospect of a catholic future queen urged James to make a further appeal to Parliament for financial support. The group was led by the earls of Suffolk and Pembroke and as the king later told the Commons, they encouraged him to think 'that my subjects did not hate me, which I know I had not deserved'.[8] His words reveal the depth of his alienation from Parliaments. However, the Privy Council was not entirely optimistic and with Salisbury dead and Northampton seriously ill, little effort was made to prepare properly for the 1614 session. The crucial position of Speaker was conferred on Ranulph Crew whose only experience of the Commons was in 1593. The new secretary of state Sir Ralph Winwood, the most senior minister present in the Lower House, was a diplomat with no previous parliamentary experience at all.

James began by rejecting any element of bargaining, which had so offended him in 1610. 'Where a contract begins, affection ceases', he reminisced wrily, adding, 'I hold the affections of my subjects to be the best purchase.' Unfortunately, the Commons returned to the most unpalatable topics of 1610, the king's uncontrollable extravagance and the impositions on trade, which they continued to regard as a threat to property rights. There was a remarkable unanimity of opinion in the Commons, with Sir Henry Montague (Recorder of London and a future chief justice) stating that 'The liberty of the kingdom is in question. That he was but a flatterer of the King that would maintain the King's right by law to impose.' The problem, as Conrad Russell has pointed out, was that 'both sides were so firmly convinced that they were legally in the right that they never fully absorbed that the other party thought differently.'[9] In addition the Commons refused to acknowledge that the king's financial straits made it unrealistic to expect him to give up impositions without an offer of alternative supply.

Another issue that caused unease was the fear of 'undertaking'. A group led by the Commons veteran Sir Henry Neville promised before the opening of the 1614 session to manage the Parliament more productively for the king. It emerged that Neville had done little more than offer some sensible advice, but the real concern probably arose from recent events. In the Irish Parliament of 1613 (see pp. 148–9), James attempted to secure a protestant majority by adding a further 84 seats to the existing 148. He insisted that by the royal prerogative, he could make as many as he liked: 'the more the merrier', he joked when addressing angry Irish members of Parliament in London in April 1614.[10] As a result, the English Commons feared that by the exercise of similar measures their independence might come under threat from the Crown.

It was clear to the king that the Commons were intent on depriving him of impositions, yet offering little but goodwill in return. It made no financial sense to conciliate them by abandoning a valuable source of income. James was particularly annoyed at a speech by the literary wit and lawyer John Hoskyns who commented that a wise prince would send strangers home, as Canute had done with his Danes. The comparison with the Scots was unmistakeable. Hoskyns also made an offensive allusion to the famous massacre known as the Sicilian Vespers when the entourage of a French king of Sicily was murdered. James dissolved Parliament after a mere nine weeks of debate and the session was dubbed the Addled Parliament, although the commission for dissolution made clear that as no acts had been passed, it was not legally a Parliament at all: as Chamberlain commented 'rather a parlee only'.[11]

The atmosphere of hostility and frustration grew even worse when the king sent four members of the Commons to the Tower, then tore up some bills and other parliamentary papers publicly in the banqueting chamber at Whitehall. He told Gondomar, the recently arrived Spanish ambassador, that the Commons was a body with no head, whose members voted without rule or order, amid cries, shouts and confusion. He was astonished that his predecessors had tolerated such an assembly, but he found it in England on his arrival and had not been able to do without it. Gondomar tactfully reminded him that he could summon and dismiss Parliaments at pleasure, at which the king brightened up. From then on, James was intent on avoiding another Parliament unless circumstances forced his hand. Instead, he fixed his hopes on a large marriage dowry and instructed his Privy Councillors to think of additional methods of money raising.

The first tactic was to appeal for a 'benevolence', a non-parliamentary tax demanded for national security, but not seen since 1546. Although a wave of protests was triggered, around £65,000 came in (not much less than a subsidy), indicating that the king still enjoyed support among his wealthier subjects. At the end of 1614, James opted for a scheme put to him by Alderman Sir William Cokayne, a smooth-talking Londoner intent on breaking into the lucrative monopoly of the Merchant Adventurers. The cloth trade expanded rapidly after the 1604 peace and was buoyant in 1614. Broadcloths (heavy, undyed woollens) dominated English overseas exports, but were finished in the Netherlands. The economic value of the final processes was very high, but the Netherlands not England benefited from the employment of skilled dyers and finishers, and from the additional profit margin when the cloths were sold on. Cokayne distributed largesse at court to obtain support for his projectors, who offered to create a dyeing and finishing capacity in England.

Cokayne convinced the king that the export of broadcloth should be phased out along with the Merchant Adventurers themselves. Additional employment would be created to benefit the realm and the customs revenues would rise by at least £40,000 annually. But the new company of 'King's Merchant Adventurers' led by Cokayne lacked the capital and expertise of the old company, and proved unable to buy up sufficient cloth to keep men in work in the clothing counties. English woollens were not as indispensable in the Netherlands as Cokayne thought. The Dutch banned all English imports and new sources of supply began to replace English broadcloths, an old-fashioned commodity whose market share was already declining. In June 1616 the king conspicuously honoured Cokayne by dining at his London house, but with exports down by about a third, and weavers' riots in Wiltshire and Gloucestershire over the summer, the project was a disaster. The old Merchant Adventurers were re-established in January 1617, although James extracted £50,000 from them for the return of their charter. The broadcloth trade improved, but never fully regained its previous position, and the outbreak of war in 1618 made trading conditions increasingly difficult. It was fortunate for English clothworkers and for the customs revenues that the 'new draperies', lighter coloured fabrics more popular than broadcloth, were in the long run able to provide increased employment and prosperity. Meanwhile, the Cokayne fiasco did not improve the reputation of the king's government either in the City of London or in the country.

In 1615 the Privy Council trawled again through various revenue-raising devices, but the majority of councillors urged concessions on impositions to facilitate a future Parliament. Then, in December 1615, the Dutch envoy Sir Noel de Caron asked if the king would be prepared to hand back the cautionary towns of Brill and Flushing in return for the sum of £250,000. This was less than half what the Dutch still owed, but the offer was cleverly timed since James was further in debt and seriously cash-strapped. The king put aside his councillors' advocacy of a Parliament but then had doubts: would the handover send the wrong signals, that England was abandoning her strong position in the Netherlands? It seems to have been the prospect of further royal expenditure that tipped the balance, for Prince Charles was coming of age and James needed to provide a suitable household for him. In May 1616 he ordered the cautionary towns to be sold and ignored calls for a Parliament.

The king's temper was tried both by the Addled Parliament and by the Somerset scandal during the winter and spring of 1616. Further irritations followed. James distrusted Sir Edward Coke, the learned but aggressive lawyer who advocated the supremacy of the English common law, which he argued was immemorial, beyond the memory or record of any beginning. To James, Coke diminished the royal position since the king saw himself as above the law and in consequence, able to expound it as well as the judges. Coke did not hesitate to criticise the Crown's discretionary powers, and further annoyed James (and successive Archbishops of Canterbury) by refusing to acknowledge that the ecclesiastical courts had a reasonable grievance when thwarted by other courts from proceeding on church matters such as tithes. These financial levies on parishioners were vital for the upkeep of the clergy, but Coke supported the rising use of prohibitions, devices removing such cases into the common law courts which were largely unsympathetic.

In 1613 James removed Coke from the position of chief justice of the Common Pleas to the equivalent position in the prestigious but less lucrative court of King's Bench, a strong hint that he should moderate his opinions. Nevertheless, James chose Coke to investigate the murder of Sir Thomas Overbury, only to find him remorseless in unearthing evidence that besmirched the court. In 1616 James and Coke clashed again, over the 'case of commendams', additional benefices that the Crown was entitled to grant to clerics who already held one living. The king wanted the judges to consult the Crown before coming to any decision in these cases but Coke refused. In the same year, he crossed Lord Chancellor Ellesmere when King's Bench threatened to bring an action against Ellesmere's court of Chancery. The king suspended Coke then dismissed him as chief justice in November 1616, the first dismissal of a judge for over a century. This cut short Coke's official career, but the legal *Reports* which he published steadily after 1600 were to prove immensely influential. James relented in 1617 and recalled Coke to the Privy Council (though not to legal office) after the fallen judge placated Buckingham by marrying his heiress daughter to the favourite's mentally defective brother. Even so, the old lawyer was to become one of the most tenacious and effective critics of the Crown in the Parliaments of the 1620s.

The Supremacy of Buckingham

By now Buckingham was well-entrenched in James's favour. In 1615–16 he became a gentleman of the Bedchamber, then master of the Horse, which entailed constant attendance on the king, and he was raised to an earldom for his willingness to accompany James to Scotland in 1617. Shortly afterwards, he was appointed to both the English and Scottish Privy Councils, and received a marquisate in 1618. Proximity to the king allowed Buckingham to promote the interests of his Villiers relatives, clients and friends, and he rapidly became the greatest (though by no means the only) noble patron at court. Among those who realised that service to the favourite was the way to promotion was the lawyer Sir Francis Bacon, son of Queen Elizabeth's first lord keeper. Bacon believed that his talents had never been properly acknowledged by his cousin Salisbury and seized the opportunity of acquiring a new and powerful patron. The downfall of the idiosyncratic and inflexible Coke led to Bacon's promotion to lord keeper in 1617, whereupon he demonstrated how much he differed in approach from his predecessor. Traditionally the lord keeper addressed the judges before they went around the country twice a year on circuit, hearing cases beyond the competence of local Justices of Peace. Bacon emphasised that the judges were lions of justice who must maintain the laws of the realm, but he added that they should equally remember that they were 'lions under the throne'.[12] Bacon would not confront the king as Coke had done.

In 1617 Principal Secretary Winwood died, whereupon James left his post unfilled and used Buckingham as his private secretary, as he had done earlier with Somerset. This gave the favourite privileged access to state information and enhanced his political standing, although the informal arrangement discomfited members of the Privy Council. Returning from Scotland, James found that councillors had censured the violent measures taken by the disgraced Sir Edward Coke to force his daughter to wed Buckingham's brother. The king reproved the Privy Council, adding that he loved Buckingham more than any other man and this was no defect since 'just as Christ had his John, so he (James), had his George'.[13] The extraordinary comparison cannot have increased councillors' respect for the king or the favourite.

The undisguised adoration bestowed by James on Buckingham fitted a pattern established in Scotland with his teenage affection for D'Aubigny. It seems almost certain that the adult relationship was physical as well as emotional, though Buckingham himself was actively heterosexual. It has been argued that James was probably 'homosocial', yearning for the warmth of a family that he lacked as a boy and enjoying male affection as a substitute. Much of his language to Buckingham – 'sweet child and wife' – supports the interpretation, although it does not counter the sexual nature of the imagery. The pair also exchanged bawdy language about the female members of the Villiers clan, another pointer to their own homosocial intimacy.[14] Buckingham knew that he and his extended family (formerly mere country gentry) were entirely dependent on the king's favour. He never made Somerset's mistake of treating James disdainfully and appeared to be genuinely fond of him, happily spending most of his time in close attendance.

The favourite soon involved James in another torrent of scandal. Lord Treasurer Suffolk and his countess, parents of the imprisoned Frances Somerset, plotted to regain favour for their family by supplanting Buckingham in the king's affections. Early in 1618 they found a handsome youth and groomed him, washing his face daily with posset-curd to beautify his complexion. Not surprisingly, the ploy kindled Buckingham's fierce anger and he determined to destroy the Howards completely. In summer 1618 he ensured that James learned of widespread allegations that creditors owed money by the Exchequer could not obtain payment without a bribe to the beautiful but rapacious Lady Suffolk. The king exiled her from London and when she disobediently returned, he told Suffolk that she risked being carted out of town like 'the vilest of her sex' – the London prostitutes.[15] Suffolk was suspended from the lord treasurership, then dismissed in July 1619.

A Star Chamber case followed in October 1619, where the Suffolks were found guilty of corruption and all the Howard clan removed from office, including Suffolk's son-in-law Lord Wallingford, master of the Wards. Lady Wallingford had been circulating defamatory libels against Buckingham, leading James to comment that Wallingford was like his father-in-law, 'altogether guided and overruled by an arch-wife'.[16] Genial, lazy and amoral, Suffolk allowed his family to enrich themselves from the royal coffers to an extent that was utterly unacceptable, even in a century that saw public office as the best way to private riches. To increase the humiliation of the court, the same year saw a further lurid Star Chamber case with accusations of incest. It involved the family of Sir Thomas Lake, who had served James for many years as secretary on his hunting trips before being promoted to a secretaryship of state. Lake joined the growing group of senior courtiers in the Tower and a fresh bunch of scurrilous libels made the rounds.

The fall of the Howards in 1619 was a turning point in the administrative history of the reign. Buckingham destroyed them primarily because they threatened him, but after their downfall there was an opportunity for change. There was little hope of reform under a lord treasurer as idle and venal as Suffolk, and his departure together with his family and hangers-on offered the possibility of better financial management. After 1618 Buckingham willingly used his considerable energies to rejuvenate what the king described as the 'ministerial' part of government. He was no longer just a favourite, but on the way to becoming a weighty politician.

5 War in Europe

In 1617 the king went on progress to Scotland (see pp. 141–2). As usual the ordinary account was in deficit, and to pay for his visit James requested from the City of London a loan of £100,000 for one year at 10 per cent interest. The lenders were so reluctant that City officials could not collect the full amount, and on the king's return the royal debt stood at £726,000. James failed to repay the capital of the loan and after another year he ceased to pay the promised interest. Not surprisingly, for the rest of his reign he was unable to raise money from the City. It was imperative to begin a programme of retrenchment and the king wrote sharply to his Privy Council, placing the responsibility for balancing his accounts entirely on them.[1]

James was easily distracted from the pursuit of economy. In January 1619 the banqueting house at Whitehall, rebuilt in 1606, was destroyed by fire. James commissioned a replacement from the architect Inigo Jones. By April Jones had devised a wooden scale model and work began on the masterly Palladian building that still survives. The king had plans to rebuild the whole palace on a grand scale, although since 1603 he had already spent around £15,000 on improvements. Only the banqueting house went ahead, aided by the economies resulting from the death of Queen Anne in March 1619 when her separate court at Denmark House was disbanded. James came to see her only three times in her last illness, but her son Charles, displaying greater affection, slept frequently in the chamber adjoining her bedroom at Hampton Court. Increasingly ignored after the rise of Buckingham, Anne was a lonely figure in her later years, but her death pointed again to her replacement by a male favourite. Popular distaste deepened for both the personal relationship between the king and Buckingham and for the Jacobean court as a whole.

Despite his neglect of the queen, James suffered an emotional blow at her demise, which cut him off even further from his past in Scotland and his earlier life as a family man. A month later the king fell seriously ill and the royal physician Sir Theodore Mayerne feared for some days that he was in mortal danger. Ill-health probably also increased his reliance on his handsome young companion. James's habit of leaning heavily on Buckingham as he walked was connected to his severe and worsening arthritis. Whether or not the king suffered from hereditary porphyria as has been plausibly suggested, his lifestyle was unhealthy. After losing his teeth he bolted his food instead of chewing it, ate no bread, and for years he drank heavily of various types of beer, ale and wine. These habits exacerbated his kidney stones, insomnia and bowel difficulties. In addition James suffered from various lasting injuries incurred on the hunting field.[2]

There were signs that the king's interest in business was fading, even in diplomacy where he prided himself on his perspicacity. In 1616 Secretary Winwood felt obliged to explain to the envoy from Savoy that his position paper was far too long: 'His Majesty would never read it for the half of his kingdom.' In January 1619 courtiers told the Venetian ambassador that the king's willingness to read through his paperwork had declined markedly since the death of Salisbury.[3] The active and creative phase of royal policy in both Ireland and Scotland was largely over by 1617 (see p. 141 for Scotland, and p. 149 for Ireland). James could not conceal his physical weaknesses on great state occasions: in 1621 he was carried to the opening of Parliament in a chair and it was feared that he would not walk again. Yet it would be wrong to see the king as broken and decrepit, for at least until 1623, when he suffered another bout of illness, he was still fully capable of asserting himself. James never became a cypher, but after 1618 his energies were declining, and from then on it was Buckingham who made fresh efforts to address the tasks of government.

The Rise of Lionel Cranfield

By 1618 it was generally accepted that the favour James showed to

Buckingham was likely to last, so those who hoped to rise in government service gravitated to his side. The exceptionally able Cranfield moved to the rising favourite after losing his first patron Northampton in 1614. In addition to helping Buckingham to increase his private income, Cranfield used the device of a subcommission of the Privy Council to investigate Household reform. He uncovered extensive waste and corruption, and in June 1618 the king was prevailed upon to sign a Book of Orders saving around £18,000 per annum. Cranfield's efforts were encouraged in September when James appointed him master of the Wardrobe, where again he found 'abuses and deceits . . . incredible'. Buckingham knew he stood to gain from backing Cranfield. As the merchant told him, 'the more desperate the King's estate is presented, the more honour . . . to rectify it and the more shall your lordship merit of his Majesty.'[4]

Cranfield also investigated the navy. Lord Admiral Nottingham, a hero of 1588, was over 80. The king was considering bestowing the title on Buckingham so Cranfield surveyed the naval accounts. Costs for ship repairs were so inflated that Cranfield wrote sardonically that it would be better for the king just to give them away. The navy needed guns, not least to fight the growing numbers of North African pirates menacing English trade, so in September Cranfield also became master of the Ordnance. Costs were reduced though most of the work was done by the hardworking naval administrator Sir John Coke. There is also evidence that Cranfield was tempted to increase his own income by a dubious land deal with the corrupt officers of the Ordnance, which weakened efforts at reform. Charges to this effect featured in his impeachment in 1624.[5]

Buckingham became Lord Admiral in 1619 and under the reform commissioners, a five-year programme was undertaken that built new warships and cut expenditure at the same time. The Privy Council was also alerted to the need to improve England's land defences, and steadily pressed the counties to modernise the arms used by the militias. In the same year, Cranfield became master of the court of Wards and a Privy Councillor, besides joining the treasury commission set up after Suffolk's downfall. To make it clear that vast peculation would no longer be tolerated, the commission insisted that the disgraced lord treasurer should be tried, though this was against the king's initial wishes. New impositions were placed on tobacco, coal and some cloths – a move Cranfield opposed as he was already conscious of the slowdown in trade – and savings of around £85,000 per annum were made. By May 1619 Lord Chancellor Bacon was so optimistic that he told the king that the ordinary account was at last in balance.[6]

By 1620, however, Cranfield's drive and energies were being spread very thinly, and his economies made him many enemies at court. He was also coming to despair of the king, to whom he wrote emphasising that the debt had increased to £900,000. James gave away one-third of the new revenues from trade to ravenous courtiers, although court pensions already swallowed up nearly a sixth of the Crown's total income. Between 1618 and 1622, his Scottish crony the marquess of Hamilton received £13,000, while at New Year 1622 a mere page of the Chamber received an annuity of £300 per year – the income of a comfortable lesser gentleman. At the same festival, the earl of Holderness, an inveterate scrounger, got a grant of £500 per year in land. When the farmers of the customs paid £16,000 in composition for the new imposition on coal, half of it went straight to Buckingham.

In summer 1622 Cranfield decided on a stop to all payments from the Exchequer, but the measure was meaningless without royal support. Deciding that his previous largesse was not enough, the king wrote to Cranfield late that year, before the birth of Buckingham's first child, to make a further gift of £20,000 towards the Villiers mansion at Burghley-on-the-Hill. He thought the favourite would also need an astonishing £10,000 for preparations for the childbed itself and an additional £3000 for the furnishing of his new London townhouse.[7] It would have been political suicide for Cranfield to oppose his patron, but a continued programme of cost-cutting would inevitably bring conflict between him and Buckingham.

Relations with Spain

Buckingham strengthened his position by winning over young Charles, created Prince of Wales in 1616. The relationship was initially uneasy, but warmed gradually until in 1618, the prince even asked the favourite to mediate in a dispute with his father. As Charles grew older, the marriage that must be arranged for him increasingly became the central theme of English diplomacy. After the difficulties with the proposed French match and the disaster of the Addled Parliament, James was convinced that only a Spanish dowry would provide the royal revenues with sufficient financial relief. Discussion began in late 1614 and in May 1615 James received the Spanish terms. These required that any children should be brought up by their catholic mother and allowed if they wished to choose her religion, without being excluded from the succession to the throne. The concession would have caused uproar in England and Scotland, but after some hesitation James decided to proceed, continuing the negotations even when he learned that Spanish theologians also insisted on toleration for English catholics. The Spanish case was expertly argued by the Conde de Gondomar, who cleverly built up a personal friendship with both James and Charles.

In July 1618 Gondomar left England on grounds of ill-heath but it was arranged that shortly after his departure, there would be less harassment of catholics under the recusancy laws. This was intended to underline the king's continued interest in the Spanish match, but by October James was irritated by the uncontrolled appearance of priests in London and the concession was cancelled. Nevertheless, the absent ambassador was still seen as a major influence on foreign policy, particularly in October 1618 when the Elizabethan sea-dog Sir Walter Raleigh was sent to the block. Raleigh had been imprisoned in the Tower since 1603 for complicity in the Bye and Main Plots, but in 1617, desperate for money, James allowed him to sail to South America in search of the fabled gold deposits of the Orinoco river. Raleigh knew he faced death if he despoiled any Spanish goods or subjects. The expedition was a disaster. Raleigh fell ill, his men attacked the Spanish-held town of San Thomé, his son was killed and there was no gold to placate the king. On the scaffold Raleigh behaved with fearless good humour and dignity, reinforcing his status as a protestant hero. The execution was seen as a base appeasement of Spain, although the king was only carrying out the threat made clear to Raleigh at the commencement of the expedition.

The Outbreak of War

The early negotiations for a Spanish bride for Charles were driven not only by the king's urgent need for a large dowry, but also by his honourable and long-standing desire to act as a bridge-builder between catholics and protestants in Europe. However, in 1618 European politics suffered a cataclysmic change. In Bohemia, a territory of the Holy Roman Empire, a majority party disavowed their recently elected ruler Archduke Ferdinand of Styria, and threw two Habsburg messengers out of a high window of the Hradschin castle – the so-called 'defenestration of Prague'. Bohemia contained a substantial number of protestants, and even catholics feared that Ferdinand, Jesuit-educated and a fierce supporter of the Counter-Reformation, would be a divisive monarch. The Bohemian crown was elective, but only in constitutional and ceremonial terms, since for centuries the Habsburg heir to the Imperial throne had been the sole candidate. To make matters worse, in 1619 the Bohemian protestants offered their throne to the Elector Palatine, husband of Princess Elizabeth. They hoped to force the Habsburgs to acquiesce in the deposition of the archduke rather than risk a costly war against a coalition of protestant powers. They miscalculated, since the insult to Ferdinand also challenged Habsburg dominance in central Europe. Bohemia voted in the delicately balanced Imperial electoral college which chose the emperor, and without its vote Habsburg control of the Holy Roman Empire was threatened.

It took some time for James to appreciate the seriousness of the situation. The Elector sent an envoy to England to solicit advice, a request which always brought out the scholar-theologian in the king. His approach to foreign policy was moralistic rather than pragmatic, and his position was doubly delicate since the Spaniards had also flatteringly asked him to mediate in the Bohemian dispute. James always hoped that his peaceful intentions together with careful explanations of his stance would be sufficient to solve problems. He later explained that he could not support his son-in-law's action because it arose from religious division in Bohemia. 'What hath religion to do to decroune a king?', James demanded. 'Leave that opinion to the Devil and the Jesuits . . . Christ came into the world to teach Subjects obedience to the king and not rebellion.'[8] It was exactly the view he maintained in *Basilicon Doron*, urging Prince Henry to treat rebellion against any prince as tantamount to rebellion at home. This academic belief in the power of his own reasoning, usually backed up by extremely partial Biblical interpretation, did no great harm as long as there were no international emergencies directly affecting his kingdoms' interests. As conflagration overtook central Europe, reason and Biblical quotations were not enough and James stood by helplessly.

In January 1619 the Venetian ambassador commented on the king's 'hatred and distaste for affairs and troublesome matters'. His long-standing interest in foreign policy had degenerated into mere curiosity: he 'likes to discuss it but not to stop him for a moment'. Badgered again in August 1620 as the situation deteriorated, James burst out petulantly that the ambassador did not know what he was talking about: 'All these troubles will settle themselves, you will see that very soon.' In September 1620 when news reached the king of the invasion of the Palatinate territories of his son-in-law, he could not be persuaded to set aside his hunting and give the crisis the sustained consideration it obviously required.[9]

Frederick did not wait for his father-in-law's answer before accepting the Bohemian crown, but took his decision only three days after his letter to James arrived in London. In August 1619 shortly after Frederick and Elizabeth arrived in their new kingdom, the deposed archduke who had become their bitter enemy became Emperor Ferdinand II. Disaster followed, as James feared it would when advising Frederick to leave well alone. protestant forces were defeated at the Battle of the White Mountain in November 1620 and the royal couple were forced to flee Bohemia. Meanwhile, in Frederick's absence large parts of his Rhineland territories were overrun by Habsburg troops under the command of the Spanish general Spinola, and by April 1621 Frederick and Elizabeth were refugees at The Hague.

The invasion of the Palatinate made the European situation far more threatening, particularly from the British perspective. In view of the grave doubts expressed by James (and shared by most other rulers) over the almost certainly illegal removal of the Bohemian crown from Archduke Ferdinand, the ejection of Elector Frederick from Prague could have been dismissed as unfortunate but hardly surprising. If the Elector had been able to return home to the Palatinate, chastened by experience, then the war might have wound down. The conquest of Frederick's own hereditary territories by catholic forces made the situation intractable, and also far more likely to inflame protestant opinion. James could no longer pretend that the troubles would soon die down.

The crucial question was whether the Spanish Habsburgs would actively support their Austrian cousins. Initially, the Spanish Council of State was unenthusiastic, but by September 1618 it decided to offer assistance. Even so, Philip III and his minister the duke of Uceda (who emerged after the downfall of Lerma) considered that a compromise between the Bohemians and Emperor Ferdinand would be wiser than war. However, Madrid was already preparing for conflict since the Twelve Years Truce of 1609 expired in 1621. Neither the Spanish nor the Dutch would negotiate an extension, and the death in July 1621 of Archduke Albert of the Spanish Netherlands silenced the last influential voice for peace. War resumed in the low countries and on the high seas, where Philip IV (who succeeded his father in March 1621) aimed to roll back the incursions the Dutch were making into formerly Portuguese territories under Spanish rule since 1580.

The outbreak of the Thirty Years War, as it became known, was the break point in James's reign. Before 1618 he could claim success on a number of fronts, even though financial stability eluded him. After the events of 1618–21, he was faced with impossible dilemmas both at home and abroad. The rashness of the Elector plunged Europe into a multi-centred war that proved difficult to contain and was appallingly costly in both lives and money. James did not support Frederick's adventure in Bohemia, but the Habsburg conquest of the Palatinate lands made Frederick and Elizabeth appear the victims of catholic aggression. Unfortunately, the king was unable to offer much practical help to his daughter and son-in-law. The landlocked Palatinate could only be reached by an expeditionary force of infantry and cavalry which would be expensive to equip and vulnerable as it marched across war-torn Europe.

Increasingly, James also found himself in difficulties at home. It was widely assumed that family ties would ineluctably lead him to assist the Elector. Many were concerned about the royal succession since the Electress was only a heartbeat away from the throne, heir to both England and Scotland if Charles died childless. Englishmen were instinctively anti-Spanish and did not understand the king's hesitant reactions. Most of them saw the conflict over Bohemia and the Palatinate not as a secular issue, but as a struggle between good and evil. James in *Basilicon Doron* argued that an honourable and just war was more tolerable than a dishonourable and disadvantageous peace: what maxim could be more applicable to the situation? Frederick and Elizabeth appeared not as the leaders of an abhorrent rebellion against a rightful ruler – James's view of their initial actions – but as heroic standard-bearers of the protestant cause. Archbishop Abbot urged intervention to show that England was awake when God called. He and others looked to the king for leadership and when it was not forthcoming, James came under attack. The French ambassador noted the animosity expressed in free speaking, cartoons and defamatory libels.[10] Imbued with religious rhetoric, Englishmen wanted to help their co-religionists in Europe. The king's reluctance undermined their trust not only in him, but also in the successful, broadly based ecclesiastical policies he had been pursuing since his accession (see pp. 155–81). After 1618–19 the religious consensus at home began to crumble, and more or less disappeared after spring 1621. Divisions widened between godly anti-Spanish protestants on the one hand, and on the other, high churchmen who saw no reason why English lives should be lost in supporting continental Calvinism.

James did not see the European situation in a confessional light. By 1618 he was the most experienced ruler in Europe and he prided himself on his Biblical motto *Beati Pacifici* (blessed are the peacemakers). He believed that a Spanish match for Charles could also achieve a solution for the Palatinate, if only he could persuade the Spanish Habsburgs to restrain the Austrians and help him prevent a devastating conflict. This delusion was purposely fostered by Gondomar, since the Spanish Council of State in Madrid considered it vital that James remained neutral. After 1620 Spain was intent on ensuring that England should not proffer military aid to the Elector. After 1621 it was even more important to stop any move by James to support the Dutch, since the Anglo-Dutch alliance of 1585 had worked to Spain's immense disadvantage. In summer 1620 the ailing Philip III instructed Gondomar to prolongue the negotiations for the English match and avoid clarifying Spanish terms. In this way, James's neutrality could be spun out for as long as possible.

Gondomar and James jointly sought to steer England in a pro-Spanish direction. To the king, the policy seemed his only hope of obtaining financial assistance as well as enabling him to bring his ecumenical influence to bear in Europe. He was also driven to look to Spain because there seemed no alternative with France unwilling to take any stand. Louis XIII was preoccupied with the fractious protestant nobility of the south-west who threatened internal stability, and as a result, was hostile to protestants both at home and abroad. For his part, Gondomar saw James as the bastion against *los puritanos*, the militant protestants who thirsted for war against Spain.

The situation in Madrid was more complex than the king appreciated. The army of Maximilian of Bavaria, the strongman of the Catholic League, was used against protestants in Bohemia while the partial conquest of the Rhineland Palatinate was achieved by Spanish troops technically under the command of the emperor. Ferdinand was also facing rebellion in Hungary, which increased his dependence on Maximilian's forces. In return for further assistance, he offered Maximilian the title of Elector, to be stripped from Frederick. After 1620 these commitments constrained Habsburg flexibility and there was much less hope of dividing the Spanish from the Austrians. Gondomar was considered by English public opinion as a wily operator out to deceive the king, a view that underestimated James's own diplomatic dexterity. It has been reinforced by the tendency of later historians to treat the ambassador's boastful and self-serving letters back to Spain as accurate accounts of his activities. Paradoxically, in Madrid Gondomar was viewed as an anglophile, so his advice carried less weight there.

James raged at the ambassador for misleading him when he heard of the Habsburg invasion of the Palatinate. In autumn 1620 the king made a formal declaration to his Privy Council that he would restore Frederick to his hereditary lands. Since it was impossible to support military action out of the royal coffers, James asked for a benevolence to be collected and sent to the Elector to pay troops. Despite public protestations of support it raised only around £30,000, less than half of the 1614 benevolence. Times were difficult, for continental war was destabilising English overseas trade, still recovering from the Cokayne project. Currency tampering in central Germany between 1617 and 1623 made the task of merchants even harder, since the disadvantageous exchange rate raised English prices and led to the collapse of the broadcloth trade. That in turn created unemployment among sheep farmers, spinners and weavers, inflicting hardship on the clothing counties. The expanding trades to Spain, the Mediterranean and the East Indies were valuable, but not yet big enough to take up the deficit.

The Parliament of 1621

In November 1620, despite Cranfield's programme of reform and retrenchment, James had no other option but to call a Parliament. Revealingly, he followed that proclamation with another one attempting to damp down the 'licentious passage of lavish discourse, and bold Censure in matters of State' all publicly directed against his government. The court was as divided as the country. A recently discovered masque, performed at Essex House in January 1621 before the king, was an unofficial attempt by his old friend the Scottish courtier James Hay Viscount Doncaster to influence James in an anti-Spanish, godly direction. Hay was usually a cautious operator intent only on his personal advantage, so his masque forms striking evidence of the depth of anxiety over the king's foreign policy at the heart of the court.[11]

Parliament met at Westminster in January 1621. James made a skilful opening speech, declaring his preference for peace, but promising he would go to war if that proved the only way to regain the Palatinate. 'My crowne, my blood, and the blood of my Sonne here shall not be spared for it', he declaimed rousingly. He regretted the lack of success of his previous Parliaments, but graciously trusted himself to the affections of his people: 'Deale liberally with me that the world may see how good and happy a sympathie there is between the King and his Subjects here'. The Commons voted two subsidies (worth about £160,000), whereupon the king thanked them for their 'free, noble and no-merchantlike dealing'. He had never forgiven or forgotten the bargaining of 1610.[12]

The optimistic beginning was continued since it was widely recognised that there was much to lose if this Parliament went the way of the others. Many in the country were already worried that the English Parliament was losing ground, just like its continental equivalents, for the seven-year gap since the 1614 Parliament (which in any case had been a disaster) was the longest since 1515. The call for annual parliaments first heard in the Commons in 1607 was made again in an anonymous tract circulating widely among the gentry. It also contained a savage attack on impositions, corrupt favourites and other objectionable features of the king's rule. Meanwhile, patents of monopoly revived as a serious grievance, since James frequently granted the patents (legal rights to the exclusive control of a commodity) to unscrupulous courtiers and others seeking his bounty. They exploited the monopoly at the expense of ordinary people.

Criticism of the patentees developed into an attack on those councillors who advised the king that the grants of monopolies were acceptable. Among these was Buckingham himself, but the scapegoat was Lord Chancellor Bacon who was accused of accepting bribes to sway his judicial verdicts. The attack on him in the Commons revived the medieval practice of impeachment, last used against a royal minister in the parliamentary session of 1450–1. Bacon later confessed his mistakes and resigned his great office rather than stand trial before the Lords. The political reality of the situation gave him no choice, for James was prepared to sacrifice his lord chancellor rather than risk having his favourite caught up in the assault on monopolies. At Easter when both Houses rose for the recess, the king spoke again of his affection for his subjects. Unexpectedly, he drew a sword from the scabbard of a nearby Scottish courtier. Joking that he was about to kill the Speaker, instead James knighted him in full Parliament to dramatise his respect for its members.

The Parliament reassembled in April. An attack in the Lords on Buckingham, deeply implicated in the granting of many of the most abusive patents, failed despite the profound hostility of many noblemen towards him. James pledged his honour to limit monopolies and the Commons refrained from blaming him openly for his admitted laxness in not ensuring that prior checks were carried out. In July after members left Westminster at the end of the first session, a royal proclamation revoked 20 monopolies and disowned another 17. The latter was a significant concession since subjects could seek a remedy at law against disowned grants. The king protested that he would have reformed these grievances earlier if he had known about them, since he was continually watching over his people, but the general view was privately expressed by Sir Thomas Edmondes, a Privy Councillor, that 'the kingdom had been undone, if we had been much longer time without a Parliament'.[13]

In July James raised Cranfield to the peerage as Baron Cranfield and in September he became lord treasurer, succeeding the venal Sir Henry Montague who had paid the king £20,000 for the office only the previous November. The advancement of the most active minister in the government appeared to indicate that the king was genuinely supportive of further financial reforms. However, Cranfield's elevation to the Lords weakened the Privy Council's influence over the Commons, where he had been a frequent speaker.

During the course of the Parliament, the council of war summoned by James estimated future expenditure. A force sent to the Palatinate would cost over £200,000 to raise and over £190,000 per annum to maintain, far more than the two parliamentary subsidies would cover. Much more money would be needed before military action could be contemplated, and given the Commons' reluctance to vote larger amounts of taxation, it was doubtful if James could raise enough. However, in June 1621 on the day that the Parliament adjourned for the summer, the Commons followed Sir James Perrot (reputedly an illegitimate descendant of Henry VIII) in a ringing statement of support for the protestant cause. 'If Religion and Right may not be restored by Treaty and peaceable means' as James hoped, they would be prepared 'to adventure the Lives and Estates of all that belong to us' to go to war for the Palatinate.[14] This seemed to promise additional supply so the Parliament was not dissolved, but prorogued until February 1622.

Meanwhile, the king was active, sending envoys to Brussels, to the exiled Frederick at The Hague and to Vienna. In January 1621 the European situation changed with the death of Pope Paul V, who had opposed the Spanish match. Then Philip III, who secretly had never thought it a practical possibility, died in March. James was encouraged, but diplomatic overtures achieved little. Frederick foolishly refused to renounce force in pursuing his claim to Bohemia, though such an acknowledgment of reality would have made negotiations with both branches of the Habsburgs far easier. At the same time, the belligerent Maximilian of Bavaria opposed any settlement that would remove the gains he had made so far, including the promise that he would receive Frederick's title of Elector. The Vienna envoy, the experienced Sir John Digby, was convinced that an immediate campaign was necessary to pressure the young Philip IV and his newly installed minister the Conde de Olivares into urging the emperor to restore the Palatinate to Frederick. By contrast, James still thought that the way forward was the Spanish match for Charles, a prospect again dangled by Gondomar who had returned to England.

Over the summer of 1621, the harvest failed and the trade slump worsened. As autumn set in, floods caused further damage. The localities could not easily afford heavy war taxation. In November 1621, as Frederick's Upper Palatinate lands on the Bohemian border were also about to fall to Maximilian, James suddenly summoned back the Parliament he had prorogued. However, he remained at Newmarket with Buckingham while the inexperienced Prince Charles sat for the first time in the Lords. James seemed intent on making threatening noises in Europe, perhaps hoping to pressurise the emperor, but gave his ministers little clear direction. They, in turn, failed to put a coherent strategy before the Commons. As Sir Edward Giles exclaimed in bewilderment, war and peace were both propounded together: 'We must fight with the Spaniards in the Palatinate and be friends with them everywhere else.'[15] The Commons were divided over strategy and offered one subsidy, in addition to the two voted earlier. Then, on 29 November, Sir George Goring (a well-known client of Buckingham) proposed that the Commons should petition the king to declare war on both Spain and the emperor unless the Palatine was restored. Assuming that a man who spoke for Buckingham must also speak for James, the Lower House was delighted to petition, but added a plea that the prince should be 'timely and happily married to one of our own religion'.[16]

The king's Spanish negotiations for his son were common knowledge and widely disliked.

Goring's motion has been extensively debated. It was moved by Goring at Buckingham's specific direction, but if James planned it, it can only have been in hopes of increasing pressure on Spain by demonstrating the backing of the House of Commons for a war. If it came from Buckingham alone, he presumably wanted to provoke a dispute that would end the Parliament and with it the hostile scrutiny to which he had been subjected. Recently, it has been claimed, on the basis of Spanish documents, that even before the recall in November 1621, James was plotting to dissolve the Parliament in order to maintain his *entente* with Spain. In a letter Gondomar depicted Goring's intrusion into the royal prerogative as a deliberate ploy co-ordinated with Buckingham. It enabled James to order the Commons to desist from discussing mysteries of state (the prince's marriage). The royal command raised again the vital issue of freedom of speech, and the Lower House replied in a Protestation that 'the Liberties, Franchises, Privileges and Jurisdictions of Parliament are the ancient and undoubted Birthright and Inheritance of the Subjects of England.'[17] As in 1604, the Commons saw themselves not as innovators, but as defenders of their ancient rights. In response, the king angrily dissolved Parliament on 28 December, ripping the Protestation out of the Commons Journal (the official record of the Lower House) in a ceremony at Whitehall before his Privy Councillors.

The Spanish evidence underlines the personal rapport that Gondomar built up with the king, the prince and the favourite, but it must be remembered that in writing to Madrid, the ambassador always wanted to emphasise his own effectiveness in ensuring that James remained pro-Spanish. Gondomar constantly overstated his influence and probably did so on this occasion. Whether or not there was a co-ordinated strategy of sabotage, he was delighted with the outcome, since without large amounts of parliamentary taxation James could not hope to assist the Elector Frederick or hinder the House of Habsburg.

It was beyond dispute that the second session of the 1621 Parliament had been mismanaged. Privy Councillors were left directionless by an absent king while suspicion of Buckingham increased. Yet many of the issues were simply intractable. The worsening of economic conditions lessened any chance that the Commons would vote enough to support military action on the requisite scale. Even if the estimates were deliberately inflated in order to lessen the pressure on James to intervene (as some historians have argued), the costs of European war were bound to be very heavy. Many of the speakers in debate were more concerned by what they saw as the catholic threat at home rather than the Habsburgs abroad. For all the rhetoric of the protestant cause, the theatre of action was far away and there was little threat to England. The Commons did not even act on the bill to make arms serviceable, which would have placed the militia musters in the counties on a statutory footing and ensured the upgrading of weaponry. Their indifference to the practicalities of self-defence demonstrated that, for all their declarations, they hardly took the threat of war seriously. At the same time, the spendthrift and unwarlike James did not inspire confidence as a military leader. By dissolving the Parliament, the king threw away the third subsidy, voted but not yet confirmed by a subsidy act. In 1610, 1614 and 1621 he dissolved in anger, as Elizabeth had never done. Since his first Parliament in 1604, he had been granted adequate supply only once, in 1606, and in 1614 the Commons refused him outright. Again, this contrasted with the queen's unfailing success in winning the subsidies she sought. Despite the high hopes at the outset that this might be a happy and harmonious Parliament, in 1621 James preferred to maintain his obdurate stance in a privilege dispute rather than offer a conciliatory gesture to safeguard the extra taxation already offered. If the Commons did not appear to give the Palatinate cause priority over other business, nor did the king.

Thereafter, it might have been sensible for James to withdraw into isolation from European affairs. He had failed to win any co-operation from the inflexible Elector, and the Commons were deeply hostile to the Spanish match on which he pinned his hopes. By dropping both the marriage and any offer of military aid to Frederick and Elizabeth, at least James would keep his kingdoms free of domestic conflict and neutral in a dreadful war. However, late in the year he shrewdly detected some renewed possibilities for peace. The allies of the Austrian Habsburgs were increasingly concerned at the emperor's reliance on Maximilian of Bavaria, the only beneficiary of three years of conflict. In late November 1621, James wrote to the widowed Archduchess Isabella, left in sole charge of the Spanish Netherlands, proposing a conference. The idea gained the support of both the Emperor Ferdinand and Philip IV of Spain. It met in Brussels between May and September 1622, aiming for a truce followed by a peace agreement. In August James released imprisoned recusants in England as a gesture of conciliation, but the conference came to an inglorious end when the victorious count of Tilly stormed the city of Heidelberg, Frederick's capital, and took it for Maximilian. The commanders in the field had paid no heed to the peace negotiations. Despairing at events, in September 1622 James wrote personally to Pope Gregory XV urging him to intervene to stop 'these calamitous discords and bloodshedds'.[18] The pope was too committed to the catholic League to respond to the king's plea. Morally admirable, the letter was unrealistic and war continued, but James had shown greater Christian leadership and insight than the papacy. To the king's lasting credit, he alone among European rulers made sustained attempts to bring hostilities to a close. If his efforts had succeeded, Europe would have been spared the following 26 years of bloody conflict.

6 The Spanish Match

By 1622 James had exhausted virtually all his diplomatic options. The attempt to raise taxation in the 1621 Parliament was only partly successful and the economies pursued by Lord Treasurer Cranfield, created earl of Middlesex in 1622, might at best balance the king's accounts, but could never produce enough for aggressive foreign action. Powerless to take decisive measures, James returned to the Spanish match as his only hope of restoring the Palatinate to Frederick and Elizabeth. To his subjects, the match merely exacerbated fears about popery and Spanish corruption, while the Overbury scandal was revived in libels deploring the absence of God's word and religious purity from the king's court.[1]

Ignoring public sentiment, the king pursued the match with fervour while Sir John Digby, recently created earl of Bristol and also committed to the plan, negotiated at Madrid. Spain was working for a cessation of arms in the Palatinate, and by autumn 1622 Bristol thought he had obtained an assurance from Philip IV that once the match was concluded, Spanish troops would join English ones in driving out Imperial forces if the handover to the Elector was resisted. The new developments encouraged James to despatch his special envoy Endymion Porter, who had close family connections with Spain. However, attitudes there were hardening, since by autumn 1622 the Conde de Olivares dominated the council. He emphasised to the young king that an English marriage would create more problems for Spain than it solved. Olivares denied to Porter that there had been any assurance that Spanish troops would help to restore Frederick against Imperial opposition. Olivares knew that the Infanta Maria was strongly averse to marrying a heretic and that Philip IV would never coerce his sister. The king had instructed him to find a way of tactfully escaping the negotiations without driving James to war. In London the Venetian ambassador noted that Bristol and Gondomar were passing on 'specious promises' about the Palatinate and the match. He warned the Venetian council that these would probably act 'as a narcotic to make [the English] sleep the more profoundly this winter'.[2]

Prince Charles was now a young man of 23 and growing restive. During the 1621 Parliament he was angered by the Commons' intrusive concern over his marriage and, like his father, he regarded their stated preference for a protestant bride as an infringement of the royal prerogative. Charles persuaded himself that he was in love with the Infanta and during 1622 discussed with Gondomar how he might win the lady he described as his 'Mistris'. Practising his novice Spanish, he jokingly addressed Gondomar as his 'alcahuete', go-between or even pimp. The prince was almost certainly unaware of the resonance of the word, but the familiar tone again testifies to the close friendship between the royal family and the ambassador.[3]

Possibly, Charles was encouraged by Gondomar to think that his personal intervention would resolve the stalemate, for the prince told him that if the ambassador sent word, he would put himself in the hands of Philip IV. In a dramatic attempt to seize the initiative, Buckingham and Charles decided to travel incognito to Spain to win the Infanta. On 17 February 1623 'Thomas and John Smith' rode to Dover, took ship for Boulogne and rode on to Paris. They reached the English embassy in Madrid on 7 March, to the joy of Gondomar who had returned to Spain, but to the shocked astonishment of Philip IV. Keen to avoid a breach with England, the king had been prepared to prolong the marriage negotiations, but the prince's arrival significantly raised the stakes.

James was already willing to concede toleration for catholics, meaning an informal cessation of persecution. Instead, the Spanish demanded the formal repeal of the recusancy laws. Olivares was hoping that the need for a papal dispensation – which he assumed would never materialise – would exonerate Spain from blame for the inevitable breakdown of negotiations. Meanwhile, he sent an envoy to Rome with instructions to block any dispensation, but to his embarrassment, one arrived in April. Gregory XV shared the widespread assumption in the catholic world that Charles's extraordinary journey meant that he intended to convert to catholicism. If so, the Spanish match was worth a papal dispensation since it would win freedom from persecution for English catholics and might even bring about the return of England to the catholic fold.

Once the papacy was aware of Madrid's underhand opposition to the match, these hopes faded and it was decided to demand new concessions before the final dispensation. They included additional religious guarantees for the Infanta and her household, and above all the prior agreement of the English Privy Council and Parliament to the terms of the marriage. Gregory XV urged Charles to return to the faith of his catholic ancestors and received a courteous reply. The anxious James, bedridden with arthritis, sent cloying letters to his 'sweet boys', assuring Buckingham that he wore his picture on a blue ribbon next to his heart and despatching a stream of gifts to him and his Villiers relatives. The favourite was promoted to a dukedom, the first non-royal with the title since 1572. The king wrote constantly to Buckingham's family, passing on news from Spain and, in turn, sent family chitchat to Madrid. Kate (Buckingham's wife) had been a little sick, but her youngest child was weaned; Sue (Buckingham's sister Lady Denbigh) supped and dined at court and was granted a ward; Kit (Buckingham's brother) should have a further £2000 out of rents due to the Crown. The king regarded them as his surrogate family, although he also begged his own 'sweet Baby Charles' to take care of himself and not to risk rash manoeuvres when tilting.[4] Meanwhile, practical measures were implemented with a catholic chapel designed by Inigo Jones under construction near St James Palace, ready for the Infanta.

Olivares was forced to admit to Philip IV that his doubts were impassable. However advantageous the terms agreed with James, how could he carry them out in defiance of English public and parliamentary opinion? When the question of the repeal of the recusancy laws was raised in 1618, Digby had proved very evasive, suggesting that a summons of Parliament to discuss the matter would bring 'muy grandes inconvinientes'.[5] Gondomar's despatches on the puritan temper of the House of Commons in 1621 also indicated that James was highly unlikely to win a legal toleration for catholics. Olivares announced that Philip III had declared on his deathbed that he never intended the match to take place. Spain could not support England to the detriment of the Austrian Habsburgs. Philip IV was nonplussed by the unexpected situation created by the prince's arrival.

In March 1623 James accepted that the journey to Madrid was the final throw of the dice. 'If my baby's credit in Spain mend not these things', he wrote, 'I will bid farewell to peace in Christendom.' The situation over the Palatinate was even more intractable than before, since in the same month, the emperor gave his indispensable ally the duke of Bavaria the title of Elector, by now stripped from Frederick. In May, desperate to get his 'sweet boys' home, James agreed to abide by whatever Charles promised in Spain. In July 1623 the king, along with his Privy Council, took an oath before Coloma the Spanish ambassador to carry out the terms of the marriage treaty which the prince and Philip IV signed in Madrid. Secret articles committed James and Charles to ensuring that Parliament revoked the recusancy laws within three years. James lamented that he had given up revenues worth £36,000 by agreeing to discharge the debts due to him from recusants.[6] By August the Spaniards made it clear that the Infanta would not accompany Buckingham and Charles back to England, though they intimated that this need not end negotiations since she might follow later. However, on both sides there was a sense of increasing unreality allied to an overwhelming desire that the prince and the duke should depart. When they finally arrived in Portsmouth in October 1623 without the Infanta, there was an immense outbreak of popular joy, with fireworks, bell ringing and street parties. The celebrations demonstrated that in pursuing the chimaera of a Spanish match, James had grown far out of touch with his subjects' deeply held convictions.

It soon became apparent that the king was faced with a further crisis. Charles and Buckingham were now inseparable friends, so the duke was set to remain in royal favour even if James should die. Both young men were convinced by their experiences in Madrid that Spain had been acting duplicitously for years, a view the king refused to accept. The Spanish envoys Coloma and Inijosa were cold-shouldered at court by the partisans of the prince and the duke. In addition, news arriving from European battlefields indicated that the House of

Austria was sweeping all before it, and must be challenged before it crushed all opposition. Counter-attack would be expensive, so a Parliament was needed. James at first denounced the advocates of a new Parliament as traitors, but he was persuaded in December 1623 to send out a summons for the following February. The reason for his caution immediately became apparent when the proclamation triggered a further outpouring of anti-Spanish and anti-catholic propaganda, not least from the Norwich clerical pamphleteer Thomas Scott, whose *Vox Populi* had been a sensation in 1620. In his *Boanerges* he prayed for the new Parliament, that its resolutions might 'extend to the glory of God . . . and the confusion of the antiChrist'. In Part 2 of his *Vox Populi*, he lavished praise on Charles and Buckingham, whose journey to Madrid delivered England from disastrous delusions about Spanish goodwill. Another popular pamphlet *Vox Coeli* depicted a heavenly conference of royalty in which Henry VIII, Edward VI, Elizabeth, Anne of Denmark and her son Prince Henry all voted against the Spanish match, with only 'Bloody Mary', the wife of Philip II, dissenting.[7] The link between anti-catholicism and anti-Spanish feeling was made explicit: no true English protestant could accept a catholic future queen.

The popularity of *Vox Populi, Boanerges, Vox Coeli* and many other pamphlets testified to the steady growth of English print culture since the late sixteenth century. As literacy rates rose, especially in London and other leading cities such as Norwich, there was an expanding market for topical and lively material. Few issues were more likely to appeal to a wide readership than the controversy over the Spanish match. The production of libels, salacious poetry, printed sermons and pamphlets all reinforced interest in current affairs and contributed to the emergence, long before the eighteenth century, of a nationwide 'public sphere' in which vigorous discussions of current topics occurred in taverns, church porches, markets and innumerable private houses. Debates were no longer confined to the House of Commons. In the proclamations of 1620 and 1621 against what he regarded as 'licentious speech', and in condemning the Lower House in 1621 for interfering in the matter of the prince's bride, James revealed that he was at odds with a significant social change taking place in his kingdoms. The king's conduct of foreign policy was increasingly seen as a matter of legitimate popular interest, not as a mystery of state. The convulsions across Europe as protestantism seemed in retreat before catholic armies raised the level of public concern. The exclusively dynastic approach that marked the king's dealings with other monarchs earlier in his reign was increasingly perceived as irrelevant and even offensive to an aroused and informed protestant opinion.

The Parliament of 1624

The prince and the duke had every intention of harnessing popular animosity to the Spanish match and using it for their purposes. Buckingham set about winning over as many supporters as he could in both the Lords and the Commons, including men who distrusted him. The accumulated distaste for the duke was particularly strong among the older members of the peerage, whose status was undermined by the steady sale of honours from which Buckingham profited. Between 1615 and 1628, the years of the favourite's ascendancy, the number of English peers rose from 81 to 126 and the number of earls increased even faster, from 27 to 65. Most of the newcomers paid money for their titles either to Buckingham himself or to the Villiers clan, and their network of clientage also spread into Ireland (see pp. 149–50). Nevertheless hostility to the duke was less powerful than hostility to Spain, and he was able to build up a party, known as 'the patriot coalition', intent on committing England to hostilities against the Habsburgs.

Buckingham and Charles wanted war, but the king and Lord Treasurer Middlesex were opposed. James balanced the opening session in February 1624 by inviting the advice of both Houses on whether the 'treaties' (negotiations) with Spain should be broken off, over both the marriage and the Palatinate. The move would not commit the king to hostilities, but might satisfy the warmongers. After their experience in December 1621, the Commons were reluctant to plunge into the dangerous waters of royal policy. Instead, they seized the opportunity to pass practical measures of legislation, most of which were bills lost at the precipitate dissolution of the 1621 Parliament.

Buckingham gave an elaborate and probably self-serving account of events in Madrid during the marriage negotiations. In the Commons this triggered speeches attacking recusants, together with a compulsory fast exemplifying protestant godliness. The Lords, led by Buckingham and Charles, were more belligerent, but only the Commons could vote taxation. The Lower House was profoundly anti-Spanish and delighted at the abandonment of the match, but a war raised complex issues even among those who favoured it. How and where would it be fought? A naval attack on Spain and her forces in the Atlantic, often described as a 'blue water strategy', aroused enthusiasm as a revival of the Elizabethan glories of Drake and Essex, but how could it bring about the restoration of the land-bound Palatinate? Many members who showed concern for the protestant cause in Europe were more immediately worried by the state of their own localities. The trade slump continued and there was increasing concern about the spread of popery in the regions. Sir Robert Phelips representing Somerset though 'Spain can do us no harm unless he have a party here in England.'[8] Once again, fear of troubles at home was more pressing than foreign affairs.

Both the Spanish match and negotiations over the Palatinate were over. The key question was what would follow. In March 1624 James told both Houses that for a war, he would need five subsidies and ten fifteenths as well as an annual subsidy and two fifteenths to clear his debts. The daunting sum shocked the Commons, but the supporters of Buckingham and Charles urged that all that was initially needed for military action was three subsidies and three fifteenths, which would bring in the respectable sum of £240,000. James accepted graciously, but warned that the money would only serve 'for a beginning'. The prince and Buckingham wanted the king to declare war, since this might encourage the Commons to vote generous supply. If no war was declared, the Lower House feared James would simply use money raised by taxation to pay off his debts. The king was firmly against being left as he commented, 'naked and without help', if he declared war, but then found no parliamentary supply forthcoming.[9] The impasse was solved by Buckingham, who suggested that the subsidy should be appropriated – specifically designated – for the war. Significantly, this manoeuvre came from the heart of the court, not from any desire by the Commons to seize the policy initiative from James. Yet there would have been no need for appropriation if the Commons and the king trusted one another over taxation. The situation was made even more complex by the obvious divergence of policy between the prince and the duke on the one hand and the king on the other. Parliament was little more than a spectator since the battle over foreign policy was fought out at court. The king was still unhappy at the lack of adequate funds in May when he adjourned the Parliament. It did not commit him to war against Spain, but equally it did not limit hostilities to the restoration of the Palatinate, as James had wished. His irritable closing speech was not well received, and in order to minimise ill-will, the lord keeper ensured that official copies of it were not distributed.

To Lord Treasurer Middlesex, any commitment to open-ended war was bound to be a financial disaster. By early April 1624, he was convinced that there was a dangerous conspiracy against him. In part, it was his own fault. Attempting to counter Buckingham's influence, Middlesex in 1622 adopted the unsuccessful stratagem tried earlier by the earl and countess of Suffolk, grooming his wife's attractive young brother to catch the king's eye. Buckingham was enraged. By 1622 the interests of the favourite and his former client were deeply at odds. Middlesex was aware that he was making little headway in his attempts to curb the wildly excessive costs of the Jacobean court, since he was opposed not only by Buckingham and his faction but also by the king himself, whose generosity could not be checked. At the same time, Middlesex was anxious to reverse the heavy drain on the royal finances caused by Ireland. Between 1604 and 1619 the subsidy sent to Dublin ran at over £47,000 annually. However, the 1622 commission to examine the state of Ireland (see pp. 150–2) uncovered Buckingham's links to the most venal officials in the Irish administration. The favourite succeeded in burying the report, which was never published, but the rift between him and Middlesex was widening.

The lord treasurer was confident that he could retain the king's support in his opposition to an expensive war. He underestimated Buckingham, who after his return from Spain began to plan the downfall of the man who tried to supplant him with another male favourite and stood in the way of an attack on the Habsburgs. On 4 April 1624 charges of corruption were laid against Middlesex in Parliament, but the only one with any substance concerned his exploitative dealings with the officers of the Ordnance. The real movers of the impeachment were Buckingham and Charles, supported by those courtiers angered when the lord treasurer's economies cut into their perquisities. Middlesex and his servants had squared the circle, saving the Crown large amounts of money while making considerable sums for themselves. By 1624 the lord treasurer's annual income was probably greater than Buckingham's. The merchant's ability to profit infuriated those whose benefits had been trimmed and also weakened his reputation for honesty. His conduct was woundingly condemned as 'ungentlemanlike'.

James did not encourage the attack on Middlesex and emphasised that the lord treasurer and Buckingham had been firm allies in the earlier movement for financial reform. However, the king was principally concerned to keep his freedom of manoeuvre at a time when he was being pushed by his son and his favourite into an unwelcome war. It seems also that James was genuinely shocked to learn of Middlesex's personal gains out of the Wardrobe, even though he had saved the Crown so much money. The lord treasurer fell not on largely unproven grounds of corruption, but as the victim of an alliance between warmongering elements at court and in Parliament. The king gave his own silent verdict when he released Middlesex from the Tower three days after the end of the parliamentary session, when Buckingham was briefly absent. In the words of his biographer, Lionel Cranfield more than anyone else had shown initiative and determination in attempting administrative reform and checking the irresponsibility of the king. James knew he had lost a good servant, but he did little to defend Middlesex from his attackers.[10]

The Final Year 1624–25

The outcome of the 1624 Parliament was ambiguous. The king was still battling to regain control of foreign policy and had not declared war. When members of the Commons left the fevered atmosphere of

Westminster, many of them began to feel that, with an end to the negotiations with Spain, perhaps all that was necessary had already been achieved. Their earlier distrust of Buckingham resurfaced, undercutting their enthusiasm for any campaign he might plan to lead. In a time of economic recession, their constituents had little money to spare for foreign adventures. To Prince Charles, however, the Commons had committed themselves to financing the conflict with Spain and he would be dishonoured if he did not persevere in it. On that divergence of interpretation, relations between the future king and the Parliaments of the years 1625–9 were to founder.

After the Parliament ended, James slowly began to regain some control over affairs. The summer of 1624 was warm, greatly relieving his arthritis. He hunted enthusiastically from May to July, one morning rousing the French ambassador at 4 a.m. to go after stags. In early August Gondomar was brilliantly pilloried in Thomas Middleton's A Game at Chess, which ran for nine packed performances at the Globe before being closed down. The play was an enthusiastic endorsement of the diplomatic revolution of 1624 in which Charles and Buckingham reversed the king's pro-Spanish policies. The theatre held around 3000 spectators, so in nine days an appreciable percentage of the population of London went to see it. James was away hunting at Rufford in the midlands and was only told of the play by the Spanish ambassador Coloma. The king instructed his secretary Conway to write at once to the Privy Council demanding angrily why they had not informed him earlier.[11]

Even before leaving Spain, Buckingham was promoting the idea of an alternative match for the prince with the French princess Henrietta Maria. The king allowed Charles and Buckingham to begin negotiations for a marriage with France, but a power shift within the French council brought Cardinal Richelieu to the forefront in April 1624. France was opposed to Habsburg dominance of Europe, and Buckingham saw the match as a means of checking the ambitions of Spain, but Louis XIII had little interest in the restoration of the Palatinate to the Elector Frederick. James may even have sensed that the French catholic princess would be virtually as unpopular as the Infanta. Pressed by Richelieu, James agreed to give a written promise to free his catholic subjects from persecution, but in general terms only rather than with the specific details required by the Spaniards. The promise was not a part of the marriage articles and was described as an *Ecrit Particulier*. Even so, it contradicted the commitment Charles made in the House of Lords that if he married a catholic princess, there would be no concessions to the English recusants.

To the Venetian ambassador, the king's policies seemed more and more obscure, since James gave little lead and rarely came to London. Anglo–Dutch relations were also under strain as a result of the massacre by Dutch forces of English merchants at Amboyna in the East Indies. However, the central fact was that no war against Spain materialised. This was due at least as much to the collapse of royal credit and the rapid exhaustion of the three parliamentary subsidies as to the delaying tactics of the king, but the silent check to the aggressive policies of Charles and Buckingham was unmistakeable. An expedition to the Palatinate, led by the German mercenary soldier Count Mansfeld, left Dover on the last day of January 1625, but it was forbidden by James to assist in relieving the Spanish seige of Dutch-held Breda (which would have struck a real blow against Philip IV). Louis XIII, who was contributing to the military costs, then forbade Mansfeld to land in France, so the troops went ashore in Holland where most of them died from hunger and infection. After an expedition that achieved nothing except loss of life and waste of money, no further war preparations were set on foot.

The improvement in the king's health proved only temporary. Severe attacks of arthritis resumed in September 1624 and James could not even write his name, he was indisposed in November and December. Aware that Buckingham was concentrating on consolidating his control of Charles to ensure his own future, the king wrote him a pathetic letter, praying 'that we may make at this Christenmass a new marriage, ever to be kept hereafter ... I had rather live banished in any part of the earth with you, than live a sorrowful widow-life without you.' [12] Even though the king was stalling the favourite's war policy, he remained emotionally dependent on him. James was pained by gout in January, but he received ambassadors and seemed deeply interested in European news. By late March 1625, the king was seriously ill with a tertian fever accompanied by fainting attacks. He aggravated his condition by excessive drinking, and finally had a stroke, followed by an attack of violent dysentery which killed him on 27 March 1625. News of James's sickness reached Buckingham as he was on his way to Paris to conclude the French match, but he at once returned to Theobalds. The disparity between the foreign policies of the monarch and of the favourite was so obvious that there was a widespread rumour that the duke had poisoned him. The slander arose because Buckingham recommended a medicine which only made the king worse, but the deeper perception of the favourite's shift to warlike plans espoused by Charles, but opposed by James, was correct. Buckingham was in tears at the king's death, but Charles comforted him with a promise that he would cherish him as his father had done. The young king's continued support of the favourite cast an immediate shadow over the new reign.

James was just short of 59 in March 1625 and had been a ruler for all but his first year of life. To the 'cradle king', the assertion of his regality was central to all his policies. Yet James showed little concern for his public image. In 1603 he succeeded a dynasty that had always been very conscious of the importance of visual representation. From the emphatic heraldry of Henry VII on his chapel at the east end of Westminster Abbey to the majestic portraits of Elizabeth in bejewelled splendour, the Tudors were accustomed to sending out images of power. By contrast, the king showed no interest in portraiture and disliked sitting for artists. When he was painted by Daniel Mytens and Paul van Somer, he appeared in rich fabrics, sometimes with his Crown and regalia nearby, but usually looked stiff or uneasy. No portrait of him approaches the imperial confidence of Henry VIII or Elizabeth.

James travelled widely across both Scotland and England, but after 1603 it was mostly for his own pleasure and recreation rather than to show himself to his subjects. He disliked crowds and could not abide the intrusiveness he was forced to endure on popular occasions. Typically, James used words not gestures for communication. His speeches in Parliament and Star Chamber, his published writings and his proclamations aimed to impress his subjects with his regal authority. Heavy reliance on print tended to restrict his message to the literate, but even those subjects who could read his words easily might be roused more to disagreement than obedience. The king's love of polemic and his enjoyment of argument could lead him to strike a boastful and self-regarding note, while his proclamations attempting to silence licentious discourse and disorderly printing were themselves evidence of his unpopularity.

Elizabeth exercised control not only over her own image, but also that of her court. By contrast the Jacobean court suffered almost from the beginning from hostile rumours about the heavy drinking and unsanitary habits of the king and his courtiers. Across Europe, hunting was the usual recreation of monarchs and their nobles, but within months of the king's accession, influential voices were complaining that James's devotion to his sports was excessive and inconvenient. These criticisms cannot be shrugged off as the result of English prejudice against the Scots, since they were often made by experienced continental ambassadors. The cultural interests of Queen Anne and Prince Henry led to a brief flowering of elegance in the royal family, but after 1612 the rise of male favourites steadily alienated public opinion. The scandals which led to the downfall of Carr and the Howards were extensively publicised and permanently tarnished the reputation of the court. The rise of Buckingham and his rapacious family increased the impression of profound corruption, and obscene libels vilified both the king and the duke. The image of James and of his court was increasingly negative.

In the days immediately after the king's death, criticism was muted. Unlike his mother Mary Queen of Scots and his son Charles I, James was not dethroned by his subjects; he died in his bed at his favourite country mansion. The corpse was brought from Theobalds to London, accompanied by grieving noblemen, courtiers, the lord mayor and aldermen. His cortege was attended by the most part of the nobility of both his kingdoms. 'The great funeral was on the seventh of May', wrote Chamberlain, 'the greatest indeed that ever was known in England. All was performed with great magnificence, but . . . very confused and disorderly. The whole charge is said to have arisen to about £50,000.'[13] In the costly confusion of magnificence and disorder the funeral may stand for much of the reign. However, the two-hour sermon was more charitable. Printed later as 'Great Britain's Salomon', it was preached by the king's old friend Bishop John Williams of Lincoln and praised him as 'the most powerful

Speaker that ever swayed the Scepter of this Kingdom'. James regarded religion and justice as the two pillars of his throne and charged his heir with the care of them. Above all, the bishop noted, 'King Solomon died in Peace, when he had lived about Sixty years . . . and so you know did King James.' The king had kept his multiple kingdoms out of the unstoppable war raging in Europe. He was widely mourned, and a popular little epitaph followed the theme of the sermon, proclaiming 'James the peaceful and the just'. For all his failings, the king had not completely lost the affection of his subjects, and despite the anti-Spanish war rhetoric of the last years, many of them were grateful to him. Under his rule they had enjoyed years of peace and low taxation, probably the lowest in Europe.

In Scotland Archbishop Spottiswode thought his subjects must 'reckon it not the least part of our happiness to have lived in his days'. The earl of Kellie mourned his sovereign. 'As he lived in peace, so did he die in peace, and I pray God our King may follow him in all his good.'[14] In retrospect the peace that James managed to keep in all his kingdoms was to seem even more precious, for Kellie's prayer for Charles I was to prove vain.

7 Monarch of Three Kingdoms

Political Ideas

In his last years in Scotland, almost certain of the English succession and enjoying a newfound sense of security, James began to reflect on the nature of his kingship. He produced two literary works, composed successively in 1597–8. *The Trew Law of Free Monarchies*, modestly described by its author as 'a pamphlet', was published anonymously (but by the king's printer) and addressed to 'my deare countreymen'. It was 'written for your weale', but James added disarmingly 'at least it is short'. *Basilikon Doron* (The King's Gift) was addressed to his heir Prince Henry and initially only seven printed copies were produced for the innermost royal circle.

These works have been pored over as the keys to the king's thinking, on which they shed a flood of light, but they emerged from very specific circumstances. They were not initially designed for an open readership, still less an English readership. Moreover, James was first and foremost an agile, practical politician rather than a theorist. He often disregarded his own advice, and there are many inconsistencies in his maxims. It may even be that he wrote as much to clarify his own mind as to communicate his thoughts. Yet the private aspect should not be over-emphasised for James already had a strong sense of his international position. As Elizabeth's closest royal relative, his youthful writings of 1587–9 were full of notions of an embattled protestant Europe. He wrote of 'this Ile' as a 'patrie' common to both Scots and English. *Basilicon Doron* seems to have been prompted by a premonition the king suffered in 1597 that he might even predecease Elizabeth and should prepare Henry for the dual succession to both thrones.

Scotland had little tradition of political theorising before the sixteenth century, so the king was establishing a novel ideological base for monarchy itself. Significantly, his main source in both tracts was the Bible rather than classical or medieval works of political ideas. The *Trew Law* began by describing 'our so long disordered, and distracted Commonwealthe'. Monarchy was 'the trew paterne of Divinitie' and using Biblical examples, James set out the divine right of kings, who must be obeyed in all things. They were elevated above all other men, but their position held commensurate risks: 'The highest bench is sliddriest to sit upon'. Kings must be fathers to their subjects, and were themselves responsible to God, 'the sorest and sharpest Schoolemaster that can be devised for them'. These vivid schoolroom images reveal that James was particularly attacking the Calvinist and contractual theories of government advanced by his old tutor George Buchanan. In contrast, James outlined a moderate theory of absolutism, sanctioned by scripture but also by reason and history. Kings possessed a monopoly of political power and could impose new law, if they came in by conquest like William of Normandy. But in settled kingdoms, they had an obligation in conscience and honour to rule according to law and in accordance with the public good. James denied that he meant to give rulers unfettered power, 'as if thereby the world were ordained only for kings'. Subjects must keep their hands clean of impious rebellion and could do nothing to remedy misgovernment, but they could rest assured that God would 'stirre up such scourges as pleaseth him, for punishment of wicked kings'. To James it was always acceptable to balance a high view of royal authority with the threat of divine sanctions against monarchs who failed in their duty. Little in this was novel, and much would have been regarded by Bible-reading contemporaries as acceptably commonplace, although lawyers in the English House of Commons would be perturbed by its substitution of divine displeasure for legal limitations on royal power. The king's assumption that monarchs, past and future, would be restrained by their fear of God's wrath was both naive and historically untenable.

By contrast with the *Trew Law*, *Basilicon Doron* was less theoretical and more practical, following a long European tradition of paternal advices. These included Charles V's supposed *Political Testament* to his son Philip of Spain, of which James was given a copy in Italian in 1592. Again, virtually all the references are scriptural. In the first edition James wrote in Middle Scots rather than the more anglicised form of his native tongue, another sign of privacy. Hoping that in time the 4-year-old Henry would enjoy 'this whole Ile, according to Gods right and your lineall discent', he produced a pithy handbook. Thinking of Henry turned his mind back to his own childhood, and the king's hatred of his old tutor came boiling up again as he lambasted the 'infamous invectives, as Buchanans or Knoxes Chronicles', whose contract theories of monarchy made them 'archibellouses of rebellion'.

Perhaps the most significant section of *Basilicon Doron* discusses the Scottish nobility, 'farre first in greatnesse and power, either to doe good or euill'. James deplored their 'fectlesse arrogant conceit of their greatnes and power' and instructed Henry never to rest 'until yee roote out these barbarous feides, that their may bee as well smoared downe, as their barbarous name is unknowen to anie other nation'. Nobles must be taught to obey the law. At the same time, Henry should 'honour them therfore that are obedient to the law among them, as Peeres and fathers of your land: the more frequently that your court can bee garnished with them, thinke it the more your honour.'

In the *Trew Law* James touched briefly on Scottish Parliaments, emphasising that kings in Scotland 'were before any estates or rankes of men within the same, before any Parliaments were holden . . . the kings were the authors and makers of the Lawes'. Parliament emerged later, and was 'nothing else but the head court of the king and his vassals'. In *Basilicon Doron* he reiterated his narrow judicial definition of a Parliament as 'the Kings head court' and counselled Henry to 'hold no Parliaments, but for the necessitie of new Lawes, which would be but seldome'. There was little place for representative assemblies in James's political philosophy, and although he had considerable success in Scotland, he lacked a theoretical vision of how to use Parliaments to his best advantage. Instead, he saw the king's coronation oath as the 'clearest, civill, and fundamentall Law, whereby the King's office is properly defined'.[1]

In fact, his view had already been outdated by events in Scotland, for he ignored both the steady rise of legislation he had overseen in the 1590s and his increasing dependency on heavy taxation voted or confirmed in Scottish Parliaments. Despite this, after 1603 James continued to insist that there was seldom much need for representative assemblies. Just as he disregarded recent changes in Scotland, he never made much effort to understand the different views of an influential group among his English subjects who were studying the distant origins of Parliament with its rights and privileges. James immediately realised that the Society of Antiquaries posed a threat, since some of them argued that parliaments were older than kings, in flat contradiction to the king's expressed views about the primacy of monarchy. However, he made no attempt to engage with the historical debate, but simply continued to insist that monarchy emerged before any other institution. Similarly, he paid little heed to the remarkable expansion of constitutional theory in sixteenth-century England, whereby sovereign power was increasingly seen as vested in the King-in-Parliament and not in the monarch alone. Both Henry VIII and Elizabeth, monarchs at least as strong and intelligent as James, successfully adapted themselves to these changing viewpoints. The king's failure to acknowledge evolving circumstances in both his kingdoms was a damaging political defect.

The most personal section in *Basilicon Doron* deals with matrimony and the respect due to wives and mothers. James described marriage as 'the greatest earthly felicitie or miserie, that can come to a man' and urged a careful choice of a godly and virtuous wife. He deplored the double standard of morality that insisted on chastity in women but not men. A husband must ensure his wife's obedience, but should treat her as 'the halfe of your selfe'. Sons must love and cherish their mothers: Henry must respect and honour Queen Anne if she were left a widow. Significantly, James included marriage and the royal family in the 'public' chapter of his book. He also went out of his way to condemn 'unreverent writing or speaking of . . . Parents and predecessours'.[2] Always sensitive to scandalous allegations about his own parentage, James emphasised that for kings, marriage and morality could not be private matters – again a counsel he later ignored.

James wrote well, scattering engaging asides throughout the text.

A king should not look like 'a deboshed waster'. Hair and nails should be short, speech natural and plain, not 'farded with artifice'. Light armour, not heavy pieces, would facilitate running away from battle if that proved necessary. Rough and violent exercises 'as the footeball' should not be used, but hunting, tennis and archery were commendable for fitness. In 'foule and stormie weather . . . may ye lawfully play at the cardes or tables'. *Basilicon Doron* retains an appealingly informal voice, although it also contains sententious political theorising, numerous contradictions and relatively second-hand advice. Later sections tended to decline into banalities. A king should always prefer peace to war, choose men of known wisdom and quality for his councillors and certainly not have a favourite, who might 'wax proud and be envied of his fellows'. He should live a life marked by moderation in all things – dress, food and recreation. Already James's practice frequently diverged from his advice, and some comments were extraordinary. The king who presided over the unparalleled collapse of the Scottish coinage transferred the blame for the debasements on to merchants who exported valuable commodities and brought home inferior ones. He advised his heir to uphold sound gold and silver currencies if only because it might be useful to debase them later. The gap between reality and theory was striking, and *Basilicon Doron* must not be read as an accurate guide to the king's policies.

The republication of *Basilicon Doron* in London in 1603 naturally enhanced its impact. The print-run was enormous for its time, producing between 13,000 and 16,000 copies. There were some changes to the original text and James composed an additional preface to the reader, intending to dispel any suspicion that he harboured 'a vindictive resolution against England' or at least against those Englishmen who had ensured the execution of Mary Queen of Scots.[3] The appearance of the book on the London market at the exact time of the accession was almost certainly masterminded by Robert Cecil and was initially intended to reassure Englishmen about their new ruler. However, in the long run the exercise perhaps went awry since the views expressed by James were often at odds with English legal and political thought. *Basilicon Doron* possibly enhanced suspicions rather than dispelling them.

Dual Monarchy in England and Scotland

For observers both at home and abroad, the events of 1603 posed pressing and complex questions about the future pattern of the king's rule. James was an experienced monarch of Scotland but when he succeeded Queen Elizabeth, he embarked upon an unprecedented experiment, bringing dynastic union to the kingdoms of England, Ireland and Scotland, together with the principality of Wales. He immediately became a ruler of far greater European consequence, and took on a much greater range and burden of responsibilities. How would he govern his novel multiple monarchy? In 1603 as he left Edinburgh, James promised his Scottish subjects that he would return every three years. This followed the advice given to Henry in *Basilicon Doron* 'once in the three yeares to visit al your kingdomes' to hear for himself their complaints and concerns.

In the early months of his English reign, the king continued to assume that he would make regular visits to Scotland. In August 1603, negotiating to purchase the manor of Southwell from the archbishop of York, James wrote that he would need somewhere about half-way to stop and hunt on his journeys north and south. However, within 12 months of his accession, a proclamation greatly improved the postal service northwards and soon around 60 royal letters a year were despatched to Edinburgh. The Scottish council *Register* shows that the king continued to take a close interest in business, but his personal presence seemed less necessary than he originally envisaged. 'This I must say for Scotland' James enthused to the English Parliament in 1607, 'Here I sit and governe it with my Pen, I write and it is done, and by a Clearke of the Councell I governe Scotlande now, which others could not doe by the sword.'[4] His words emphasised his government's effectiveness even in his absence.

James had no intention of appointing a viceroy for Scotland, but he needed experienced senior ministers. At first the king's right-hand man was Alexander Seton earl of Dunfermline, one of the cost-cutting Octavians in 1596. However, when faced with the revival of Presbyterian grievances in 1606 (see p. 164) James thought Dunfermline lacked firmness. He replaced him with his old friend Sir George Hume, lord treasurer of Scotland from 1601 and later earl of

Dunbar. The king also created him Baron Home of Berwick in the English peerage, though he never took his seat in the House of Lords. Dunbar travelled regularly between London and Edinburgh, and in summer he followed the king on his hunting expeditions, although he thought them largely a waste of time. 'I have no news to send you but that we are all become wild men wandering in a forest from the morning till the evening', he wrote resignedly to Salisbury in August 1607 from Beaulieu in Hampshire. By diligent attendance on the king, Dunbar kept him abreast of events in his northern kingdom while at the same time keeping the Scottish Privy Council under firm control. Right up to his death in 1611, he embodied the king's policy of maintaining an integral political connection between his two kingdoms.[5] Thereafter, Dunfermline returned to his previous position and remained as the king's most trusted minister until his death in 1622. James was fortunate to find two men of such high calibre and devotion to his service. Dunbar, in particular, played a vital role in ensuring the stability of Scotland in the early years after the king's departure.

The Scottish Privy Council, dominated by a core of office holders, gradually emerged as an able group of officials intent on increasing royal control rather than merely maintaining it at the level achieved by 1603. The steady decline of violence in Scottish politics continued, with an act of 1604 laying down heavy penalties for those found guilty of feuding. This was followed by a more restrictive act in 1609. In an attempt to put teeth into the legislation, James decided to introduce Justices of the Peace on the English model, although as late as 1625 they were present in less than a quarter of Scottish shires. However, little could be done about the tradition of hereditary sheriffs drawn from the landowning nobility, although the king explicitly condemned them in *Basilicon Doron*. Despite these limitations, the council kept its grip on events. The sensational execution of Lord Maxwell for murder in 1613 sent a clear signal that aristocratic violence would not be allowed to re-emerge in the king's absence.

The new context of the regnal union allowed James to tackle the perennial problem of Border raiding. He strengthened his administration there from the 1580s onward, and as king of England strove 'utterlie to extinguishe as well the name as substance of the bordouris', creating instead a peaceful region of 'middle shires'. Between 1603 and 1611 a series of good harvests eased hardship, and in 1605 a joint Anglo-Scots commission was created to stabilise the six Border counties, using a small force of mounted troops. The involvement of Dunbar, himself a Borderer and intent on expanding his estates in the region, ensured vigorous action up to 1611. There was considerable improvement, although Northumberland continued to suffer from malefactors who fled across the Border from Scotland. Cranfield's economies led to the shortsighted dissolution of the cavalry force in 1621, while bad harvests inflicted misery on the Border counties between 1622 and 1625. Nevertheless, the dual monarchy slowly brought some stability and by the end of the reign, the main problem for Border magistrates was sheep-stealing rather than the murderous raids of earlier years.[6]

When James left Edinburgh for London in 1603, his own kingdom was still in the process of state formation. His government exercised little real authority in the remote parts of Scotland, although trading contacts with the Highlands were steadily increasing. In *Basilicon Doron* he condemned his Gaelic-speaking subjects, dividing them into 'barbarous' (the highlanders of the mainland) and 'utterly barbarous' (the western and northern islanders). In fact Gaeldom formed a distinct entity; linguistic, religious, economic and cultural influences were interwoven to create a pastoral, clan-based society far different from that of the settled lowlands. Gaeldom also crossed the Irish sea, which served as a pathway rather than a barrier. Since the thirteenth century, informal migration and settlement had planted Gaelic-speaking communities of Scottish descent in north-eastern Ireland.

In 1596 James demonstrated his intention of tackling the problems of the Islands and Highlands by attempting to plant lowlanders on the Isle of Lewis. It failed, but in *Basilicon Doron* the king expounded a policy of colonisation whereby 'answerable In-lands subjects' would reform and civilise those remote parts. Another attempt at plantation in 1605 also failed, as did an attempt on the Isle of Harris. Then in 1608 an expedition under the command of Lord Ochiltree was sent to subjugate the Western Isles. The key item on the royal agenda, confirmed by the Scottish Parliament, was the security and collection of the royal rents. With great ingenuity Ochiltree captured a number of Highland chiefs without a pitched battle. The Scottish council thereafter pursued a policy of co-operation, consolidated by an agreement worked out on the island of Iona in 1609 between Andrew Knox (recently appointed bishop of the Isles) and the majority of the chiefs. Known as the Statutes of Iona (or Icolmkill), the agreement recognised the chiefs' authority over their followers, but also made them agents of royal order against violence. The Gaelic culture of fighting and feasting was undermined by restrictions on alcohol and on the size of the lords' households. They were also to abandon their residual catholicism and embrace the protestant kirk, educating their eldest sons in schools in the lowlands.

At first the Statutes of Iona seemed little more than empty aspirations. Fratricidal struggles between the chiefs continued, with the Campbells driving out the Macdonalds in Islay and Kintyre. In 1616 the Privy Council restructured the earlier agreement and the impact of royal rule was increased, although it still relied on the devolved government of the chiefs. Almost as valuable was the gradual introduction of Gaelic-speaking ministers, who made a reality of the parish system and turned it into a powerful agent of social order. Acting as an enforcer of cultural uniformity, the kirk could become an effective arm of the state rather than a contender against it. Lawlessness was endemic until the late seventeenth century, but in retrospect the years betweeen 1596 and 1625 were the pivotal moment of change in the Western Isles.

The Scottish Privy Council only met with determined resistance on Orkney, where sheer distance from Edinburgh allowed Earl Patrick, a distant royal cousin, to rule as a princeling. He disregarded the Statutes of Iona and was at odds with Bishop James Law of Orkney, a commissioner of the peace for the Northern Isles since 1610 who became a royal revenue collector in 1612. 'Black Patie' was imprisoned in 1609, released but then hanged in 1615 after a brief rebellion. Patrick's bitter enemy the earl of Caithness was used by the Scottish Privy Council to reduce the island and execute the insurgents, but the rich earldom of Orkney was retained by the Crown. Ruthlessly, the council sent Caithness himself into exile in 1623 after he fell into debt and contemptuously disregarded the Edinburgh legal proceedings brought by his creditors.

The processes of strengthening central government that James began in the 1590s continued steadily after his departure. The low-lands continued to provide the core of royal revenues and royal administrators, but by 1625 the powers exercised from the capital over the whole of Scotland were greater than ever before. The taming of previously anarchic frontier regions was one of the greatest achievements of the early Stuart monarchy.[7]

These victories were not won without some cost. In 1621 a new political divide was visible in the Scottish Parliament. The earl of Rothes and Lord Balmerino, among others, found themselves blocked by a phalanx of Privy Councillors, bishops and court noble-men voting for measures – heavy taxation and the Five Articles of Perth – that commanded little support in the country. Religious and political principles came together to oppose an autocratic Crown and its tax-subsidised courtiers, and to demand more representative Parliaments and freer General Assemblies. The correlation between courtiers and opponents in 1621 was to be paralleled in 1638 when the parliamentary opponents emerged as covenanting leaders.[8]

The king's initial hopes for a fuller Anglo-Scottish Union of both law and Parliaments came to nothing. However, he defended his plans as 'a perfect child, yet . . . no man', and the metaphor of gradual growth was an apposite one. Over the course of time and in more informal arenas, James had more success with his policies. He expanded the Scottish peerage by over half after 1603, and there was an initial flurry of Anglo-Scottish marriages. James also encouraged many Scots noblemen to spend time in England, and the Jacobean court became distinctively British, with an Anglo-Scottish court elite gradually emerging, dominated by the Lennox Stewarts and the Hamiltons, with the Erskines, Douglases, Murrays and Kers also prominent. Many of them participated in the management of Scottish affairs from London, sometimes earning English titles as well as grants of property and office from James. These courtier-nobles have been described by their historian, Keith Brown, as shar-ing 'a high view of monarchy, a preference for episcopal church government, and a commitment to some idea of Great Britain'.[9] Some also developed links with Irish noble families. The vast major-ity of the Scottish nobility remained untouched by 'Briticisation', but

James might reasonably pride himself on initiating a long-term process whereby his nobilities might grow more friendly and familiar with each other. Prince Henry enthusiastically created a group of young 'Scoto-Britons' around him, and his premature death was a real setback for further integration, since the English nobility much preferred him to his father. Sadly, after 1625 Charles I made little effort to continue the work of King James and Prince Henry in promoting mutual acculturalisation.

Acting in concert with his competent Scottish Privy Council, James made vigorous efforts to maintain and enhance all that he had achieved before 1603. Yet Scotland was bound to suffer once it became an absentee monarchy. The king remarked wistfully in 1607 that 'I doe not alreadie know the one halfe of them by face, most of the youth now being risen up to bee men, who were but children when I was there'. Scots feared that the regnal union would transform their future kings into Englishmen. Instead, James quickly realised that the change of generations would make him lose contact with his Scots. For a king who excelled at personal kingship, time and distance undermined his sureness of touch in man-management, previously the strongest aspect of his rule. His rich experience of Scotland, which sustained his dual monarchy in the early years after 1603, was inevitably a declining asset as the reign progressed. The Privy Council grew more expert than the king in handling business and deflected ill-informed royal interventions. 'Alas, Sir', the earl of Mar remarked in 1626 to Charles I, perhaps revealing more than he intended, 'a hundred times your worthy father has sent down directions which we have stayed, and he has given us thanks for it when we have informed him of the truth'.[10]

Despite his long absence, in 1617 James triumphantly revitalised his contacts in Scotland. In December 1616 just after the great Overbury-Howard scandals rocked his court, he felt in need of refreshment. The king wrote to the Scottish council of his 'salmon-like instinct' to see once again the place of his birth and breeding. On learning of his proposed visit, the council embarked on a series of measures designed to ensure that the roads, lodgings and stabling, together with other necessary amenities such as plenty of deer and wildfowl for hunting, should all be in good order when James came north. The journey would also remind the English court and people that the king was not theirs alone: the Scots shared equally in the regnal union. Both sides had declined a closer rapprochement, but Scotland remained a proud kingdom, not an English colony.

The king's English courtiers begged him on their knees not to undertake a progress of unprecedented length and expense. Queen Anne had no desire to go north and James did not seize the opportunity to introduce his heir Charles to the Scottish people. In retrospect that was a grave mistake, since the prince succeeded to the throne of Scotland in 1625 with hardly any memories of his native kingdom and no personal sense of its different traditions. The sole courtier who readily agreed to travel to Scotland was the new favourite George Villiers. James promptly raised him to an earldom by way of thanks. Financed by a loan reluctantly made by the City of London and by the proceeds of selling another flurry of knighthoods, James set out from Theobalds in March 1617. Travelling slowly north he crossed the Tweed in May and stayed mostly in Holyrood House in Edinburgh, although the royal party also visited Glasgow, Stirling, Dundee, Aberdeen and St Andrews. The king's plan to refurbish the chapel at Holyrood in the style of the more elaborate chapels royal of his English palaces caused dismay, with even the Scottish bishops protesting at what they saw as idolatrous paintings and sculpture (see pp. 165–6) but little else disturbed the harmonious atmosphere.

The smooth organisation of the visit was a credit to the Scottish council particularly the treasurer depute, Sir Gideon Murray, who masterminded the preparations. James was delighted with the hospitality offered to him and at Dunglass demanded of his followers, 'Tell me My Lordes did you feid so well sence you cam from London?.' He was warmly received wherever he went and by August when he turned south again it was clear that the visit had been a great success, although it cost a staggering £228,846 Scottish.[11] However, there were strains present in Scotland which the king's visit did nothing to solve. Religion was already a sensitive issue. Resentment was growing at the rapid expansion of the Scottish peerage, seen as dishonouring the ancient nobility. At the same time, the king's vast generosity to only a handful of Scots was creating a 'court and country' divide between those who had benefited from the dual monarchy and those who had not. By the mid-1630s those divisions had widened further.

Ireland

Gaeldom was not limited to the more remote parts of Scotland, for a clan-based social structure and Gaelic-language culture linked the Scottish west coast with the north-east coast of Ireland. Effective English rule extended little further west or north than a strip of land known as the Pale surrounding Dublin, which served as the administrative capital, and a few port towns such as Cork and Galway. The Old English in Ireland were descended from the Angevin adventurer-conquerors of the twelfth century, and the Old English FitzGerald earls of Kildare largely monopolised the office of lord deputy in the early sixteenth century. Most of the inhabitants of the countryside were labelled as mere, or Gaelic, Irish or 'The Irishry'. They spoke no English and looked to their clan chieftains for leadership. In 1541 Henry VIII took the title of 'King of this land of Ireland', replacing the previous status of Ireland as a lordship. In an attempt to extend the reach of the Tudor court, Henry ennobled some clan heads, including the leader of the powerful O'Neills who became earl of Tyrone, but Anglicisation hardly touched the rest.

The Reformation brought further divisions since Ireland did not follow England in rejecting catholicism. Under Elizabeth the Crown committed itself to a harsh policy of protestantisation and Anglicisation together with the expropriation of land for incoming English settlers. After a series of disturbances, a major rebellion finally broke out in 1596 under Hugh O'Neill third earl of Tyrone, whose ancestral lands dominated Ulster. Coincidentally, it was in the same year that the poet Edmund Spenser published the second part of his great epic *The Faerie Queen* together with his *View of the Present State of Ireland*, which called for the destruction of Gaeldom and systematic English colonisation. Spenser and his family were among the recent 'undertakers' (expropriators of Irish land) in Munster, another area English settlers were attempting to colonise. They were burned out of their castle in 1598 and fled Ireland to die in poverty in London.

Well before his accession to the English throne James became increasingly aware of the importance of Ireland in British affairs. The Elizabethan struggle to assert effective control over Ireland generated guerrilla warfare that provided employment opportunities for mercenaries known as redshanks or gallowglasses. Between the 1560s and the 1590s, around 25,000 Scots served in the conflict against English expansionism. Large numbers of them came from the Western Isles and on their return, they dramatically destabilised the social structure of their homeland, becoming a violent parasite class living off the farming clansmen.

Tyrone cherished hopes that the King of Scots would abandon many of Elizabeth's Irish policies as soon as he inherited the English throne. The earl kept in contact with James even at the height of the rebellion, or Nine Years War as it is known in Irish history. However, in 1601–2 the English government successfully pressured James to stop the flow of west highlanders across to Tyrone's rebel forces in Ulster. The king also offered Scots military aid to Elizabeth in 1601 when Spanish forces landed in Kinsale. It was graciously declined, but the gesture reinforced James's loyalist credentials in the eyes of the queen and her government.

After Tyrone's surrender in 1603, the Irish economy was in ruins, and the debasement of the coinage during the war years made recovery far harder. On his way south from Edinburgh, James was lobbied on the issue by the soldier Sir Henry Danvers, and he decided to act despite Cecil's worries about the shortage of silver available to upgrade the coins. By September 1603 the new coinage was ready, a prompt response that underscored the king's concern for Irish affairs. For the first time a fixed rate of exchange was established with the English coinage also circulating in Ireland. These measures stimulated a swift improvement in both internal and external trade.

There was also a brief attempt at a broader Anglo-Irish conciliation under Elizabeth's victorious general Lord Mountjoy who remained in office as Lord Deputy until June 1604. Mountjoy was convinced that a lenient settlement would be the most effective way to return Ulster to peace and prosperity. Tyrone was restored to his lands and his ally Rory O'Donnell was created earl of Tyrconnell in September 1603. Unfortunately, the far-sighted policy of reintegration was left with few supporters after Mountjoy's return to England and his premature death there in April 1606.

Sir Arthur Chichester, who became lord deputy in 1604 largely in the absence of other candidates, was a servitor, one of those Englishmen who had served the Crown in Ireland in a military capacity. Like most of his colleagues, he disagreed with Mountjoy's policy of reconciliation, instead seeing Tyrone's defeat as an opportunity for further colonisation. Chichester thought that the earl's estates should have been sequestered not restored, and tenures on them granted to unemployed soldiers. Thereby, English influence and control would be extended into the heartland of the rebellion. The lord deputy despised the native Irish, describing them as 'beasts in the shape of men', and thought that the only way to 'civilise' Ireland was by bringing in new settlers.

From 1604 on, Chichester's administration set its face against the local power-bases of Tyrone and Tyrconnell. At the same time, a new English bishop, George Montgomery, took over the conjoint three dioceses of Derry, Raphoe and Clogher. Formerly the dean of Norwich, the new bishop began a vigorous campaign to restore to his bishopric lands and revenues currently in the possession of the two Irish earls. Chichester and the servitors were staunchly protestant and disapproved of the tolerance traditionally shown to the catholic Old English, let alone the Gaelic nobility. In Montgomery they had a new ally in their campaign of harassment.

After 1605 the energetic legal imperialist Sir John Davies, Solicitor-General of Ireland from 1603 and promoted to Attorney-General in 1606, began imposing English land law on Ulster. He had the firm backing of both Chichester and the king, for Sir Thomas Lake reported to Salisbury from Royston that James read the Irish letters diligently while taking note of particular points: 'He approves exceedingly, of reducing of the Irish to the English tenures.' Some of the approval was no doubt due to the prior efforts of Salisbury himself, who acted as patron and supporter at court of Chichester and his party. In a tract written in 1612, Davies argued that the settlement of Ireland required firstly the assertion of the primacy of central government. Then a national system of jurisdiction must be established, parallel to that of England, with the introduction of fixed units of landholding, unlike the Irish system of shared control of grazing land. The adoption of arable farming instead of stockholding, together with English laws of property and inheritance, would complete the 'civilising' process.[12]

Davies's plan was in line with the king's earlier thinking. In the *Trew Law* James supported the civil law doctrine whereby conquest led to the sequestration of lands, and in *Basilicon Doron* he advocated policies of plantation, which he had already tried to put into effect in Scotland. These were plantations organised and imposed by the state, but the king was also in favour of the commercial plantations that his subjects, the wealthy merchants of London, were beginning to create on the eastern seaboard of North America. In 1607 the settlement at Jamestown, named in honour of the king, marked the beginnning of the revived colony of Virginia and with it, the commencement of a far greater British empire, although initially it seemed of less importance than developments in Ulster.

By 1607 the earl of Tyrconnell was weary of the struggle against Chichester's regime and Spanish archival sources reveal that he was preparing to become a soldier or pensioner in the service of Spain. Tyrone, however, was both much wealthier and much tougher, so it came as a bolt from the blue when in September 1607, both Tyrone and Tyrconnell fled into exile along with many of their followers. It is possible that they went with some intention of seeking additional military support from Spain before returning to try to reclaim their lands, but if so they were unsuccessful. In December their extensive estates were declared escheated (forfeited) to the Crown. The flight of the earls, more than the surrender of 1603 itself, marked the end of the old order: thereafter, the prospects for the native Irish of Ulster looked bleaker and for the servitors, far brighter.

After 1607, for the first time, there was a possibility of a wholesale plantation. A brief rebellion of the Irishry led by Sir Cahir O'Doherty in 1608 allowed the Crown to confiscate additional lands. Chichester suggested that Scots protestants should join Englishmen in the project of plantation, for his earlier military service made him aware that Ulster and western Scotland shared much the same economy and polity.

Marriage alliances also linked the ruling familes of Ulster and

Scottish Gaeldom. However, Chichester thought in terms of local and piecemeal settlements that would not expropriate large numbers of native proprietors, a scheme more pragmatic and flexible than the policies subsequently followed. The king was immediately convinced that a policy of settlement could transform Ireland, despite its general lack of success in the Scottish islands. He was already keen on a strategy of uprooting the Grahams, the most troublesome of the Scottish Border clans, and resettling them in Roscommon. The ruffianly Grahams were unlikely to be civilising agents, but their transplantation (which at least helped the Borders) prefigured later policies of using British colonies to resettle undesirables not wanted at home. More important to James, protestantism was still a missionary enterprise in Scottish Gaeldom, and if the Gaels on both sides of the North Channel were held down by a policy of protestant plantation, his rule in two of his three kingdoms would be strengthened.

After 1609 the notion of plantation in Scotland was dropped, but in Ulster it proceeded with the same aim of controlling and pacifying the outlying Gaelic regions. The scheme for the six escheated counties treated the native landholders much less favourably than Chichester had proposed, with most of the land set aside for incoming colonisers. In time, it was hoped, plantation would transform Ulster from a conquered province garrisoned by a costly English army into a civilised protestant settlement. James took a close personal interest, for the project would forward his ideal of a 'greater Britain'. Sir Alexander Hay, secretary of the Scottish Privy Council, was also enthusiastic since it provided opportunities for impover ished, land-hungry Scots to hack out their own farms in Ulster. In the words of the leading Irish historian Nicholas Canny, 'the first distinguishing feature of the Ulster plantation was that it was to be a "British" effort', the first major enterprise of James's united monarchy.[13]

Despite an impressive flow of both English and (especially) Scots tenant farmers into Ulster, there were never enough settlers to corral the native Irish into restricted areas which could easily be controlled. To the irritation of the king, who wanted Chichester to discipline those undertakers who failed to fulfil their obligation to bring sufficient labour with them, the Irish remained as under-tenants. It was

cheaper for the undertakers to use the locals than to import additional settlers. Control over the economy passed to the newcomers,
but the plantation created a hostile catholic underclass who laboured
on the land while resenting the protestant head tenants. From the
beginning, the seeds of future conflict were sown.

The new plantation also destabilised Old English dominance over
the rest of Ireland. Traditionally an Irish Parliament met in Dublin,
although under Poynings law of 1494, it could not be summoned
except by the English Crown. The Old English were accustomed to
dominating the assembly, but in autumn 1611 as part of the plantation process, James sent Lord Carew to visit Ireland and submit recommendations. Carew advised the king to increase protestant
representation by adding 84 parliamentary seats to the existing 148.
Thirty-eight new members were to be assigned to Ulster, by creating
new boroughs that were either mere villages or simply areas designated for later plantation. This blatant gerrymandering created a
protestant majority of 32 and destroyed the control previously exercised by the catholic Old English. They also learned that a bill was
proposed that would banish Irish priests and fine catholic laymen
accused of sheltering them. In future the packed Dublin Parliament
would not be able to block anti-catholic laws applicable to both the
native Irish and the Old English. A petition was sent to James, asking
for a free Parliament and the repeal of those recusancy laws already
in existence. The king was assured that such a policy would win him
the hearts of his Irish subjects forever.

James paid no heed, so when the Dublin Parliament met in May
1613, the catholic peers excused themselves from the opening ceremony and sent a deputation to the king. The Old English in the
Lower House refused to accept the members returned from the new
Ulster boroughs. There was an unseemly brawl over the choice of
Speaker, with the catholic candidate sitting in the Speaker's chair
with his protestant rival Sir John Davies in his lap. In April 1614 at an
audience in London James berated the Old English petitioners as
being 'Parliament recusants . . . never before heard of'. He thought
they were 'but half-subjects . . . you that have an eye to me one way
and to the pope another way', and he sharply reproved them for
tumultuous, reckless behaviour. However, three months later James

decided on a compromise, reducing the new protestant majority in the Commons to only six members, and withdrawing the proposed anti-catholic legislation. His move quieted agitation, and once back in Dublin in the new session of Parliament, the Old English were studiously polite and business-like. In April 1615 they joined in a novel vote of parliamentary taxation. Nevertheless, the king was coming to the conclusion that the Irish Parliament was more trouble than it was worth. Although the long-term consequence of his actions in 1614 was to turn the assembly permanently into a predominantly protestant body, he dissolved it in August 1615 and never summoned another. His attitude to the Irish Parliament increasingly typified his weary view of the kingdom as a whole. On his first visit to the newly-created English office for state papers, James was so struck by the bulk of Irish records that he commented that there was more ado with Ireland than all the world besides.[14]

After eleven years' service, Chichester left office in 1615 and withdrew to his estates around Dungannon. Knowing the king's commitment to the plantation ideal, he built up a model settlement in Tyrone's former stronghold, expending much of his fortune to create an example for other servitors.[15] In 1616 James appointed another leading Ulster undertaker to replace Chichester as lord deputy. Sir Oliver St John, created Viscount Grandison in 1621, was a client of the rising favourite George Villiers, baron and later duke of Buckingham. By 1616 Buckingham had captured the heights of the Irish bureaucracy and St John was active in pushing forward the Ulster plantation as well as enforcing anti-catholic measures. These further alienated the Old English while St John's reliance on the favourite forced him into numerous conflicts of interest as the latter gained increasing control over Irish business. Buckingham was intent on building up a lucrative Irish patrimony for the Villiers family and clientage, although he was anxious to keep the extent of his interests concealed. The Irish peerage ballooned from 24 in 1616 to 99 by 1630 as titles were sold, and nearly all of the newcomers seem to have obtained their honours by gift or purchase from the Villiers family. To take only one example, Randall Macdonnell gave the favourite £5000 in 1620 for his earldom of Antrim.[16] The exploitation of Irish patronage and revenues by 'Villiers Enterprises (Ireland)

Unlimited', in the words of their historian, made it impossible to improve relationships with the Old English. At the same time, the dominance of Buckingham at court cut off those channels of communication that the Old English previously used to appeal directly to the monarch on Irish affairs. In any case, the king himself regarded the sale of honours, such as the new order of Irish baronets created in 1619, as part of his policy of British social engineering. Most of the recipients were Englishmen, with payoffs to Buckingham. If the profits largely went to the favourite, James was behind the long-term aim of establishing a new ascendancy throughout Ireland, at once British and protestant, and happy to allow Buckingham to act as a major agent.[17]

The central problem of Ireland, as far as the English government was concerned, was its drain on the Westminster treasury. Recent research indicates that from 1604 to 1619, the subsidy sent from England was over £47,000 per annum. Small sums of money were raised from the farming-out of the Irish customs in 1613 for an annual rent of £6000, but in 1618 the farm was granted to Buckingham on condition he passed over half the profits. Once again the Villiers ascendancy drained away revenues that might have contributed to either the Irish or the English Exchequer. The English Parliament of 1621 attacked corruption and royal prodigality in Ireland, so Buckingham secured Grandison's discreet recall in 1622. He did not oppose a parliamentary commission of enquiry which forwarded the reform agenda of the lord treasurer, Lionel Cranfield earl of Middlesex, though it rapidly revealed the incompetence and parasitism of the Irish administration. Cranfield boasted to Buckingham that he would make Ireland self-sufficient and save England £20,000 per year, and he proposed a series of reforms which might have had some effect. In addition, he attempted to put some vigour into the officials of the Irish Exchequer. There seems good ground for thinking that by the last years of James's reign less subsidy was required from England.

Unfortunately, these attempts at reform appeared to undermine the Villiers connection in Ireland and only contributed to Cranfield's own impeachment and downfall in 1624. Another Buckingham client, Henry Cary Viscount Falkland, became Lord Deputy in late 1622 and made further attempts to increase Irish revenues through the establishment of a court of Wards on the English model. He also revived Chichester's briefly implemented policy of enforcing the recusancy laws. Both these measures further alienated the Old English landowners, who saw the court of Wards as an attack on their feudal tenures. It also effectively debarred their heirs from inheriting as long as they remained catholic. Unpopular policies like these brought in relatively small amounts of money and when relations with Spain broke down after 1623, they looked likely to imperil Ireland's internal stability and the country's loyalty to the English monarchy. The threat of another Kinsale re-emerged. James intervened in 1624 to inhibit the Dublin government from pursuing a policy of religious persecution. In November 1625 a memorandum from a senior English official in Dublin mixed its metaphors, but forcefully made the point that Spain wished 'to have the backdoor of Ireland kept open as a bridle upon England'. He urged that political discontent should be met by amendment and reform that would pre-empt pleas for Spanish assistance.[18] Thereafter, Falkland was increasingly under attack and his lord deputyship ended in disgrace in 1629.

By the 1620s the new shape of Ireland could be discerned. In 1622 the commissioners appointed to survey the state of the country compiled a lengthy report, assessing progress particularly on the Ulster plantation. It was never published, largely because it indicted Buckingham's clients in Ireland for ravenously pursuing their own economic interests. It also posed so many questions about present and future royal policies that the issue of further plantations dominated Irish affairs from 1622 to 1641. Nevertheless, the survey stands as a record of how much had changed since 1603. English law was steadily replacing Irish, English counties were introduced as the unit of local government, and the merchant companies of the City of London, already coerced into investing very large sums of money, were building new ports at Derry and Coleraine. Both towns were substantial places, and by 1626 the rental incomes from them were beginning to give the London companies a decent return on their investment. As ports, they promised to bring prosperity by encouraging trade in agricultural commodities and thereby increase Irish contacts with the outside world.

The 1622 commissioners also pointed to enduring problems.

Native Irish cultural and economic influences remained predominant across the country. catholicism was still the religion of virtually all the Gaelic Irish and the Old English. The deeper aim of reforming the Irish population on the English model of civility had comprehensively failed, while the divide between Ulster and the rest of Ireland was already entrenched. At the same time, the undertakers in Ulster had failed to bring in sufficient numbers of settlers, so the plantation there remained dependant on Gaelic Irish agricultural labour. The Dublin government was neither efficient nor popular enough to command loyalty across the country, and the Old English, formerly the key supporters of the Crown, were weakening in their loyalty.

It would be easy with the knowledge of hindsight to deplore virtually all aspects of Jacobean policy in Ireland as deeply misguided and ultimately doomed to failure. The six Irish lords representing Old English opinion who urged James in 1613 to win the hearts of his subjects by calling a free Parliament and repealing the recusancy laws were almost certainly right. Yet to the king both policies were unthinkable, despite his leniency to the catholic community in England. Equally, it must be emphasised that in 1625 no-one could have predicted the Irish uprising of 1641. A strong case can be made for the Jacobean achievement. In the 1590s famine stalked the country with thousands of deaths in Ulster during the Nine Years War. By contrast, after 1603 Ireland was mostly peaceful and famine disappeared. Ordered conditions fostered the economy. The country was more prosperous than it had been for centuries, and Irish towns were steadily growing, with significant communities of artisans, merchants, moneylenders and chapmen. They and other itinerant peddlers linked town and countryside, distributing goods and building up networks of internal trade. As Lord Deputy St John once cynically observed, 'The love of money will sooner effect civility than any other persuasion whatsoever.'[19]

It should be admitted that internal peace was being bought in Ireland partly at the price of high levels of emigration, with large numbers of young men going abroad to enrol in continental catholic armies. At the same time, a major transfer of land-holding was under way. In 1600 most land was owned by the Old English and the native Irish, but by 1641 the Old English, the Irish and the New British settlers were roughly equally balanced, each owning about a third of the country. Nevertheless, looking back from the perspective of the 1620s to the 1590s, those who administered Ireland could reasonably pride themselves on their achievement. In April 1621 when the record of Buckingham and his clients came under attack in the House of Commons, James at once intervened to defend both his favourite and his own record. He insisted that he was no 'Idle nor sleepinge kinge' and he considered his reforms in Ireland 'one of his master peices'. This was over-optimistic, but Lionel Cranfield, a shrewd observer, noted how much more land was worth in Ireland in 1621 than in 1603.[20]

The king could also point to the increasing levels of social integration as the Old English, and even the Irish nobility, were gradually taking on a dual identity. Through wardships and intermarriage, many leading families such as the FitzGerald earls of Kildare acquired English educations and English wives, as well as links with Scottish noble families. The process began under Elizabeth but accelerated after 1603. One of the most striking links was formed early in James's reign when Frances Walsingham, the widowed countess of Essex, married the fourth earl of Clanricarde, the effective ruler of County Galway. They resided for much of the year on his substantial estates in Kent. Thereafter, the families of Devereux and Bourke remained closely intertwined, and Lord Clanricarde was created first earl of St Albans in the English peerage in 1628.[21] Like their Scottish counterparts, the leaders of Irish society were experiencing not exactly anglicisation, but rather a slow process of 'Briticisation' that created a new mental world for many of them. The integration of elites was only just beginning, but the Jacobean peace brought a hitherto-unknown degree of contact and intermingling between at least some of the great landowning families of the three kingdoms.

Both Scotland and Ireland enjoyed peace and rising prosperity between 1603 and 1625. At the same time, they continued to exhibit all the problems that Conrad Russell has identified as intrinsic to multiple kingdoms: resentment at the king's absence, problems over the disposal of offices and the sharing of war costs, conflicts over trade and colonies, foreign intervention and religion.[22] The smooth running of an imperial monarchy covering England, Scotland and Ireland inevitably encountered immense structural obstacles, many of them still not overcome today. It is only when we come to appreciate those entrenched difficulties that we can appreciate that – flawed as it was – King James's achievement after 1603 as monarch of three kingdoms was both pioneering and impressive.

8 Supreme Governor

Puritanism and Godliness

As king of Scotland James devoted sustained attention to the affairs of the kirk, aiming to establish the measure of royal control never imposed during his minority. His efforts disposed him to have a high regard for the English church, whose Supreme Governor (the title given to the Crown in the 1559 religious settlement) enjoyed extensive powers without any parallel in Scotland. In 1603 James was confident that he could fill his English role effectively.

In the revised 1603 edition of *Basilicon Doron* (see p. 135) intended for his English subjects, James added a new preface identifying 'two extremities' of religion. One was 'to beleeve with the Papists, the churches authority, better then your owne knowledge'. Rome considered that its authority included the power to depose secular princes, a claim James abhorred and thought that other Christian monarchs should also oppose. However, he was usually prepared to acknowledge that Rome was a true church in its essential doctrines. Here he differed from most godly protestants, who regarded catholicism as the exact opposite of true religion, the Antichrist predicted in the Bible.

The king's other 'extremitie' was to 'leane with the Anabaptists, to your owne conceits and dreamed revelations'. In the original edition, James roundly condemned 'Puritaines, verie pestes in the Church and Common-Weale', but in 1603 the king explained that the label of Puritan belonged only to 'the Anabaptists, called the Family of Love', Brownists and such like. Their distinctive features were contempt for 'the civill magistrate', an attitude which undermined orderly society, and intolerance towards those who did not agree with them on all minutiae of doctrine. On this very narrow definition, English 'Puritans' were a tiny and uninfluential minority.

The king was well aware, however, that the English church contained many who regarded themselves as 'the godly', the description they preferred to 'Puritan', which had originated as a term of abuse. They had little in common with sects like the Anabaptists or the Family of Love, and historians usually label them 'moderate puritans'. Reaching out to this substantial group, James emphasised that he equally loved and honoured 'the learned and grave men' of both his churches, although he knew that to some (English moderate puritans and Scottish Presbyterians alike), the English bishops 'smell of a Papall supremacie, that the Surplise, the corned cap, and such like, are the outward badges of Popish errours'. The king regarded these as matters of indifference, but was prepared to listen to other viewpoints if expounded 'by patience, and well-grounded reasons'. James wanted to distinguish between radical troublemakers who wanted major structural changes in the English church, and moderate puritans whose views might differ from his, but who conformed to the established worship of the Elizabethan Prayer Book.[1]

This judicious statement, reflecting the king's Scottish experience of balancing moderates against radicals, made an impact in 1603 and was frequently remembered thereafter. His acceptance of 'well-grounded' argument indicated a willingness to consider cautious reform, in contrast to Elizabeth's inflexibility. As James rode south, he was presented with the Millenary petition, allegedly signed by a thousand English clergy. Puritan petitioners were also active in the counties, particularly Northamptonshire and Sussex. Flatteringly addressed to 'our physician to heal these diseases', the petition set out the grievances of moderates. It called for the reform of allegedly 'popish' ceremonies in the Prayer Book, including the sign of the cross in baptism, the giving of the ring in marriage, and bowing in church at the name of Jesus. The petitioners disliked the Elizabethan obligation laid on clergymen to wear the cap and surplice, but urged stricter sabbath observance, including more sermons. Perhaps aware of the king's fondness for theological discussion, they suggested proceeding 'by conference among the learned'.[2]

James listened, despite the anxieties of his senior churchmen that he might be undermining their authority by opening issues to debate. He decided on a formal conference between nine bishops led by

Archbishop Whitgift, and five academic representatives of puritanism. They met on 14 January 1604 at Hampton Court, with James presiding. He emphasised his commitment to episcopacy, twice repeating his maxim: 'No bishop, no king.' He required all clergy to acknowledge his supremacy over church and state. They must subscribe to the three articles of religion formulated by Whitgift in 1583 even though they had been found objectionable by an earlier generation of puritans. James balanced these demands, however, by promising to address some long-standing abuses such as pluralism (which led inevitably to absenteeism from some parishes). He agreed to reform the court of High Commission, detested by puritans whom it often targeted. He made it clear that he strongly supported preaching – 'we meane to plante preachers' – while altering some minor features of the Prayer Book. The most constructive puritan suggestion was for a new translation of the whole Bible. James personally drew up detailed instructions to the team of translators, to ensure that the new version was as inclusive and eirenic as possible. It must not contain marginalia, which could draw attention to divisions over interpretation. The resulting masterpiece of Jacobean prose known as the Authorised or King James Version was completed in 1611 and remains in regular use around the world.[3]

Moderate puritans welcomed the piecemeal concessions offered at Hampton Court, but subscription to the new canon 36 in 1604 (incorporating Whitgift's three articles) was inevitably contentious. Whitgift died in February just after the conference concluded, and was succeeded at Canterbury by the energetic, tough-minded Richard Bancroft bishop of London. James was persuaded to grant troubled clergy a period for reflection before they subscribed. In some cases where the king or Bancroft pushed too hard for conformity, the Privy Council, led by Cecil, smoothed over difficulties. The last thing the English councillors wanted was an outbreak of religious bitterness at the beginning of the reign. Around 75 beneficed ministers were deprived for refusing to subscribe, together with probably a larger number of lesser fry such as chaplains, lecturers and curates.

Efforts to reform pluralism came to little, since the problem was primarily legal and financial. It has been calculated that 3849 livings (out of 9224) were impropriated by lay patrons, mostly landowners. This meant that laymen collected the parish tithes, but paid only a fraction of them over to the vicar. Many livings were too poor to attract a well-qualified clergyman, but two or more held together might provide adequate maintenance. Massive legal reform at the expense of the gentry would have been necessary to change the system, so absenteeism necessarily continued. However, the king ended the pernicious looting of the lands and revenues of bishoprics by courtiers and others that had taken place under Elizabeth. In the 1610 Parliament, he repeated his willingness to accept minor reforms over the misuse of excommunication, and in 1611 he acted upon some of the common lawyers' objections to High Commission, clarifying the definition of the court's jurisdiction.

It gradually became clear after Hampton Court that what the king required was not full ceremonial conformity but loyalty, obedience and goodwill. Only those clergy who openly defied royal or episcopal authority would incur penalties. Under this benign regime, the radical Presbyterianism of the 1580s and 1590s virtually disappeared, and only two obdurate ministers were deprived for nonconformity between 1610 and 1625. 'Godly reformation' ceased to imply ecclesiastical restructuring and focused more on creating a well-educated preaching ministry. The king was a connoisseur of sermons and considered that the English church lacked high-quality preaching. After 1603 he prided himself on the outstanding quality of sermons at court, which would set an example to the nation. His endorsement of the preaching ministry won widespread approval, as did his permission for the resumption under episcopal licence of the 'prophesyings' or clerical training exercises banned by Elizabeth in 1576. The king's own anti-papal writings reassured moderate puritans, as did his patronage of evangelical (Bible-emphasising) clergy such as Toby Matthew, archbishop of York 1606–28, and George Abbot, archbishop of Canterbury 1611–33. As Patrick Collinson has commented, 'This rising tide of consensual, evangelical Calvinism all but submerged the old differences between conformity and nonconformity.'[4]

Unlike Elizabeth, James had a high personal regard for clerics and told his son Charles in 1619 that bishops were the best companions for princes. James chose his English bishops carefully, partly because they were staunch royal supporters in the House of Lords. He filled episcopal vacancies promptly, where Elizabeth often left them empty for months or even years in order to collect their revenues for the Crown. The king often preferred royal chaplains whom he already knew personally, and at least 25 of the 40 bishops consecrated between 1603 and 1625 had served him. James took considerable personal interest in the chapel royal. The Hampshire gentleman Sir Richard Paulet attended communion at Whitehall palace in 1610, while he was serving as a member of the House of Commons. He was surprised when a courtier came up afterwards to take his name, explaining that the king required a list of all those who communicated. James spent around £7000 per year on musicians at court, a generous provision that covered their occasional performances at entertainments and masques, but their most regular employment must have been in the chapel royal.

The king also ensured a wide spectrum of doctrinal opinion in the English church. Most of his bishops were Calvinist in theology, but not all. The great court preacher Lancelot Andrewes bishop of Winchester was not a Calvinist; nor was Richard Neile, a skilled administrator who rose from being chaplain to Robert Cecil via the deanery of Westminster to the bishopric of Durham. Provided non-Calvinists did not enter into public disputation on certain issues, they could rise to high office. Theological differences occasionally led to friction, but allowed the king to deploy balanced teams on projects such as the translation of the Bible. His inclusive policy over appointments produced a broadly based, theologically flexible church, in which it was tacitly accepted that contentious issues which might breach the king's carefully established harmony must be put aside. Until around 1620 the atmosphere remained cordial.[5]

The charge made by an earlier generation of historians that the Jacobean episcopate was indifferent, negligent and secular cannot be sustained. Most bishops were diligent in overseeing their dioceses. They preached regularly, held confirmations of children and young people (a popular event in the parishes), and on their visitations disciplined clergy accused of sexual or alcoholic misconduct. Rising educational standards allowed bishops to be more selective when ordaining candidates for the ministry. Six bishops were named to the Privy Council, another area where James broke with Elizabethan practice. James Montagu of Winchester, an old friend who helped the king edit his collected works, became a Privy Councillor after accompanying him in 1617 on progress to Scotland. The letter-writer John Chamberlain commented on Montagu's promotion that 'the clergie was not so stronge at the counsaile table these many years.' The new councillor celebrated with a house-warming feast at his recently redecorated episcopal palace in Southwark for all those who had travelled north with him.[6]

James strove for balance, but he could not eradicate deep-seated differences. One of the key fault lines was over attitudes to popery. By 'popery' moderate puritans usually meant anything that reminded them of catholicism, including not only elaborate services, but also old-established pastimes such as maypoles or stage-plays. Ben Jonson's Zeal-of-the-land Busy in *Bartholomew Fair* stingingly caricatured that bossy, interfering and even hypocritical aspect of puritanism. Another divide came over predestination, for moderate puritans cherished their conviction that they were among God's elect. To them, predestination was the central Calvinist doctrine. By contrast anti-Calvinists (later to be called Arminians or Laudians) downplayed predestination. Not only was it a complex matter – Lancelot Andrewes called it *abyssus magna* – but it could be divisive, since assured Calvinists tended to lack charity towards those deemed un-elect. Anti-Calvinists tended to be less censorious of traditional sports and community activities. They also pointed to the fact that the Elizabethan Thirty-Nine Articles did not commit the English church to full predestinarian Calvinism, and gloried instead in the liturgical grandeur of the Prayer Book.

Despite these frictions, James skilfully kept his options open and promoted men of talent. By the middle years of the reign the church was free from extremist agitation, while possessing a distinguished episcopate and an educated preaching ministry. With the parallel improvement of standards in the Scottish kirk, it seemed possible by 1624 to boast that 'the clergy of Britain is the wonder of the world'.[7] By then, however, bitter divisions were already resurfacing.

catholics

In 1603 when distinguishing between radical and moderate puritans, James also divided catholics into extremists and moderates. He loathed the Jesuits, regarding them as 'venomed wasps and fire-brands of sedition', but he was convinced that most lay catholics were loyal subjects, particularly those he later described in the House of Lords in 1610 as 'ancient papists'. He was less trusting of recent converts or 'apostates'. After the Gunpowder Plot, the king devised an Oath of Allegiance, trusting that those who were 'popishly affect-ed [but] retained in their hearts the print of their natural duty towards their sovereign' would distance themselves from potential and actual traitors like Guy Fawkes. Often treated as evidence for James's ecumenism, the oath more recently has been seen as a subtle and powerful device undermining catholics' loyalty to Rome, for it denied the pope's powers of deposition and absolution.[8] Paul V expressly forbade catholics to take it, provoking James to write an *Apologie* (explanation) for the oath, published in English, French and Latin in 1607–8. The king attached great importance to the issue, but most catholics thereafter avoided the oath.

The failure of his overture did not turn James into a persecutor. In 1606 after fresh anti-catholic legislation in Parliament, a royal procla-mation emphasised that although the king's recent experience of catholic treachery would more than justify the harshest measures, he continued to prefer that Jesuits and seminary priests should simply leave the realm. This would avoid what he detested, 'the effusion of blood'. Even more striking was his leniency in 1608 when addressing the judges before they left to conduct the county assizes. Those priests who remained in England despite the proclamation ordering them to depart were to be dealt with flexibly, provided they showed no hint of violence. 'The King's woord was "No torrent of blowd: poena ad paucos"', (penalties to the few), recorded Sir Francis Bacon.[9]

James genuinely considered that the English recusancy laws, imposing the death penalty for religious belief, were barbaric. He wrote firmly to Robert Cecil just after his accession that he regarded persecution 'as one of the infallible notes of a false church'. In the secret correspondence before 1603, he assured Lord Henry Howard he would not persecute 'any that will be quiet and give but an outward obedience to the law'. A crypto-catholic, Howard took the king at his word and sedulously attended the chapel royal. As earl of Northampton he was a patron of many other catholics up to his death in 1614 and in his final months, was secretly received back into the Roman church by a Spanish chaplain sent by Gondomar. Later, Buckingham's many catholic connections, particularly among his womenfolk, also indicated a *de facto* toleration at court. In the counties gentlemen prepared to conform, even though suspected of catholicism, could take their place in royal service far more easily than had been possible before 1603. Crypto-catholics like Sir George Shirley of Northamptonshire aimed for acceptance by buying a baronetcy in 1611 and working hard in the onerous and unpaid offices of local government. When his puritan neighbours targeted Shirley in the anti-recusant drive of 1618, the midlands magnate Thomas Cecil earl of Exeter sprang to his defence, writing to the Privy Council in praise of Shirley's tireless efforts over the county musters.[10]

It must be remembered, however, that James's tolerance of catholics was often limited and grudging. After a brief period of relaxation at the beginning of the reign, the recusancy fines were re-imposed when the catholic community emerged in unexpected strength. There were about 40,000 catholics in England in 1603, and James did not want or expect their numbers to increase. Even those who took the Oath of Allegiance were not exempted from the recusancy laws, although there were wide disparities of enforcement at the local level and in some counties catholics were barely affected. The Exchequer gradually began to regard recusants as a financial resource, and instead of punitive fines designed to force them to convert or face bankruptcy, officials opted for a steady mulct that profited the royal finances. The policy was pragmatic, but some catholic families fell into hardship. At moments of crisis like 1610, with the assassination of Henri IV, James became fiercely anti-catholic and there was a sustained campaign particularly around London. The number of priests imprisoned and executed dropped sharply after the king's accession, but the death penalty did not disappear: 19 suffered during his reign, most of them at periods of diplomatic crisis.

The House of Commons consistently pressed for harsher treatment of both clerical and lay catholics, and not surprisingly in 1606 after the Gunpowder Plot, the government accepted tougher measures when the Lower House demanded them. Salisbury assured the Spanish ambassador these were merely meant 'in terrorem' – to frighten – but in 1610 a further act made the Oath of Allegiance compulsory for all office holders. It also established financial penalties for the husbands of recusant wives. Despite these measures, there were further complaints about laxity towards catholics in the Parliament of 1614, which suggests that most local magistrates had ignored the new regulations. catholic numbers grew steadily and by 1625 stood above 50,000, while the number of priests increased disproportionately to the laity. catholics were also prominent among the nobility, who acted as well-placed spokesmen; inevitably this provoked suspicions of undue influence. Probably, the growth in numbers arose from the long-term impact of the catholic mission to England begun in the 1570s, but to godly protestants it seemed instead the inevitable outcome of the king's casual attitude towards repression.

The Scottish Church

In *Basilicon Doron* James characterised the Scottish Reformation as 'inordinate' and 'not proceeding from the prince's order'. Many of his actions, such as his steady re-establishment of Scottish episcopacy after 1596, were designed to lead the kirk into greater harmony with the English church as well as increasing royal control. James believed that monarchy was divinely ordained, and he held that the apostles themselves instituted bishops in the early church. He supported the English Church as he found it under Whitgift: largely Calvinist in doctrine but episcopal in organisation. The Scots, however, regarded their kirk as setting a purer example of Reformation as well as contributing to their distinctive nationhood. In 1604 in deference to Scottish anxieties, messengers from James assured the commissioners of the General Assembly that a union of churches was not part of the agenda of Union. The Parliament held later that year in Edinburgh passed an act excluding the kirk from the scope of the Union commissioners. Even so, there were rumours around the time of Bancroft's promotion to the see of Canterbury in October 1604 that the king would have liked to make him Primate of Great Britain, not just England, but held back for fear of offending the Scots. More tactfully, James moved for what John Morrill has characterised as 'congruity', providing for each national church 'all those marks of a true church which the leaders of each thought to be necessary'.[11]

In pursuit of congruity, in England James encouraged the preaching ministry. The Scottish church still lacked full episcopacy, which he was intent on implementing. By the end of 1605, nine commissioners of the General Assembly were bishops, enough to form a quorate meeting, and in the Scottish Parliament of 1606 the bishops' finances were strengthened when the revenues of their dioceses, removed in 1587, were restored to them. However, the policy aroused some opposition. In March 1605 Archbishop Spottiswode of Glasgow wrote to James to warn him that there were daily invectives against the bishops in Edinburgh's pulpits. The king decided to forbid the forthcoming meeting of the General Assembly at Aberdeen, but when large numbers of ministers turned up in July 1605, they agreed to dissolve only after setting a date for the next meeting. Chancellor Dunfermline approved of the ministers' moderate action, but the king was led to believe that they were defying him. He concluded that Dunfermline had shown weakness and sent Dunbar north to deal with the issue. Dunbar thereafter became the king's most trusted Scottish minister, but it may well be that Dunfermline was more in touch with grass-roots Scottish opinion. He was aware of the growing tide of opposition and if James had appreciated his moderate strategies, the later difficulties with the kirk might never have arisen. The disagreement with Dunfermline can be seen as one of the earliest indications that the king was losing his sureness of touch in Scottish affairs.[12]

Eight leading Presbyterian critics of the royal polices were then summoned to London, including Andrew and James Melville, and subjected to a rota of sermons on the twin themes of godly princes and godly bishops. Unlike at Hampton Court, James had no intention of compromising and eventually the recalcitrant Melvilles were sent into exile. In 1610 a decisive General Assembly in Glasgow restored the boundaries of pre-Reformation dioceses. Dunbar ensured that moderate ministers were present by paying their travel expenses. The synods then became episcopal courts and two courts of High Commission on the English model were established (later merged into one) to increase the bishops' control over their clergy. In December 1610 three Scottish bishops were consecrated in London, but to avoid any overtones of superiority neither of the English archbishops acted as consecrators. On their return these bishops consecrated their brethren, thereby reintroducing the apostolic succession (which the English church had kept in 1559–60) to Scotland.

Scottish bishops still differed greatly from their English counterparts. They remained moderators of synods and presbyteries rather than autonomous rulers of their dioceses, with little of the socio-legal status or palatial accommodation that English bishops still enjoyed. James was motivated almost as much by secular as by ecclesiastical factors. His bishops would strengthen his position in the Scottish Parliament, and he wanted them to increase the flow of information coming to him from distant regions like the Highlands. His practical concerns were not appreciated by the kirk and from 1606 onward, sharp criticisms of royal policies were heard in Scotland.

When Bancroft died in 1610, James was careful over the choice of his successor at Canterbury. The appointment in 1611 of George Abbot, Dunbar's chaplain who accompanied him to Scotland in 1608, was influenced by the king's appreciation that Abbot's plain, Bible-emphasising churchmanship was very acceptable to Scots. Royal sensitivity, however, began to fade soon afterwards, and in 1612 a draft plan was sent to Scotland aiming to bring the kirk 'so neir as can be' to the English model. James was moving from congruity towards 'Anglo-centric convergence', in Morrill's term, and in Star Chamber in 1616 he even extolled the English church as 'sureliest founded upon the word of God, of any Church in Christendom', a far cry from his dismissal of it in 1590 as 'an evill said masse in English'.[13] Before the king's journey north in 1617, changes were made to the chapel at Holyrood palace. An organ (not used in Scottish churches since the Reformation) was installed and wooden statues were carved, although the Scottish bishops' hostility to images made James draw back from erecting them. However, the king took three

English bishops north and the Whitsuntide communion was celebrated in full English style, with communicants kneeling to receive
the consecrated bread and wine. There were protests from ministers
who flocked to Edinburgh when Parliament met in June, but a greater
outcry greeted the king's five new Articles, secretly prepared in 1616
and unveiled to the synods in July 1617. Only bishops were to carry
out confirmations; the five greatest pre-Reformation holy days
(Christmas, Good Friday, Easter, Ascension and Whitsunday) were to
be reinstated; most contentious of all, everyone must receive communion while kneeling. Sunday was the only holy day acknowledged
by the kirk, and kneeling was regarded as indicating acceptance of
the popish doctrine of transubstantiation. Anxiously, the synods
remitted the Articles to a General Assembly, but when one followed
at St Andrews in November 1617, most of the Five Articles were
remitted again, indicating their unacceptability.

In England, James had come to regard kneeling at communion as
an essential demonstration of his subjects' acceptance of his powers as
Supreme Governor. He wrote angrily to Archbishop Spottiswode in
December 1617, 'Either we and this church here [in England] must be
held idolatrous in this point of kneeling, or they reputed rebellious
knaves in refusing the same.' At Perth in 1618 the unhappy bishops
forced the Five Articles through a General Assembly, but a substantial
minority of ministers voted against them. The Scottish Parliament ratified the Articles in 1621, but despite unprecedented levels of government management, they passed more narrowly than before. Already,
the Articles had sparked a sharp exchange of views in print, begun by
David Calderwood, the most prolific Presbyterian propagandist of his
generation. It continued until 1638, and its impact on Scottish political
thought was immense. As its historian has commented, 'It would be a
short step from disobedience to resistance'.[14]

After 1621, the Scottish bishops with the tacit support of the
Scottish Privy Council gradually backtracked on the enforcement of
the Articles. Yet, for the first time since the Reformation, the kirk was
experiencing widespread lay resistance. By insisting on kneeling,
James more than doubled the number of lay Nonconformists and
increased the level of absenteeism from worship. The Five Articles of
Perth undermined acceptance of the strict discipline administered by

the kirk courts and split the clergy, many of whom were as opposed to the king's policies as their parishioners. In 1625 as Easter approached, the dying James was still insisting on kneeling and demanding that non-compliant ministers should be deprived. Only the lack of enforcement by the bishops and the Privy Council prevented divisions from worsening still further.

Historians have disagreed in their assessments of the situation in the kirk at James's death. Some consider that the Scots might gradually have come round to the Five Articles although in view of the evidence this seems over-optimistic. Others have argued that the king left the kirk in crisis. Charles I went on to create many more problems for himself, but it seems fair to conclude that the ecclesiastical situation inherited in Scotland by the youthful and inexperienced monarch was an extremely difficult one. In 1638 when the commissioners of the Scottish church convened at Glasgow in the wake of the National Covenant opposing Charles I, they emphasised 'the uniformity of worship which was in the kirk before the Articles of Perth'. They deplored 'the great rent which entered at that time, and hath continued since'. The prime responsibility for that 'great rent' must rest on the shoulders of King James, not his son.[15]

Religion in Ireland

Henry VIII and Edward VI imposed the royal supremacy over the church on their Celtic territories of Ireland and Wales as well as England. They succeeded in Wales but failed in Ireland. Although the Crown pursued increasingly protestant policies, both the Old English and the native Irish remained catholic. The Nine Years War led by Tyrone was explicitly in defence of the old faith, and his successful appeal for Spanish help reinforced the perceived religious divide between Ireland and England. protestantism did not take root, not least because the native clergy of the newly established Church of Ireland showed little commitment to the Reformation and could barely read the authorised services. In the opinion of Archbishop Thomas Jones of Dublin, many of them were 'fitter to keep hogs than serve in the church'.[16] They had nothing to offer the catholic majority of their fellow countrymen.

The failure to create an effective protestant church during Elizabeth's reign gave catholics a breathing space. Traditional belief survived largely unchallenged, both among the Old English and the Gaelic Irish, and by the late sixteenth century, Counter-Reformation teaching and literature (including poetry) was beginning to reinvigorate Irish catholicism. Seminary priests, mostly trained in the Spanish Netherlands at the University of Louvain, joined the friars in proselytising, particularly amongst the townspeople of the Pale (the area around Dublin) and other urban centres such as Cork. In the absence of protestant schools, catholic schoolmasters built up a clientele in the towns, ensuring that the younger generation would also be brought up as catholics.

Successive English lords deputy in Dublin faced an insuperable dilemma. The protestant statutes of 1560 proscribed catholicism, but the Old English refused to accept that catholicism and loyalty to the English Crown were incompatible. In any case, it was impossible to enforce protestant conformity on an overwhemingly catholic population, in both town and countryside, without causing extreme resentment that might feed into active rebellion. In 1603 it was widely, if naively, hoped by Irish catholics, as by their English co-religionists, that the accession of the son of the martyred Mary Queen of Scots would bring freedom of worship. In Irish towns there was an immediate upsurge of confrontational public activities such as masses and processions, with Jesuits and other priests moving around openly. In some places protestants were expelled and formerly catholic churches reclaimed and re-consecrated. Firm but flexible, Mountjoy refused to allow public demonstrations of catholicism, but agreed to allow private worship until he received further instructions. However, in October 1605 the king published a proclamation denouncing the presumption that he would allow toleration and commanding Irish priests to quit the realm by December. Lord Deputy Chichester, convinced that the state must insist on protestant conformity, briefly began to implement the recusancy fines authorised since 1560, but used previously only as a threat. This was a step too far; most protestant churches were ruinous and even those who were willing to attend services could not find any. In April 1607 the English Privy Council forced Chichester to retreat, since he was alienating the prosperous and urbanised Old English families who possessed many influential connections at court. Though the Gunpowder Plot made it increasingly difficult for the Old English to argue that their adherence to catholicism was a private matter, the king seems only to have wanted to demonstrate his capacity for enforcing conformity if necessary and in appropriate circumstances.[17]

After 1603 James was personally committed to the support of Irish protestantism, which he saw a as a prime vehicle of 'Briticisation' in his third kingdom. He filled Irish bishoprics with Englishmen and Scots, but added generously to the endowments of Trinity College Dublin (founded in 1592) to enable it to train Irish protestant clergy. In January 1604 he ordered a survey of clerical livings in the Pale and of the conditions of the grammar schools, then made the bishops responsible for creating a wider educational network. As with the established Church of England, he strove particularly to encourage a preaching ministry. 'The king', wrote Salisbury, 'knows well that true religion is better planted by the word than by the sword.'[18] James also insisted that remuneration for both bishops and parish ministers should be a legal requirement in the land-grants that shaped the Ulster plantation.

The king was building on a process of improvement that was already in train. A rise in clerical standards in the protestant Church of Ireland began in the 1590s, and continued for the next 50 years. The older generation of unsatisfactory clergy was gradually replaced by ministers who were university educated, English-speaking and committedly protestant. Yet the notable improvement in quality which has even been described as a 'second Reformation' had far less impact than was hoped, for the structural problems were acute. Large numbers of churches remained too dilapidated to be usable. Benefices were poor and unattractive, and extensive lay control also tended to bring the new clergy into conflict with landowners who were often absentee Dublin merchants.

There was a facile optimism in the early years of the reign that Irish catholicism was more a matter of habit than conviction, and could easily be undermined. Sir John Davies, Attorney-General of Ireland, commented sardonically that there were many Irish saints, but 'No

man ever heard or read of an Irish martyr.' However, despite rising
clerical standards, the king's hopes of weaning the natives from popery proved vain. In November 1611 Lord Deputy Chichester wrote to
Salisbury that the pope had more hearts than the king.[19] In response,
the level of activity against catholics increased, and steady pressure as
well as the appointment of protestant lawyers ensured that all the
judges in Ireland were conformable in religion by 1613. The disquali-
fication of catholic lawyers was enforced, the county commissions of
the peace purged of catholics wherever possible, and in 1618 an
attempt was made to tighten and standardise recusancy proceedings.
However, in 1623 the minimal enforcement of protestant conformity
was suspended as Prince Charles left for Madrid to negotiate for the
Spanish Infanta. Many of the Old English and Irish who had begun to
attend their protestant parish churches thereupon ceased to do so.
Despite the increasingly protestant regime in Dublin, Irish catholicism survived and prospered at the grass-roots, not least because the
machinery of the state was not strong enough to repress such a substantial majority. The Counter-Reformation succeeded in revitalising
Irish catholicism and a well-educated, active catholic ministry pursued the aims of the Council of Trent. These were often at variance
with Irish customs and social organisation, and ironically were
imbued with notions of civility very similar to those which the
English were intent on enforcing. After 1618 resident catholic bishops
were appointed from Rome, which strengthened the organisation of
the dioceses, and the new appointees were all committed Tridentine
reformers. The Spanish match, besides lessening the pressures of
protestant conformity, aroused renewed hopes that James would
concede toleration or that Philip IV would demand it in the marriage
settlement.

Over the years 1603–25, the Church of Ireland increasingly limited
its ministry to the English and Scottish newcomers who were
expanding their tenancies in Ulster and the Irish midlands. The
Prayer Book was translated into Gaelic in 1608 and a few exceptional
protestant ministers learned to speak the language, but made little
impact on traditionally-minded country people. They clung to their
old-style catholic faith which focused on images, shrines and devotion to the saints. Protestantism, with its demand for lay literacy and

its emphasis on individual spirituality, was ill-suited to a society still only semi-literate and largely clan-based. By the end of the king's reign, it was clear that Irish protestantism had failed as a missionary endeavour. The divide between the overwhelmingly protestant inhabitants of England and Scotland, and the catholic majority in Ireland (both Old English and Gaelic-speaking) was not only unbridged but had widened further.

A divide also grew up between English and Irish protestantism. The theological articles of 1615, which formed the Church of Ireland's statement of faith, were more strongly Calvinist and predestinarian than the Thirty-Nine Articles of the English church. Both English and Scottish Nonconformist clergy were welcomed in the Church of Ireland, which managed to adopt many of those puritan practices that James forbade at Hampton Court. Its unadorned services also appealed to the preferences of those settlers in Ulster who were accustomed to the Scottish kirk, and a similarly unofficial adoption of many Presbyterian practices gradually took place. The Church of Ireland's emphasis on the godly who knew themselves to be among the Calvinist elect could also be seen as providing an elitist and colonial ideology particularly suitable for the plantation areas. The Irish protestant church helped to create a community of incomers, its separate identity constructed from a potent blend of religious and racial attitudes. As both Gaelic culture and catholicism were steadily identified with political disloyalty, Irish protestants were increasingly filled with a visceral fear of the threat posed by an overwhelmingly catholic majority. Until 1641 an uneasy harmony prevailed, but by 1625 all the aspects of religious division that were to bedevil the future history of Ireland were visibly in place.

Witchcraft

King James's interest in witchcraft, sparked during his honeymoon visit to Denmark, was well known in England in 1603. His *Daemonologie* of 1597 was immediately reprinted in two English editions, and a new statute reinforcing the 1563 act against witches was passed in the 1604 Parliament. No direct evidence links the act to James, but his accession must have highlighted the issue. Between

1605 and 1608, he was personally involved in a notorious case when a young Oxfordshire woman named Anne Gunter was claimed by her family to have been bewitched by malevolent neighbours. The king skilfully brought her to confess that her overbearing and quarrelsome father had taught her various tricks, including swallowing pins, and forced her to take drinks concocted to induce fits. James was delighted by his success in unmasking the imposture, and did not punish Anne. When Sir John Harington had a private audience in 1607, the king talked at length about witchcraft and confessed that he had read books in the hope of foretelling the future. In 1616 at Leicester James exposed another set of fraudulent accusations, saving six alleged witches from death and rebuking the judges for having hanged nine already. English assize judges were already cautious and sceptical when faced with witchcraft evidence and the incident presumably made them more so. There were individual cases, but no further witchcraft panics until 1633–4.[20]

Religion and Social Culture

On his return from Scotland in 1617, James rode through Lancashire. He found a quarrel in progress, with local magistrates attempting to impose a stricter sabbatarianism on the crypto-catholic gentry and ordinary folk. This entailed curbing their traditional leisure pursuits such as wrestling, shooting, ten-pin bowling and football. In *Basilicon Doron* James urged that days should be appointed 'for delighting the people with publicke spectacles of all honest games, and exercise of armes . . . for entertaining friendship and heartlinesse'. So he at first backed the devotees of Sunday sports, but provoked further friction when enthusiasts assumed that royal support allowed them to disrupt and harass their churchgoing neighbours. In an attempt at a middle way, the king published in May 1618 a further Declaration (or Book) of Sports for all England, insisting that games should not be played until after church attendance. Unexpectedly, this too provoked hostility; to moderate puritans the Crown was still supporting the forces of disorder (the sporting multitude) against the sober and godly. Abbot persuaded the king to withdraw the instruction that the declaration should be read in churches. The Lancashire outcry must reflect not only the widespread presence at grass-roots level of profoundly divergent religious assumptions, but also the rising tension between the middling sort with their puritan-suffused vision of a disciplined social order, and an older, more festive neighbourly culture that survived in outlying areas.[21]

Ecumenism

All contemporaries agreed that King James disliked both religious persecution and war. In youth, he suffered the political consequences of religious strife between warring factions in Scotland, and he later managed to reconcile them with considerable, although not universal, success. As a mature king he promoted reconciliation among the churches of Christendom, not least because he knew that religious divisions exacerbated volatile political situations. He was amicably in contact with Gregory XIII and Clement VIII before 1603, primarily to ensure that the papacy would not back an alternative candidate for Elizabeth's throne. James revived the idea of a General Council of Christendom, to emphasise how much all the Christian churches had in common. In his proclamation of February 1604, ordering catholic priests to leave England, James urged 'a generall Councell free and lawfully called' and promised his support for it. He repeated the call for 'a generall Christian union . . . as . . . we might meete in the middest' when addressing Parliament in March 1604. The king patronised ecumenical reformers such as the Huguenot Pierre du Moulin. He was deeply interested in the national synod of the French Huguenots at Tonneins in 1614, which accepted du Moulin's scheme to create first a united Calvinist front, then win over the Lutherans, and finally to confer with Rome. The disappointing outcome showed that both the king and du Moulin underestimated the depth of the divisons they faced.

In 1616 James welcomed to England the renegade catholic cleric Marc'Antonio de Dominis, archbishop of Spalato, whose unconventional views included a vision of more or less independent bishoprics not subservient to the Roman papacy, but all sharing the ancient faith of the church. The king warmed to the old man's passion for reuniting Christendom and was saddened when he left his new benefices in the English church and returned home to Italy.[22] James also believed that Christendom could best reunite under the auspices of monarchs like himself. His powerful vision of unity and sense of God-given vocation underlay his efforts at ecclesiastical reform in all his kingdoms. After the Hampton Court conference, he saw himself as a new Constantine, presiding over a Europe-wide debate. He was fascinated by the events of 1606 when catholic Venice defied the papacy, and told the ambassador that it was only the mutual jealousies of princes, and not the will of Christ, that allowed the papacy to be so overwheening. He offered the Doge his enthusiastic support, even giving the Venetian ambassador a lengthy and learned lecture on the iniquity of papal claims to depose temporal princes. He was delighted when Venice expelled the Society of Jesus: 'O blessed and wise Republic', he exclaimed, 'the Jesuits are the worst and the most seditious fellows in the world. They are slaves and spies, as you know.'[23]

Although he constantly attacked the papal deposing power, James also held out an olive branch. He offered the prospect that Rome could enjoy universal recognition and respect as Christendom's oldest see. It has been conclusively established that James was sincere, persistent and adroit in his ecumenical policies. He achieved some better relationships among the protestant churches, though sometimes his plans were 'imaginative but naive'.[24] However, his plans for a General Council were fruitless (as he occasionally admitted), since successive popes thought the proposal both impossible and unnecessary. Instead, they interpreted James's overtures as signs that he might turn catholic. Clement VIII in 1605 prayed for two hours every night for the conversion of the king and his dominions.

The middle years of the multiple monarchy saw rising hopes of European peace, especially after the Twelve Years Truce of 1609 between Spain and the Dutch. However, after the assassination of Henri IV in 1610, James was the only leading monarch to whom protestants could appeal whenever tensions arose with catholic powers. In 1615 he thought that 'not only the good estate of my own people but even the estate of religion throughout all Christendom . . . almost wholly, under God, rests now upon my shoulders'.[25] By the outbreak of the Thirty Years War James was incontestably the leading ruler among the European reformed churches. He also reached out to the Greek Orthodox Church, regarding it as preserving a purer form of early Christianity than catholicism.

The Rise of Arminianism

James asserted both his protestant credentials and his status as a continental arbiter in November 1618, when he sent a delegation of churchmen to Holland. The king had urged the calling of a national synod, rather on the model of Hampton Court, to settle a dispute that was wracking the United Provinces. The theologian Jacob Arminius (1559–1609) attracted followers by opposing the extreme predestinarian views espoused by Dutch Calvinists. Instead, Arminius emphasised the importance of human willpower in overcoming sin and the need for spiritual modesty to balance Calvinist assurance. Christians should not presume on salvation, but concentrate on leading a devout and charitable life.

For complex theological reasons, James opposed Arminian views for some years before the situation reached crisis point. In 1612 he opposed the appointment of Conrad Vorstius, the professor of theology who succeeded Arminius at Leiden University. Vorstius's followers rapidly became embroiled in bitter political frictions. Prince Maurice of Nassau, second son of William the Silent and captain-general of the seven United Provinces, was hostile to Johan van Oldenbarneveldt, advocate of Holland (the most powerful province and a vigorous competitor against English economic interests). Oldenbarneveldt was seen as a supporter of Arminius and Vorstius while Prince Maurice opposed them. James feared that the tolerant attitudes of Arminius's followers might permit a resurgence of pro-Spanish catholicism in the Netherlands, while deepening theological divisions might even dissolve the political union between the seven provinces. He also considered Maurice (uncle of the Elector Palatine) as the rightful leader of the republic. At the same time, the king urged the English churchmen to suggest moderate positions, 'which may tend to the mitigation of heat on both sides'.[26] He added one Scots cleric to the delegation in December 1618.

The British visitors were influential in moderating some of the extreme Calvinist positions, and the synod's decrees were not out of line with a Biblical theology common to all reformed European churches. Unfortunately, once the decrees were approved, the Dutch authorities carried out a purge on Arminian clergy in the United Provinces, as much for political as religious reasons since there was a genuine fear that religious war might break out. James supported the political party of Prince Maurice, and Calvinists in England assumed in consequence that he was in favour of the repression of all Arminian views. In fact, the king was anxious to prevent similar disputes breaking out in England, and it soon become plain that his views would differ significantly in an English context.

The marriage of Princess Elizabeth and the Elector Palatine was the first step in the king's grand design for a network of dynastic alliances bridging the religious divide. The second was his attempt to conclude a Spanish match for his son. Especially after the outbreak of European war in 1618, the policy succeeded only in arousing deep anti-catholic feeling in both England and Scotland. From the beginning, the king's creation of a delicately balanced, inclusive church at home was crucially dependent on peace abroad. It was the 1604 Treaty of London that gave James vital room for manoeuvre on religious issues, since peace with Spain severed the link between English catholics and the threat of potential Spanish invasion to support them. It also silenced those ardent protestants who saw the adoption of godly policies (including the persecution of catholics) as essential in ensuring God's support in time of Spanish attack. The king successfully quieted differences of religious viewpoint, but only so long as there were no acute divisions over foreign policy. After 1618, divisions emerged when it seemed plain to many protestants that Englishmen must go to the aid of their co-religionists abroad who were under catholic attack.

Thereafter, James became increasingly divorced from public opinion. Most of his subjects saw religion and foreign policy as two sides of the same coin. They could not reconcile what was seen as his pro-Calvinist stance at Dort with his policy on the Spanish match. Speaking in Latin to ensure confidentiality, the archbishop of Canterbury in January 1619 agreed with the Venetian ambassador that the king was far too trusting. 'The preparations of the Spaniards were only too true and all should fear them . . . his king would do well to look more sharply after them because prosperity finally terminates in pain.'[27] As the corantoes (pamphlet accounts) outlining the defeats suffered by continental protestants began to arrive in England, an increasing tide of criticism – in the pulpit, in published tracts and in the underground circulation of libellous verse – flowed against the king. His worries deepening, in 1621 Archbishop Abbot arranged for a tract against the match to the Infanta to be presented to Prince Charles. He spoke out against including toleration for catholics in the proposed Spanish marriage treaty: and in 1623, in a letter he almost certainly wrote to James but disavowed, he referred to the Roman Church as the Whore of Babylon. It was the archbishop's sad destiny to find himself leading a vociferous ecclesiastical faction again the king who had promoted him in 1611. Abbot was the most senior, but far from the only churchman to criticise the Supreme Governor's fixation with a pro-Spanish policy.

As criticism heightened, the king's old fears of radical puritanism reawakened. He had not faced such a barrage of religious criticism since his early days in Scotland. When moderate evangelical clergy told him uncomfortable truths, James turned instead to pro-Arminian bishops like Andrewes and Neile who praised his peace-loving diplomacy. They were careful never to advocate an explicitly anti-Calvinist theology, but they emphasised that 'popularity', which in seventeenth-century usage meant whipping up public support, was a hallmark of the puritan faction. James had always been aware of the dangers of disorderly preaching, and in December 1620 he instructed the bishop of London to call his diocesan clergy before him and order them in the king's name not to meddle in their sermons with the Spanish match nor any other matter of state. This was followed by a general proclamation against licentious speech.

As James was to find, nothing seemed able to stop the flood of critical pamphlets and libels. The first to make a great impact was a tract by the Norwich rector Thomas Scott, entitled *Vox Populi*, in which ambassador Gondomar was shown bragging that he was powerful enough to silence any preacher who dared attempt a critical sermon against Spain. Between 1620 and 1622 a series of ministers included the noted Ipswich preacher Samuel Ward were punished for speaking out. In 1622, faced by an increasingly bitter divide in English opinion, James issued his Directions to Preachers, ordering clergy under the rank of dean to steer clear of inflammatory topics. Among these he included predestination, which moderate puritans took to be the central tenet of reformed religion. James issued similar instructions to preachers in 1604, but in the inflamed circumstances of 1622, forbidding discussion of predestination seemed like an attack on a crucial protestant truth. The Directions further undermined trust in the king's policies, but failed to silence public debate. The king had no better success with a series of prosecutions in Star Chamber, backed up by a further proclamation against scandalous books and pamphlets in September 1623.

It was inevitable that the negotiations for the Spanish match would also impact upon Scotland and Ireland. It was part of the acute dilemma of the Stuart monarchs that they not only ruled three kingdoms with different religious settlements, but that each kingdom was also internally divided over religion between a majority and a minority. In Scotland as in England, suspicion of the king's foreign policy arose largely from the realisation that it would inevitably involve concessions to an unpopular catholic minority. These fears stiffened opposition to the Five Articles of Perth, described by dissident clergymen as 'the sound of the feet of popery at the doors'. The growing habit of obedience to royal authority, so carefully nurtured by Maitland, Dunbar and Dunfermline, was undermined when many Scots saw in the king's policies an affront to their deepest religious beliefs. In 1621 Dunfermline himself expressed his disquiet.[28]

In Ireland, where the majority of the population was catholic, the response was entirely different, but equally threatening to the peaceable good order that James had tried to implement since 1603. Among the papers of Gondomar, recalled back to Madrid in 1622, is a document addressed to King Philip IV of Spain. Entitled 'The Appeal of the catholics of Ireland', it can be dated to 1623. The authors pointed resentfully to the failure of the constable of Castile's negotiations in 1604 to secure any concessions for all those catholics ruled by James VI and I in his multiple territories. They went on to urge Philip IV to seize the opportunity of the Spanish match to make a lasting religious and constitutional settlement in Ireland, which must include freedom of conscience and open catholic worship. The Appeal also demanded the return of land confiscated from the exiles of 1607 (Tyrone and Tyrconnell with their followers), a measure that would have overthrown the protestant plantation of Ulster. Lastly, the Irish catholics requested a fair Parliament in Dublin, summoned in accordance with medieval precendents, a clear condemnation of the king's gerrymandering.[29]

The petition makes clear the Irish catholics' deep alienation from Jacobean policies. It illustrates once again that James could not espouse any general policy with religious repercussions without risking conflict in each of his three kingdoms. If the Spanish match had been concluded, its promise of toleration for English catholics could hardly have been withheld from their Irish and Scottish co-religionists. That, in turn, would have greatly exacerbated fears within the protestant communities. Ireland would have been destabilised almost immediately, and in Scotland the ferment over the Five Articles of Perth would have grown worse. After 1618 the king's pro-Spanish foreign policy placed immense strain on the religious harmony of all his multiple kingdoms, not just England. Bishop Joseph Hall, a perceptive observer, feared in 1622 that 'there needs no prophetical spirit to discern by a small cloud there is a storm coming towards our Church'.[30]

It is easy to condemn James after 1618 as wilfully deluded. Yet his attempts at diplomatic intervention in the Thirty Years War stemmed from his Christian abhorrence of the carnage. At home, the influence of anti-Calvinist prelates at court, although increasing after 1618, should not be over-emphasised. In 1624, when the controversial Arminian cleric Richard Montagu published his tract *A New Gagg for an Old Goose*, he judged it would be acceptable to James to minimise the differences between the Church of England and Rome, and to emphasise the similarities. But he thought he could probably count on no more than five bishops to support him; the majority of them were still evangelical and pro-Calvinist. James was reluctant to promote the aggressively anti-Calvinist William Laud, giving him only the minor bishopric of St David's. When Buckingham pressed Laud's claims, the king perceptively responded, 'Take him to you. But on my soul you will repent it'. The cleric who was probably closest to James in his last years was the affable John Williams, bishop of Lincoln, the first ecclesiastic since Wolsey to hold the legal office of lord keeper of the Great Seal. Worldly-wise and careful to keep to the middle of the clerical road, Williams was congenial to the king who enjoyed his company. It was he, not Andrewes or Neile, who preached at James's funeral in 1625. It was only after 1625 that attitudes among the episcopate began to tip much further in the Arminian direction.

It also seems unlikely that these rising tensions immediately destabilised English parish life. There is evidence that 'Prayer Book protestantism' was becoming deeply rooted, since by 1625 at least three generations of English people had grown familiar with its services. The dignity with which they clothed the universal human rites of passage – baptism, marriage, burial – was appreciated, and clergy who arbitrarily imposed their own versions of services, or failed to carry out their duties, could find themselves at visitation time accused by their parishioners before the bishop. Sacred time and sacred space, experienced in their familiar parish church, were cherished by many who were not necessarily 'godly' in the usual puritan sense. At the same time, moderate puritans had little to fear in most dioceses until after 1625. Nevertheless the rising atmosphere of contention after 1618 was bound to percolate slowly downwards.

The king's rule over his churches was characterised by three defining aspects. In Scotland his policies aimed above all to re-establish royal control over the kirk and bury the pernicious doctrine of the 'two kingdoms', sacred and secular, that denied the monarchy any role in the church. In England, James usually worked for the widest range of agreement he could achieve. His ecclesiastical policies brought about nearly two decades of broad consensus that began to crumble only when confronted by an intractable religio-political conflict in Europe. In Scotland, stress fractures became visible earlier, with the introduction of the Five Articles of Perth, and it was the discretion and common sense of his Scottish bishops, who quietly ignored the royal orders concerning strict enforcement, that kept the church from open division. In Ireland, it is arguable that the religious situation was already too intractable by 1603 for James to achieve very much. By the end of the reign, Ireland was clearly divided into a catholic majority and a protestant, settler minority. Nevertheless it is important to realise that when James died, it was still possible to argue that his three kingdoms, for all their tensions and divisions, remained the best example in Europe of a harmonious and stable protestant coalition. By contrast, the French Huguenots were faced with an increasingly hostile state, and in the Netherlands the dispute over Arminianism nearly caused civil breakdown. The Thirty Years War brought utter misery and destitution to large areas of protestant Germany and the end of protestantism in Bohemia. In contrast, James made largely successful efforts to create a consensus. Already by the 1630s, his even-handedness was favourably contrasted with the more autocratic and pro-Arminian policies of his son. To those who had to endure the 'War of the Three Kingdoms', it was hardly surprising that the years when James presided over his churches as Supreme Governor came in retrospect to seem like a golden age.

Conclusion

Too often James VI and I has been viewed as merely a King of England with some appendages. Until recently, this gross Anglocentrism contributed to a lack of interest in the real dimensions of his multiple monarchy and distorted historical understanding of both his problems and his achievements. A similarly Anglocentric approach ignored, or at best underestimated, the crucial differences between England and the other kingdoms over which James ruled. The boundaries of the English state were fixed before the Norman Conquest and under the Tudors, the control exercised by central government was highly effective by sixteenth-century standards. Under Henry VIII, Wales was brought under the English system of parliamentary representation and the co-operation of the Welsh elite thereafter ensured the success of the protestant Reformation. By contrast, large areas of Scotland and Ireland were only just emerging from a more fluid period of devolved governance, in which the centre wielded far less influence over the outlying regions. In both these kingdoms the Jacobean monarchy was still battling to assert a degree of effective control that the Tudors could take for granted in England.

From the time that James emerged from his minority in Scotland, his attention was focused on his claim to the English throne. His success in peacefully achieving that goal was the high point of his rule in all three kingdoms. He came to the English throne with a profound conviction that he was an experienced king who needed no instruction on how to rule over the much larger, wealthier and more complex monarchy he had worked for so many years to inherit. His new subjects were grateful that he was an adult monarch whose young family promised an end to all their long-standing anxieties over the succession. In many areas the king's knowledge and acquired skills served them very well; James was perceptive, for example, in choosing able and experienced men in both church and state.

In other ways, however, after 1603 the king's earlier Scottish successes were as much a hindrance as a help, since they inculcated a striking degree of complacency. Convinced that he had little to learn, James failed to appreciate that the differences between English and Scottish monarchy were as important as the similarities. The king's self-confidence misled him severely in his handling of English Parliaments. Accustomed to the very different Parliament of Scotland, James never bothered to acquire the management techniques necessary to achieve harmony and consensus in the English context. The parliamentary system that he inherited was under strain, with its tax system needing reform if the nation was to preserve its security when faced with the steadily rising costs of military action. Undoubtedly, James faced complex problems not of his making. However, the king failed to understand that, for all the wealth that he saw on his way south from Edinburgh, England unlike Scotland was just emerging from a lengthy and burdensome war. The Crown needed time to recover and could not support disproportionate expenditures on the court and courtiers. Just as he had done in Scotland, the king made little, if any, attempt to keep control of his finances. He thereby made it impossible for his ministers to argue that the Crown needed to increase its income and that the safety of the realm would be imperilled if the problem was not tackled. James did not listen when administrators of the calibre of Salisbury told him that the English monarchy could not guarantee national security without good relations with Parliaments, since they alone could provide the finances necessary for war. Similarly, James refused to accept that members of the House of Commons were following strong medieval precedents when they refused to vote taxes for royal expenses that did not arise from commonwealth matters.

Under Elizabeth the tax system was already inefficient, yet it had proved possible to wage a long and victorious war against Spain – with multiple theatres of conflict – that was overwhelmingly financed by parliamentary supply. The 18 years between 1603 and 1621 scarcely seem long enough to posit a complete breakdown in English military capacity. The crucial difference was that the queen enjoyed her subjects' confidence that when they were taxed, the money was necessary for national survival and would not be wasted. On both counts that confidence was lacking under James. Spanish and Venetian ambassadors regularly saw what the king refused to acknowledge; that without a well-managed and supportive Parliament the standing of the English Crown in Europe was negligible, because it could deploy little or no military or naval force.

In foreign policy, monarchs of Scotland played a far less pivotal role in European affairs than their English equivalents. Scotland had never been at war with Spain and had hardly been touched by the Dutch revolt, so James underestimated the forces of English animosity towards the Habsburgs still present after the peace of 1604. He ignored the rising public agitation over a catholic bride for his heir, even in 1612 when his own son opposed the marriage under negotiation for him. By 1616–17 the king's willingness to master complex issues of foreign policy was fading. Although he consistently and honourably sought to act as a peacemaker, after 1618 he pursued ill-advised and contradictory goals, relying merely on Spanish protestations of goodwill and failing to appreciate Spain's very different goals. The king's unrealistic pursuit of the Infanta was also heavily influenced by his need for a large dowry, which stemmed from the financial chaos which he had brought upon himself. It is true that after 1618, James was faced with a situation of vast difficulty; after the Habsburg conquest of the Palatinate in 1620, the intractability of the European situation posed a problem for all European statesmen and not just the king. It was his misfortune that his last years were overshadowed by a conflict that created daunting and arguably insoluble difficulties for his monarchy, but the Spanish match was never likely to offer any effective solution.

When we widen our historical horizon from just England and include both Scotland and Ireland, it is easier to appreciate both the strengths and the weaknesses of Jacobean multiple monarchy. One of the most delicate issues was the existence in each of the three kingdoms of different religious majorities and minorities. England and Scotland were both transformed by the Reformation, but their churches tended to be as conscious of the differences between them as of their shared protestantism. Both countries had significant catholic minorities labouring under penal legislation, which posed numerous political as well as religious challenges. By contrast, the population of Ireland, both Gaelic and Old English, was overwhelmingly catholic, but increasingly entry to the ruling elite was confined to protestants. Irish catholics, like those of Scotland and England, were regularly alerted to the prospects for toleration at home as the king between 1603 and 1625 sought a catholic bride for his heir; this made them chafe all the more at legal restrictions imposed on them.

Despite these myriad problems, the king achieved his greatest successes in balancing religious conflict, at least until the last years of his reign. The Church of England, in particular, flourished as a broad-based, inclusive national church that was competently administered by well-educated clergy who enjoyed the respect of their flock. Radical Presbyterianism was brought under control in Scotland and a *modus vivendi* was achieved with the kirk, again until the 1620s brought fresh problems. In all three kingdoms, catholic militancy faded and ceased to be a threat to the person of the monarch or the stability of the state, although catholic grievances still simmered. These were significant achievements, particularly when set against the background of religious turbulence in Europe.

It is only recently that the realisation that Jacobean monarchy was *multiple* and not merely dual has led historians to devote serious attention to Ireland. Unlike the relationship between England and Scotland, the relationship between England and Ireland had always been that of a superior to an inferior kingdom. James inherited the pattern and never questioned his powers to transform Ireland, if necessary by ignoring the wishes of most of its inhabitants. In the flawed and incomplete process characterised as 'Making Ireland British', the Jacobean plantation of Ulster occupies a central place. Englishmen like Chichester were not the only ones to profit, for Scots such as James Hamilton first earl of Abercorn carved out very large estates that laid the foundations of enduring family fortunes. However, as more and more political power and economic advantage were tranferred to protestant incomers, it became steadily more difficult to continue peaceable co-existence with a catholic majority that was suffering increasing encroachment. The plantation eagerly supported by the king was fraught with incalculable consequences, not merely for Ireland but also for the peoples of the wider Atlantic archipelago. Yet if James burdened Ireland with the plantation system, his administration in Dublin also presided over considerable economic recovery and growth; freedom from war and famine; and the creation of an expanding educational network. Jacobean Ireland was more prosperous and more stable than ever before. Religion was more divisive there than anywhere else in the multiple monarchy, but the revitalisation of the Jacobean Church of Ireland, with its educated clergy, and the invaluable contribution of the continental Counter-Reformation to Irish catholicism, culture and civility, were considerable bonuses. Neither would have been possible without the stability brought by Jacobean rule.

Since the time of the earl of Clarendon, opinion has been divided on the question of responsibility for the outbreak of civil war in England in 1642. Historians such as Lawrence Stone, who emphasised long-term economic and political causes going back even before 1603, have lost ground over the last 30 years to those who follow Clarendon in seeing nothing in 1625 that would lead inexorably to civil war. They argue that James left all his kingdoms in peace at his death, and that the disasters that followed between 1625 and 1629 showed the wisdom of his inactivity. James saved the lives of thousands of his subjects, and spared the purses of hundreds of thousands more, by refusing to enter the European armed conflict.

These points are persuasive, although his peace policy produced deep divisions in English and Scottish public opinion and undermined much of the king's achievement in settling religion. In other areas, too, his legacy was less benign. In Scotland, forceful Jacobean policies led to considerable friction by the 1620s. The Five Articles of Perth were dangerously ill-advised and aroused a hostility that revived the radical Presbyterian movement that the king had taken such pains to root out. By 1621 the divisions within the Scottish Parliament seem to indicate that many of the battle-lines of the Scottish revolution had already been drawn. The king had lavished vast sums of money on Scottish courtiers, to the great displeasure of his English subjects, but he failed to reap political gains from his expenditure since he had not distributed his bounty judiciously or evenly. The result was the creation of a sharp division between a very small minority of Scots who profited and the great majority who did not. The polarisation antedated the accession of Charles I, though his insensitivity widened it further.

The Scots took up arms against Charles I in 1637, the Irish in 1641, and the English last of all in 1642. Since the monarchy was the sole political institution the three kingdoms had in common, Charles must bear the major share of responsibility. Yet if we accept that civil war was far from inevitable in 1625, James cannot be exonerated completely since he had aroused abiding grievances in each of his kingdoms. The opportunity for peaceful evolutionary change was present in England in 1603, but had lessened considerably by 1625. The benefits of much that the king had achieved in Scotland before 1603 were dissipated by his failure to address the escalating problems of absentee monarchy and his ill-conceived attempt to force the kirk to adopt English-style practises. In Ireland the plantation of Ulster was to have a strongly negative impact unforeseen by its creators. The result in all three kingdoms was that Charles I inherited a more complex and less flexible situation than his father. Nevertheless, the Jacobean achievement, although flawed, was remarkable. The accession of James in 1603 created a multiple monarchy that endured until the creation of the Irish Free State in 1922. The various peoples of the three kingdoms began to grow closer together culturally and through intermarriage, a process fostered by the Crown. The bitter hostility born of centuries of warfare between England and Scotland faded considerably. Vigorous overseas expansion in both trade and colonies pointed forward to an imperial future in the East Indies and the New World. The Atlantic archipelago began its long transformation from a purely geographical expression to a social and political entity. Whatever the frictions between its component parts, a sense of unity of interests grew steadily over the following centuries. The reign of James VI and I was arguably the most formative in British history.

Notes

Introduction

1. Quoted in Jenny Wormald, 'James VI and I: Two Kings or One?' *History* (1983) pp. 190–1.
2. Edward Hyde earl of Clarendon, *The History of the Rebellion and Civil Wars in England* ed. D. W. Macray (Oxford 1888) vol. 1, pp. 3–4.
3. D. Harris Willson, *King James VI and I* (London 1956) pp. 424–5.
4. Jenny Wormald, 'James VI and I, *Basilikon Doron* and *The Trew Law of Free Monarchies*: The Scottish Context and English Translation', in *The Mental World of the Jacobean Court* ed. L. L. Peck (Cambridge 1991) pp. 36–54.
5. John Morrill, 'The fashioning of Britain', in *Conquest and Union: Fashioning a British State* ed. Steven G. Ellis and Sarah Barber (London 1995) pp. 8–39.

1 'The Bright Star of the North'

1. Bergeron, *Royal Family, Royal Lovers: King James of England and Scotland* (Columbia and London 1991), p. 1.
2. Jenny Wormald, 'Tis True I am a Cradle King', in *The Reign of James VI* ed. Julian Goodare and Michael Lynch (East Linton 2000).
3. Maurice Lee, *Great Britain's Solomon: James VI and I in His Three Kingdoms* (Urbana and Chicago 1990) p. 32.
4. Michael Lynch, *Scotland: A New History* (Edinburgh 1991) p. 221.
5. *Calendar of State Papers, Scotland* vol. 5, pp. 180–1.
6. The 'Castalian band' of James's 1598 sonnet probably referred to the Nine Muses. P. Bawcutt, *Scottish Historical Review* (2001) pp. 254–9.
7. D. H. Willson, *King James VI and I* (London 1956) p. 36. *Calendar of State Papers Relating to the Affairs of the Borders of England and Scotland* vol 1 p.82
8. For the poem and cryptogram, Caroline Bingham, *James VI of Scotland* (London 1979) pp. 64–5, 191–2.
9. Alan R. MacDonald, *The Jacobean Kirk, 1567–1625* (Aldershot 1998) pp. 22–3.
10. Julian Goodare, *State and Society in Early Modern Scotland* (Oxford 1999) p. 193.

11. Lee, *Great Britain's Solomon* p. 57.
12. *HMC Salisbury* vol. 3, pp. 59–61.
13. Conyers Read, *Mr Secretary Walsingham and the Policy of Queen Elizabeth* (New York 1978) vol. 2, pp. 202–25.
14. G. P. V. Akrigg, *Letters of King James VI and I* (Berkeley and Los Angeles) p. 82.
15. BL Cotton MS Julius F vi. f.76v.
16. Julian Goodare, 'James VI's English Subsidy', in *The Reign of James VI* ed. Goodare and Lynch.
17. Akrigg, *Letters* p. 88.
18. J. H. Burns, *The True Law of Kingship: Concepts of Monarchy in Early Modern Scotland* (Oxford 1996) pp. 258–60.
19. Alan F. Westcott, *New Poems by James I of England* (New York 1966) pp. 2, 26.
20. Ibid., pp. 124–6.
21. Akrigg, *Letters* p. 215.
22. *Daemonologie* (1597) p. 81.
23. Akrigg *Letters* p. 220.
24. Jenny Wormald, 'Ecclesiastical Vitriol: The Kirk, the Puritans and the Future King', in *Reign of Elizabeth I: Court and Culture in the Last Decade* ed. John Guy (Cambridge 1995) p. 177.
25. MacDonald, *Jacobean Kirk, 1567–1625* p. 64.
26. Johann P. Sommerville, *King James VI and I: Political Writings* (Cambridge 1994) p. 26
27. *CSP Scottish, 1571–1603* vol. 13 pt 1, p. 243.
28. Macdonald *Jacobean Kirk* p. 85.
29. Sommerville, *Political Writings* p. 29.
30. Jenny Wormald, *Court, Kirk and Community: Scotland, 1470–1625* (London 1981) p. 151.
31. Ian B. Cowan 'The Darker Vision of the Scottish Renaissance: The Devil and Francis Stewart', in *The Renaissance and Reformation in Scotland* ed. Cowan and Duncan Shaw (Edinburgh 1983) p. 139.
32. *CSP Scottish 1597–1603* pp. 138, 161.
33. Willson, *King James VI and I* p. 47.
34. *CSP Scottish, 1589* vol. 10 p. 3.
35. Sir Robert Sangster Rait, *The Parliaments of Scotland* (Glasgow 1924) is outdated but has not been replaced. Goodare, *State and Society in Early Modern Scotland* and 'Parliamentary Taxation in Scotland' *Scottish Historical Review* vol. 68 (1989).
36. *CSP Scottish* vol. 9, p. 650. Wormald, *Court, Kirk and Community* p. 161.
37. *CSP Scottish* vol. 10, p. 509. Wormald, 'Two Kings or One?', p. 198.
38. *CSP Scottish, 1597–1603* vol. 13, pt 1, p. 551.
39. Sommerville, *Political Writings* p. 56.
40. Howard Nenner, *The Right to be King: The Succession to the Crown of England, 1603–1714* (Chapel Hill 1995) p. 57.

41. *CSP Scottish, 1597–1603* p. 136.
42. *CSP Scottish, 1597–1603* pt 2, p. 631.
43. Logan Pearsall Smith, *Life and Letters of Sir Henry Wotton* (Oxford 1907) vol. 1 pp. 314–15.
44. Lynch, *Scotland: A New History* pp. 237, 244.

2 The English Throne

1. Akrigg, *Letters* pp. 175, 182–4.
2. James F. Larkin and Paul L. Hughes (eds) *Stuart Royal Proclamations* vol 1 *Royal Proclamations of King James I, 1603–1625* (Oxford 1973) pp. 1–3.
3. Akrigg, *Letters* pp. 208–9.
4. *Commons Journal* vol. 1, p. 142. *HMC Salisbury* vol. 15, pp. 8–11.
5. John Nichols (ed.) *The Progresses of King James I* vol 1 pp. 128–32.
6. *CSP Venetian* vol. 10, pp. 48–50.
7. R. Malcolm Smuts, *Culture and Power in England, 1585–1685* (Basingstoke 1999) pp. 52–3.
8. Larkin and Hughes (eds) *Stuart Proclamations* pp. 18– 19.
9. *HMC Salisbury* vol. 16 p. 415.
10. Leeds Barroll, *Anna of Denmark, Queen of England: A Cultural Biography* (Philadelphia 2001) p. 161.
11. F. L. G. von Raumer, *History of the Sixteenth and Seventeenth Centuries* (London 1835) vol. 2, pp. 206, 209–10.
12. Lee, *Great Britain's Solomon* p. 114. Conrad Russell, 'The Anglo-Scottish Union 1603–1643: A Success?', in *Religion, Culture and Society in Early Modern Britain* ed. Anthony Fletcher and Peter Roberts (Cambridge 1994) p. 241.
13. *Commons Journal (CJ)* vol. 1, pp. 142–3.
14. Ibid., p. 178
15. Ibid., p. 171. Akrigg, *Letters* pp. 235–7.
16. Wallace Notestein, *The House of Commons, 1604–10* (New Haven and London 1971) p. 133
17. John Phillips Kenyon, *Stuart Constitution, 1603–1688* (2nd edn Cambridge 1986) pp. 29–37.
18. Larkin and Hughes, *Stuart Royal Proclamations* p. 97
19. *CJ* vol. 1, pp. 332–3. N. E. McClure (ed.) *The Letters of John Chamberlain* (Philadelphia 1939) vol. 1, p. 241.
20. Croft, 'Libels, Popular Literacy and Public Opinion in Modern England', *Historical Research* (1995) vol. 68, p. 277. K. Brown, 'The Scottish Aristocracy, Anglicisation and the Court, 1603–38', *Historical Research* (1993) vol. 36, p. 557.
21. *CJ* vol. 1, p. 358.
22. Theodore Rabb, *Jacobean Gentleman: Sir Edwin Sandys, 1561–1629* (Princeton 1998) p. 130.

23. *HMC Portland* vol. 9, p.113.
24. Howard Colvin, *The History of the King's Works* (London 1982) vol. 4, pp. 769–78

3 Early Years in England

1. Akrigg, *Letters* pp. 221–2.
2. Pauline Croft, 'Fresh Light on Bate's Case' *Historical Journal* (1987) vol. 30.
3. Pauline Croft, 'A Collection of Treatises and Speeches of the Late Lord Treasurer Cecil', Royal Historical Society, *Camden Miscellany* (1987) vol. 29, pp. 273–8.
4. S. R. Gardiner, *Parliamentary Debates in 1610* (London 1862) pp. xi–xx.
5. L. M. Hill 'Sir Julius Caesar's Journal' *Bulletin of the Institute of Historical Research* (1972) vol. 45, pp. 320, 322
6. Croft, *A Collection* p. 255. Akrigg, *Letters* pp. 269–71.
7. Brown, 'The Scottish Aristocracy, Anglicisation and the Court, 1603–38', p. 557.
8. E. R. Foster, *Proceedings in Parliament 1610* (2 vols New Haven 1966) vol. 2, p. 11.
9. G. L. Harriss, 'Medieval Doctrines in the Debates on Supply, 1610–1629', in *Faction and Parliament: Essays on Early Stuart History* ed. K. Sharpe (Oxford 1978).
10. Johann P. Sommerville, *Royalists and Patriots: Politics and Ideology in England, 1603–1640* (Harlow 1999) pp. 115–19.
11. Pauline Croft, 'The Parliamentary Installation of Henry Prince of Wales' *Historical Research* (1992) vol. 65.
12. *CJ* vol. 1, pp. 431–2.
13. Foster, *Proceedings in Parliament 1610* vol. 2, p. 388.
14. Akrigg, *Letters* pp. 316–17.
15. Croft, *A Collection* p. 313.
16. Pauline Croft, 'The Catholic Gentry, the earl of Salisbury and the Baronets of 1611' in *Conformity and Orthodoxy in the English Church, c.1560–1660* ed. Peter Lake and Michael Questier (Woodbridge 2000).
17. Sommerville, *Political Writings* p. 133.
18. W. B. Patterson, *King James VI and I and the Reunion of Christendom* (Cambridge 1997) pp. 91–7.

4 The Rise of the Favourites

1. Linda Levy Peck, *Northampton: Patronage and Policy at the Court of King James I* (London 1982).
2. *HMC Hastings* vol. 4, p. 230.
3. Akrigg, *Letters* pp. 336–7.

4. Ibid., pp. 335–40.
5. Ibid., pp. 343–5.
6. Anne Somerset, *Unnatural Murder: Poison at the Court of King James* (London 1997) p. 265
7. Alastair Bellany, *The Politics of Court Scandal in Early Modern England: News, Culture and the Overbury Affair, 1603–1660* (Cambridge 2001) pp. 74–135.
8. Maija Jansson, *Proceedings in Parliament 1614* (Philadelphia 1988).
9. Jansson, *Proceedings 1614* pp. 17, 431. Conrad Russell, *The Addled Parliament of 1614: The Limits of Revisionism* (Stenton Lecture, University of Reading 1992) p. 7
10. *Calendar of Carew Manuscripts, 1603–24* pp. 288–92.
11. McClure, *Chamberlain Letters* (2 vols Philadelphia 1939) vol. 2, p. 207.
12. James Spedding, *The Works of Francis Bacon* vol. 12, pp. 201–2.
13. Roger Lockyer *Buckingham: The Life and Political Career of George Villiers, First Duke of Buckingham, 1592–1628* (London 1981) p. 43
14. Ibid., p. 22: Akrigg, *Letters* pp. 373, 386–7, 409, 420, 431, 436, 442.
15. S. R. Gardiner, *History of England, 1603–1642* (5 vols, London 1864–6) vol. 3, p. 185
16. McClure, *Chamberlain Letters* vol. 2, p. 207.

5 War in Europe

1. Akrigg, *Letters* pp. 361–2.
2. A. L. Goodall, 'The Health of James VI of Scotland and Ist of England' *Medical History* (1957) vol. I.
3. *CSP Venetian* vol. 14, p. 314, vol. 15, p. 428–9.
4. Menna Prestwich, *Cranfield* p. 229, Lockyer, *Buckingham* p. 72.
5. Young, 'Illusions of Grandeur and Reform'.
6. Prestwich, *Cranfield: Politics and Profits under the Early Stuarts* (Oxford 1996) p. 248.
7. Akrigg, *Letters* pp. 381–2.
8. W. Notestein, F. H. Relf and H. Simpson *Commons Debates 1621* (7 vols, New Haven 1935) vol. 6, p. 370.
9. *CSP Venetian* vol. 15, 1617–19, pp. 428–9, vol. 16, 1619–21, p. 377. McClure, *Chamberlain Letters* vol. 2, p. 317.
10. Larkin and Hughes, *Stuart Royal Proclamations* p. 496 n. 1.
11. Larkin and Hughes, *Stuart Royal Proclamations* pp. 519–20. Timothy Raylor, *The Essex House Masque of 1621* (Pittsburg 1999).
12. Notestein, Relf and Simpson, *Commons Debates 1621* vol. 6, pp. 370–71, vol. 5, p. 466.
13. Robert Zaller, *The Parliament of 1621* (London 1971) p. 100.
14. Ibid., p. 137.

15. Conrad Russell, *Parliaments and English Politics, 1621–29* (Oxford 1979) p. 125.
16. *CJ* vol. 1, p. 652. Lockyer, *Buckingham* p. 190.
17. Brennan C. Pursell, 'James I, Gondomar and the Dissolution of the Parliament of 1621' *History* (2000) . Zaller, *Parliament of 1621* p. 178.
18. Patterson, *Reunion of Christendom* pp. 311, 313.

6 The Spanish Match

1. Bellany, *Politics of Court Scandal* p. 252
2. *CSP Venetian* vol. 17, p. 502.
3. Glyn Redworth, 'Of Pimps and Princes: Three Unpublished Letters from James I and the Prince of Wales relating to the Spanish Match' *Historical Journal* (1994) vol. 37.
4. Akrigg, *Letters* pp. 389–92, 401, 403, 405, 410.
5. S. R. Gardiner, *El Hecho . . . Narratives of the Spanish Marriage Treaty* (London 1862) p. 141.
6. Akrigg, *Letters* pp. 394, 421.
7. Thomas Cogswell *The Blessed Revolution: English Politics and the Coming of War, 1621–24* (Cambridge 1989) pp. 287–292.
8. *CJ* p. 752.
9. Lockyer, *Buckingham* pp. 186–90.
10. Prestwich, *Cranfield* pp. 449, 467.
11. PRO, SP14/171/39, 12 August 1624.
12. Lockyer, *Buckingham* p. 233.
13. McClure *Chamberlain Letters* vol. 2, p. 616.
14. Robert Ashton, *James I by His Contemporaries* (London 1969) pp. 20–1. Lee *Government by Pen* pp. 219–20.

7 The Monarch of Three Kingdoms

1. Sommerville, *Political Writings* pp. xviii–xix, 1–84. J. H. Burns, *The True Law of Kingship* (Oxford 1996) pp. 242, 250, 257–9, 277–8.
2. Burns, *True Law of Kingship* pp. 250, 277–8.
3. Jenny Wormald 'James VI and I, *Basilicon Doron* and *The Trew Law of Free Monarchies*', in *The Mental World of the Jacobean Court* ed. Linda Levy Peck (Cambridge 1991) p. 51.
4. PRO, SP14/3/27. *CJ* vol. 1, p. 358.
5. Croft, 'Robert Cecil and the early Jacobean Court', in Peck, *Mental World*. Jared R. M. Sizer, "The Good of this Service Consists in Absolute Secrecy" *Canadian Journal of History/Annales canadiennes* (2001) vol. 36, pp. 230–257.

6. S. J. Watts, *From Border to Middle Shire: Northumberland, 1586–1625* (Leicester 1975), Goodare and Lynch, *Reign of James VI* pp. 205, 221.
7. Jane H. Ohlmeyer in Nicholas Canny, *The Origins of Empire: British Overseas Enterprise to the Close of the Seventeenth Century* (Oxford 1998) pp. 132–3, 144.
8. Goodare, 'The Scottish Parliament of 1621', pp. 41–7.
9. *CJ* vol. 1, p. 367. Keith H. Brown, *Kingdom or Province?* p. 35 and 'Courtiers and Cavaliers', in *The Scottish National Covenant in its British Context* ed. John Morrill (Edinburgh 1990).
10. Sommerville, *Political Writings* p. 166. Maurice Lee, *Government by Pen: Scotland under James VI and I* (Urbana, Chicago and London 1980) p. 115.
11. Nichols, *Progresses of King James I* vol 3 p. 309. William A. McNeill and Peter G. B. McNeill, 'The Scottish Progress of James VI, 1617' *Scottish Historical Review* (1996) vol. 75.
12. *HMC Salisbury*, vol. 18, p. 314. Hans S. Pawlisch, *Sir John Davies and the Conquest of Ireland: A Study in Legal Imperialism* (Cambridge 1985).
13. Nicholas Canny, *Making Ireland British, 1580–1650* (Oxford 2001) pp. 187–97.
14. *CSP Carew 1603–24* p. 290. *CSP Domestic 1623–25, Addenda 1603–25* p. 555.
15. Ciaran Brady, 'England's Defence and Ireland's Reform: The Dilemma of the Viceroys', in *The British Problem c.1534–1707: State Formation in the Atlantic Archipelago* ed. Brendan Bradshaw and John Morrill (London 1996) p. 109.
16. Lawrence Stone, *The Crisis of the Aristocracy 1558–1641* (Oxford 1966) p. 104. Victor Treadwell, *Buckingham and Ireland, 1616–1628* (Dublin 1998) p. 109.
17. Treadwell, *Buckingham* pp. 48, 107, 299.
18. *CSP Ireland 1625–32*, p. 47, 'Memorandum on the present state of Ireland'.
19. Canny, *Making Ireland British* p. 248. Clark, 'The Irish Economy', *New History of Ireland* vol. 3 *Early Modern Ireland, 1534–1691* ed. T. W. Moody, F.-X. Martin and F. J. Byrne (Oxford 1991) pp. 169, 174.
20. Zaller, *Parliament of 1621* p. 118. Prestwich, *Cranfield* p. 332.
21. Patrick Little, 'Blood and Friendship: The Earl of Essex's Protection of the Earl of Clanricarde's Interests 1641–1646' *English Historical Review* (1997) vol. 112.
22. Conrad Russell, 'The British Problem and the English Civil War'.

8 Supreme Governor

1. Sommerville, *Political Writings* pp. 6–7
2. Joseph Robson Tanner, *Constitutional Documents of the Reign of James I* (Cambridge 1930) p. 53
3. Kenneth Fincham, *Prelate as Pastor: The Episcopate of James I* (Oxford 1990) pp. 62, 124–5, 212–3, 241.

4. Patrick Collinson, 'The Jacobean Religious Settlement: The Hampton Court Conference', in Tomlinson *Before the English Civil War* p. 50

5. Kenneth Fincham and Peter Lake, 'Ecclesiastical Policies', in *The Early Stuart Church 1603–42* ed. Kenneth Fincham (London 1993).

6. McClure, *Chamberlain Letters* vol. 2, pp. 101, 114.

7. Patrick Collinson, *The Religion of Protestants: the Church in English Society, 1559–1625* (Oxford 1982) p. 92.

8. Michael C. Questier, 'Religion, Loyalism and State Power . . . the Jacobean Oath of Allegiance', *Historical Journal* (1997) vol. 40.

9. Spedding, *Bacon* vol. 11, pp. 90–1.

10. Akrigg, *Letters* pp. 205, 207. Peck, *Northampton*. Croft, 'Catholic Gentry, Salisbury and the Baronets of 1611' in Lake and Questier, *Conformity and Orthodoxy* pp. 272–3.

11. John Morrill, 'A British Patriarchy?', in Fletcher and Roberts, *Religion and Culture in Society*.

12. MacDonald, *Jacobean Kirk* p. 111–13

13. Sommerville, *Political Writings* p. 210. MacDonald, *Jacobean Kirk* p. 156.

14. Akrigg, *Letters* p. 363–4. John Ford, 'Conformity in Conscience: The Structure of the Perth Articles Debate in Scotland, 1618–38' *Journal of Ecclesiastical History* (1995) vol. 5.

15. MacDonald, *Jacobean Kirk* pp. 168–70. John Ford, 'The Lawful Bonds of Scottish Society: The Five Articles of Perth, the Negative Confession and the National Covenant', *Historical Journal* (1994) vol. 37, p. 45.

16. *CSP Ireland 1606–1608* p. 242.

17. Canny, *Making Ireland British* p. 174.

18. *CSP Ireland 1603–1606* p. 590.

19. Ibid., pp. 153–4, 166.

20. James Sharpe, *The Bewitching of Anne Gunter* (London 1999).

21. Sommerville, *Political Writings* p. 31. Patrick Collinson 'Elizabethan and Jacobean Puritanism as Forms of Popular Religious Culture', in *The Culture of English Puritanism* ed. Christopher Durston and Jacqueline Eales (Basingstoke 1996).

22. Patterson, *Reunion of Christendom* pp. 221, 225–9.

23. *CSP Venetian 1603–1607*, pp. 360–1.

24. Patterson, *Reunion of Christendom* pp. 194–5.

25. Akrigg, *Letters* p. 338

26. Patterson, *Reunion of Christendom* p. 265

27. *CSP Venetian* vol. 15, p. 443

28. Maurice Lee *Government by Pen* pp. 181, 211.

29. Glyn Redworth, 'Beyond Faith and Fatherland: The Appeal of the Catholics of Ireland, c.1623' *Archivium Hibernicum* (1998) vol. 52.

30. Collinson, *Religion of Protestants* p. 90.

Select Bibliography

Simon Adams 'Spain or the Netherlands? The Dilemmas of Early Stuart Foreign Policy', in Howard Tomlinson (ed.) *Before the English Civil War*
—— 'The Road to La Rochelle: English Foreign Policy and the Huguenots, 1610–1629' *Proceedings of the Huguenot Society of London* vol. 22, 1975
—— 'Foreign Policy and the Parliaments of 1621 and 1624', in Kevin Sharpe (ed.) *Faction and Parliament*
G. P. V. Akrigg (ed.) *Letters of King James VI and I* (Berkeley and Los Angeles 1984)
J. D. Alsop 'The Privy Council Debate and Committees for Fiscal Reform, September 1615' *Historical Research* vol. 68, 1995
Robert Ashton *James I by His Contemporaries* (London 1969)
—— *The Crown and the Money Market* (Oxford 1960)
Leeds Barroll *Anna of Denmark, Queen of England: A Cultural Biography* (Philadelphia 2001)
Priscilla Bawcutt 'James VI's Castalian Band: A Modern Myth' *Scottish Historical Review* vol. 80, 2001
A. W. Beasley 'The Disability of James VI and I', *The Seventeenth Century* vol. 10, 1995
Alastair Bellany *The Politics of Court Scandal in Early Modern England: News, Culture and the Overbury Affair, 1603–1660* (Cambridge 2001)
—— 'Raylinge Rymes and Vaunting Verse: Libellous Politics in Early Stuart England, 1603–1628', in Kevin Sharpe and Peter Lake (eds) *Culture and Politics in Early Stuart England*
David M. Bergeron *Royal Family, Royal Lovers: King James of England and Scotland* (Columbia and London 1991)
—— *King James and Letters of Homoerotic Desire* (Iowa City 1999)
Brendan Bradshaw and John Morrill (eds) *The British Problem c. 1534–1707: State Formation in the Atlantic Archipelago* (London 1996)
Brendan Bradshaw and Peter Roberts (eds) *British Consciousness and Identity: The Making of Britain, 1533–1707* (Cambridge 1998)
Ciaran Brady 'England's Defence and Ireland's Reform: The Dilemma of the Irish Viceroys, 1541–1641', in Bradshaw and Morrill (eds) *The British Problem c. 1534–1707*
Keith M. Brown *Kingdom or Province? Scotland and the Regnal Union, 1603–1715* (Basingstoke 1992)

—— *Bloodfeud in Scotland, 1573–1625* (Edinburgh 1986)

—— 'The Scottish Aristocracy, Anglicisation and The Court, 1603–38' *Historical Journal* vol. 36, 1993

—— 'Noble Indebtedness in Scotland between the Reformation and the Revolution' *Historical Research* vol. 62, 1989

—— 'Aristocratic Finances and the Origins of the Scottish Revolution' *English Historical Review* 1989

—— 'Courtiers and Cavaliers', in John Morrill (ed.) *The Scottish National Covenant in its British Context*

Glen Burgess *The Politics of the Ancient Constitution* (London 1992)

—— *Absolute Monarchy and the Stuart Constitution* (New Haven and London 1996)

—— 'The Divine Right of Kings Reconsidered' *English Historical Review* vol. 325, 1992

—— (ed.) *The New British History: Founding a Modern State, 1603–1715* (1999)

J. H. Burns *The True Law of Kingship: Concepts of Monarchy in Early Modern Scotland* (Oxford 1996)

Calendars of State Papers Ireland, Scottish, Venetian, Carew

Calendar of State Papers Domestic James I

Nicholas Canny (ed.) *The Origins of Empire: British Overseas Enterprise to the Close of the Seventeenth Century* (Oxford 1998)

—— *Making Ireland British, 1580–1650* (Oxford 2001)

Charles H. Carter 'Gondomar: Ambassador to James I' *Historical Journal* vol. 7, 1964

—— *The Secret Diplomacy of the Habsburgs 1598–1625* (1964)

Thomas Cogswell *The Blessed Revolution: English Politics and the Coming of War, 1621–24* (Cambridge 1989)

—— 'A Low Road to Extinction? Supply and Redress of Grievances in the Parliaments of the 1620s' *Historical Journal* vol. 33, 1990

—— 'Phaeton's Chariot: The Parliament Men and the Continental Crisis in 1621', in J. F. Merritt (ed.) *The Political World of Thomas Wentworth Earl of Strafford, 1621–1641* (Cambridge 1996)

—— 'England and the Spanish Match', in Richard Cust and Ann Hughes (eds) *Conflict in Early Stuart England* (London 1989)

Patrick Collinson *The Religion of Protestants: The Church in English Society, 1559–1625* (Oxford 1982)

—— 'The Jacobean Religious Settlement: The Hampton Court Conference' in Howard Tomlinson (ed.), *Before the English Civil War*

—— 'Elizabethan and Jacobean Puritanism as forms of popular religious culture', in Christopher Durston and Jacqueline Eales (eds) *The Culture of English Puritanism*

Commons Journal vol. 1

Howard Colvin *The History of the King's Works* vol. 3, pts 1 and 2, 1485–1660 (London 1957, 1982)

Ian B. Cowan and Duncan Shaw, (eds) *The Renaissance and Reformation in Scotland* (Edinburgh 1983)

Pauline Croft 'Annual Parliaments and the Long Parliament' *Bulletin of the Institute of Historical Research* vol. 59, 1986

—— 'Wardship in the Parliament of 1604' *Parliamentary History* vol. , 1983

—— 'Parliament, Purveyance and the City of London 1589–1608' *Parliamentary History* vol. , 1985

—— 'Fresh Light on Bate's Case' *Historical Journal* vol. 30, 1987

—— 'A Collection of Treatises and Speeches of the Late Lord Treasurer Cecil' *Royal Historical Society, Camden Miscellany* vol. 29, 1987

—— 'The Religion of Robert Cecil' *Historical Journal* vol. 34, 1991

—— 'The Reputation of Robert Cecil: Libels, Political Opinion and Popular Awareness in the Early Seventeenth Century' *Transactions of the Royal Historical Society* 6th series vol. 1, 1991.

—— 'Serving the Archduke: Robert Cecil's Management of the Parliamentary Session of 1606' *Historical Research* vol. 64, 1991

—— 'The Parliamentary Installation of Henry Prince of Wales' *Historical Research* vol. 65, 1992

—— 'Robert Cecil and the Early Jacobean Court', in Linda Levy Peck (ed.) *The Mental World of the Jacobean Court*

—— 'Libels, Popular Literacy and Public Opinion in Early Modern England' *Historical Research* vol. 68, (1995)

—— 'The Catholic Gentry, The Earl of Salisbury and the Baronets of 1611', in Peter Lake and Michael Questier (eds) *Conformity and Orthodoxy in the English Church, c. 1560–1660* (Woodbridge 2000)

Neil Cuddy 'The Revival of the Entourage: The Bedchamber of James I, 1603–1625', in David Starkey (ed.) *The English Court: From the Wars of the Roses to the Civil War* (London 1987)

—— 'Anglo-Scottish Union and the Court of James I' *Transactions of the Royal Historical Society* 5th series vol. 39, 1989

Richard Cust and Ann Hughes (eds) *Conflict in Early Stuart England: Studies in Religion and Politics 1603–1642* (London 1989)

D. M. Dean and N. L. Jones (eds) *The Parliaments of Elizabethan England* (Oxford 1990)

Gordon Donaldson *Scotland: James V to James VII* (Edinburgh and London 1965)

Christopher Durston and Jacqueline Eales *The Culture of English Puritanism, 1560–1700* (Basingstoke 1996)

J. H. Elliott *The Count-Duke of Olivares* (New Haven 1986)

—— and L. W. Brockliss *The World of the Favourite* (London 1999)

Steven G. Ellis and Sarah Barber *Conquest and Union: Fashioning a British State, 1485–1725* (Harlow 1995)

Lori Anne Ferrell, *Government by Polemic* (Stanford 1998)

Kenneth Fincham *Prelate as Pastor: The Episcopate of James I* (Oxford 1990)

—— (ed.) *The Early Stuart Church, 1603–1642* (London 1993)

—— and Peter Lake 'The Ecclesiastical Policy of King James I' *Journal of British Studies* vol. 24, 1985

—— 'Ramifications of the Hampton Court Conference in the Dioceses, 1603–1609' *Journal of Ecclesiastical History* vol. 36, 1985

—— 'Prelacy and Politics: Archbishop Abbot's Defence of Protestant Orthodoxy' *Bulletin Institute of Historical Research* vol. 61, 1988

Anthony Fletcher and Peter Roberts (eds) *Religion, Culture and Society in Early Modern Britain* (Cambridge 1994)

Alan Ford *The Protestant Reformation in Ireland, 1590–1641* (Dublin 1997)

John D. Ford 'Conformity in Conscience: The Structure of the Perth Articles Debate in Scotland, 1618–38' *Journal of Ecclesiastical History* vol. 46, (1995)

—— 'The Lawful Bonds of Scottish Society: The Five Articles of Perth, The Negative Confession and the National Covenant', *Historical Journal* vol. 37, (1994)

E. R. Foster *Proceedings in Parliament 1610* (2 vols New Haven 1966)

Bruce R. Galloway *The Union of England and Scotland, 1603–08* (Edinburgh 1986)

—— and Brian P. Levack *The Jacobean Union: Six Tracts of 1604* (Edinburgh 1985)

S. R. Gardiner *History of England, 1603–1642* (vols 1–5, London 1864–86)

—— *Parliamentary Debates in 1610* (London 1862)

—— *El Hecho . . . Narrative of the Spanish Marriage Treaty* (London 1869)

Julian Goodare *State and Society in Early Modern Scotland* (Oxford 1999)

—— and Michael Lynch (eds) *The Reign of James VI* (East Linton 2000)

—— 'Parliamentary Taxation in Scotland, 1560–1603' *Scottish Historical Review* vol. 68, 1989

—— 'The Scottish Parliament of 1621' *Historical Journal* vol. 38, 1995

Christopher Grayson 'James I and the Religious Crisis in the United Provinces 1613–19', in Derek Baker (ed.) *Reform and Reformation: England and The Continent c.1500–c.1750* (Oxford 1979)

John Guy *The Reign of Elizabeth I: Court and Culture in the Last Decade* (Cambridge 1995)

G. L. Harriss 'Medieval Doctrines in the Debates on Supply, 1610–1629', in K. Sharpe (ed.) *Faction and Parliament: Essays on Early Stuart History* (Oxford 1978)

J. H. Hexter (ed.) *Parliament and Liberty: From the Reign of Elizabeth to the English Civil War* (Stanford 1992)

—— 'The Apology of 1604', in Richard Ollard and Pamela Tudor-Craig (eds) *For Veronica Wedgwood These: Studies in Seventeenth-Century History*

Historical MSS Commission . . . Marquess of Salisbury

R. W. Hoyle (ed.) *The Estates of the English Crown 1558–1640* (Cambridge 1992)

Maija Jansson *Proceedings in Parliament, 1614* (Philadelphia 1988)

Peter Lake 'Constitutional Consensus and Puritan Opposition in the 1620s: Thomas Scott and the Spanish Match' *Historical Journal* vol. 25, 1982

James F. Larkin and Paul L. Hughes *Stuart Royal Proclamations: Royal Proclamations of King James I, 1603–1625* (Oxford 1973)

Maurice Lee Jnr *Great Britain's Solomon: James VI and I in His Three Kingdoms* (Urbana and Chicago 1990)

—— *James I and Henri IV: An Essay in English Foreign Policy, 1603–1610* (Urbana 1970)

—— *Government by Pen: Scotland under James VI and I* (Urbana, Chicago and London 1980)

Brian P. Levack *The Formation of the British State: England, Scotland and the Union, 1603–1707* (Oxford 1987)

Eric Lindquist 'The Failure of the Great Contract' *Journal of Modern History* vol. 57, 1985

—— 'The King, the People and the House of Commons: the Problem of Jacobean Purveyance' *Historical Journal* vol. 31, 1988

David Lindley *The Trials of Frances Howard: Fact and Fiction at the Court of King James* (London 1993)

Roger Lockyer *Buckingham: The Life and Political Career of George Villiers, First Duke of Buckingham, 1592–1628* (London 1981)

—— *The Early Stuarts: A Political History of England 1603–1642* (Harlow, 2nd edn 1999)

Albert J. Loomie *Spain and the Jacobean Catholics* (Catholic Record Society 1973)

—— *Spain and the Early Stuarts, 1585–1655* (Aldershot 1996)

—— *Toleration and Diplomacy* (Philadelphia 1963)

Michael Lynch *Scotland: A New History* (Edinburgh 1991)

—— 'Preaching to the Converted? Perspectives on the Scottish Reformation', in *The Renaissance in Scotland: Studies in Literature, Religion, History and Culture* (Brill 1994)

Alan R. MacDonald *The Jacobean Kirk, 1567–1625* (Aldershot 1998)

Allan I. MacInnes 'Early Modern Scotland: The Current State of Play', and Michael Lynch 'Response' *Scottish Historical Review* vol. 73, 1994

Roger A. Mason (ed.) *Scots and Britons: Scottish Political Thought and the Union of 1603* (Cambridge 1994)

N. E. McClure (ed.) *The Letters of John Chamberlain* (2 vols Philadelphia 1939)

Peter E. McCullough *Sermons at Court: Politics and Religion in Elizabethan and Jacobean Preaching* (Cambridge 1998)

William A. McNeill and Peter G. B. McNeill 'The Scottish Progress of James VI, 1617' *Scottish Historical Review* vol. 7, (1996)

T. W. Moody, F.-X. Martin and F. J. Byrne (eds) *A New History of Ireland* vol. 3 *Early Modern Ireland 1534–1691* (Oxford 1991)

John Morrill, Paul Slack and Daniel Woolf *Public Duty and Private Conscience in Seventeenth-Century England* (Oxford 1993)

—— (ed.) *The Scottish National Covenant in its British Context* (Edinburgh 1990)

—— 'A British Patriarchy? Ecclesiastical Imperialism under the Early Stuarts', in Anthony Fletcher and Peter Roberts (eds) *Religion, Culture and Society*

David George Mullan *Episcopacy in Scotland: The History of An Idea, 1560–1638* (Edinburgh 1986)

Howard Nenner *The Right to Be King: The Succession to the Crown of England, 1603–1714* (Chapel Hill 1995)

Andrew D. Nicholls *The Jacobean Union: A Reconsideration of British Civil Policies Under The Early Stuarts* (Westport, CT 1999)

Mark Nicholls *Investigating the Gunpowder Plot* (Manchester 1991)

W. Notestein, F. H. Relf and H. Simpson, *Commons Debates, 1621* (7 vols New Haven 1935)

Richard Ollard and Pamela Tudor-Craig *For Veronica Wedgwood These: Studies in Seventeenth-Century History* (London 1986)

Jane H. Ohlmeyer 'The Civilisinge of those rude partes': Colonisation within Britain and Ireland, 1580s–1640s', in Nicholas Canny (ed.) *The Origins of Empire*

G. Dyfnallt Owen *Wales in the Reign of James I* (Woodbridge 1988)

Graham Parry *The Golden Age Restored: The Culture of the Jacobean Court* (Manchester 1981)

W. B. Patterson *King James VI and I and the Reunion of Christendom* (Cambridge 1997)

Hans S. Pawlisch *Sir John Davies and the Conquest of Ireland: A Study in Legal Imperialism* (Cambridge 1985)

Linda Levy Peck (ed.) *The Mental World of the Jacobean Court* (Cambridge 1991)

—— *Northampton: Patronage and Policy at the Court of James I* (London 1982)

—— *Court Patronage and Corruption in Early Stuart England* (London 1990)

—— 'For a King not to be Bountiful were a Fault' *Journal of British Studies* vol. 25, 1986

Michael Perceval-Maxwell *The Scottish Migration to Ulster in the Reign of James I* (London 1993)

—— 'Ireland and the Monarchy in the Early Stuart Multiple Kingdom' *Historical Journal* vol. 34, 1991

John Platt 'Eirenical Anglicans at the Synod of Dort', in Derek Baker (ed.) *Reform and Reformation: England and the Continent, c.1500–c.1750*

Menna Prestwich *Cranfield: Politics and Profits under the Early Stuarts* (Oxford 1996)

Brennan C. Pursell 'James I, Gondomar and the Dissolution of the Parliament of 1621' *History* vol. 85, 2000

Michael C. Questier 'Sir Henry Spiller, Recusancy and the Efficiency of the Jacobean Exchequer', *Historical Research* 1993

Michael C. Questier 'Religion, Loyalism and State Power in Early Modern England: English Romanists and the Jacobean Oath of Allegiance' *Historical Journal* vol. 40, 1997

B. W. Quintrell 'The Royal Hunt and the Puritans' *Journal of Ecclesiastical History* vol. 31, 1980
—— 'The Practice and Problems of Recusant Disarming, 1585–1641' *Recusant History* vol. 17, 1984–5
Theodore K. Rabb *Jacobean Gentleman:Sir Edwin Sandys, 1561–1629* (Princeton 1998)
Glyn Redworth 'Of Pimps and Princes: Three Unpublished Letters from James I and The Prince of Wales Relating to the Spanish Match' *Historical Journal* vol. 37, 1994
Glyn Redworth 'Beyond Faith and Fatherland: The Appeal of the Catholics of Ireland, c.1623' *Archivium Hibernicum* vol. 52, 1998
Robert Ruigh *The Parliament of 1624: Politics and Foreign Policy* (Cambridge, MA 1971)
Conrad Russell 'Divine Rights in the Early Seventeenth Century', in John Morrill, Paul Slack and Daniel Woolf (eds) *Public Duty and Private Conscience*
—— 'The Anglo-Scottish Union, 1603–1643: A Success?', in Anthony Fletcher and Peter Roberts (eds) *Religion, Culture and Society in Early Modern Britain*
—— 'Parliamentary History in Perspective, 1604–1629' *History* vol. 61, 1976
—— *Parliaments and English Politics, 1621–29* (Oxford 1979)
—— 'The nature of a Parliament in Early Stuart England', in Howard Tomlinson (ed.) *Before the English Civil War*
—— 'English Parliaments, 1593–1606: One Epoch or Two?', in D. M. Dean and N. L. Jones (eds) *The Parliaments of Elizabethan England* (Oxford 1990)
—— *The Addled Parliament of 1614: The Limits of Revisionism* (Stenton Lecture, University of Reading 1992)
—— (ed.) *The Origins of the English Civil War* (London 1973)
—— *The Causes of the English Civil War* (Oxford 1990)
—— 'The British Problem and the English Civil War' *History* vol. 72, 1987
James Sharpe *The Bewitching of Anne Gunter* (London 1999)
Kevin Sharpe 'Private Conscience and Public Duty in the Writing of James VI and I', in John Morrill, Paul Slack and Daniel Woolf (eds) *Public Duty and Private Conscience in Seventeenth-Century England* (Oxford 1993)
—— and Peter Lake (eds) *Culture and Politics in Early Stuart England* (London 1994)
—— 'The King's Writ: Royal Authors and Royal Authorship in early modern England', in Sharpe and Lake (eds) *Culture and Politics in Early Stuart England*
—— (ed) *Faction and Parliament* (Oxford 1973)
Jared R. M. Sizer 'The Good of this Service Consists in Absolute Secrecy: The Earl of Dunbar, Scotland and the Border, 1603–1611' *Canadian Journal of History/Annales canadiennes* vol. 36, 2001
A. G. R. Smith (ed) *The Reign of James VI and I* (London 1973)
—— 'Crown, Parliament and Finance: The Great Contract of 1610', in P. Clark, A. G. R. Smith and N. Tyacke (eds) *The English Commonwealth, 1547–1640* (Leicester 1979)

R. Malcolm Smuts *Culture and Power in England, 1585–1685* (Basingstoke 1999)
—— *Court Culture and The Origins of a Royalist Tradition in Early Stuart England* (Philadelphia 1987)

Anne Somerset *Unnatural Murder: Poison at the Court of King James* (London 1997)

Johann P. Sommerville *King James VI and I: Political Writings* (Cambridge 1994)
—— 'The Ancient Constitution Re-Assessed: The Common Law, the Court and the Languages of Politics in Early Modern England', in R. Malcolm Smuts (ed.) *The Stuart Court and Europe: Essays in Politics and Political Culture* (Cambridge 1996)
—— *Royalists and Patriots: Politics and Ideology in England 1603–1640* (Harlow 1999)
—— 'The Royal Supremacy and Episcopacy Jure Divino, 1603–1640' *Journal of Ecclesiastical History* vol. 34, 1983

David Starkey *The English Court: From the Wars of the Roses to the Civil War* (London 1987)

David Stevenson *Scotland's Last Royal Wedding: The Marriage of James VI and Anne of Denmark* (Edinburgh 1997)

Roy Strong *Henry Prince of Wales and England's Lost Renaissance* (London 1986)

David Thomas 'Financial and Adminstrative Developments', in Howard Tomlinson (ed.) *Before the English Civil War*

Howard Tomlinson (ed.) *Before the English Civil War: Essays on Early Stuart Politics and Government* (London 1983)

Victor Treadwell *Buckingham and Ireland, 1616–1628* (Dublin 1998)

Alison Wall *Power and Protest* (London 2000)

S. J. Watts *From Border to Middle Shire: Northumberland 1586–1625* (Leicester 1975)

Allan F. Westcott *New Poems of James I of England* (New York 1966)

D. H. Willson *King James VI and I* (London 1956)

W. L. Woodfill *Musicians in English Society from Elizabeth to Charles I* (Princeton 1953)

Jenny Wormald *Court, King and Community: Scotland, 1470–1625* (London 1981)
—— 'James VI and I: Two Kings or One?' *History* vol. 68, 1983
—— 'James VI, James I and the Identity of Britain', in Brendan Bradshaw and John Morrill (eds) *The British Problem c.1534–1707*
—— 'Ecclesiastical Vitriol: The Kirk, the Puritans and the Future King of England', in John Guy (ed.) *The Reign of Elizabeth I: Court and Culture in the Last Decade*
—— 'The Creation of Britain: Multiple Kingdoms or Core and Colonies?' *Transactions of the Royal Historical Society* 6th series vol. 2, 1992
—— 'Gunpowder, Treason and Scots' *Journal of British Studies* vol. 24, 1985
—— 'Tis True I am a Cradle King': The view from the Throne', in Julian Goodare and Michael Lynch (eds) *The Reign of James VI*

Michael B. Young *Servility and Service: The Life and Work of Sir John Coke* (London 1986)

—— *King James VI and I and the History of Homosexuality* (Iowa 1999)

—— 'Illusions of Grandeur and Reform at the Jacobean Court: Cranfield and the Ordnance' *Historical Journal* vol. 22, 1979

George Yule 'James VI and I: Furnishing the Churches in his Two Kingdoms', in Anthony Fletcher and Peter Roberts (eds) *Religion, Culture and Society in Early Modern Britain*

Robert Zaller *The Parliament of 1621* (London 1971)

Note

The following items appeared too late to be cited, but they are valuable in reinforcing and amplifying points already made in the text.

Judith M. Richards 'The English Accession of James VI: "National" Identity, Gender and the Personal Monarchy of England' *English Historical Review* vol. 117, June 2002, pp. 513–35

The British Union: A Critical Edition and Translation of David Hume of Godscroft's 'De Unione Insulae Britannicae', ed. and trans. Paul J. McGinnis and Arthur H. Williamson (Aldershot 2002)

Royal Subjects: The Writings of James VI and I, ed. Daniel Fischlin, Mark Fortier and Kevin Sharpe (Detroit 2002)

Index